THE POLITICS OF PRIVACY IN CONTEMPORARY NATIVE,
LATINX, AND ASIAN AMERICAN METAFICTIONS

The Politics of Privacy in Contemporary Native, Latinx, and Asian American Metafictions

COLLEEN G. EILS

THE OHIO STATE UNIVERSITY PRESS
COLUMBUS

Copyright © 2020 by The Ohio State University.
All rights reserved.

Library of Congress Cataloging-in-Publication Data
Names: Eils, Colleen G., author.
Title: The politics of privacy in contemporary Native, Latinx, and Asian American metafictions / Colleen G. Eils.
Description: Columbus : The Ohio State University Press, [2020] | Includes bibliographical references and index. | Summary: "Explores contemporary metafictions by writers of color and Indigenous writers, such as Viet Thanh Nguyen, David Treuer, Monique Truong, Rigoberto González, Nam Le, and Stephen Graham Jones, and how they engage visibility, privacy, and access in relation to a post-9/11 US and histories of racial and colonial politics"—Provided by publisher.
Identifiers: LCCN 2020011497 | ISBN 9780814214220 (cloth) | ISBN 0814214223 (cloth) | ISBN 9780814278239 (ebook) | ISBN 081427823X (ebook)
Subjects: LCSH: Privacy in literature. | Politics and literature—United States. | Marginality, Social, in literature. | American fiction—21st century—History and criticism. | English fiction—21st century—History and criticism. | American fiction—Minority authors—History and criticism. | American fiction—Hispanic American authors—History and criticism. | American fiction—Asian American authors—History and criticism.
Classification: LCC PS374.P647 E37 2020 | DDC 810.9/8—dc23
LC record available at https://lccn.loc.gov/2020011497

Other identifiers: ISBN 9780814256008 (paper) | ISBN 0814256007 (paper)

Cover design by Susan Zucker
Text design by Juliet Williams
Type set in Adobe Minion Pro

∞ The paper used in this publication meets the minimum requirements of the American National Standard for Information Sciences—Permanence of Paper for Printed Library Materials. ANSI Z39.48-1992.

To Dan

CONTENTS

Acknowledgments   ix

INTRODUCTION   1

CHAPTER 1   Ethnographic Surveillance and the Limits of Looking   29

CHAPTER 2   Omniscient Surveillance and the Politics of Visibility After 9/11   65

CHAPTER 3   Selling/Out and the Commodification of Difference   105

CHAPTER 4   Textual Archives and Anti-Documentary Desire   143

CONCLUSION   179

Works Cited   189
Index   199

ACKNOWLEDGMENTS

This book of literary criticism represents my sincere reckoning with how I ought to read literature and approach scholarship and teaching. The correctives, support, and alternatives offered by peers, mentors, and students throughout the years, therefore, course through its chapters. I don't know that I have it right but am grateful for the conversations along the way and for those still to come.

I especially appreciate my community from Austin, particularly Jim Cox and Domino Perez, whose warmth and support remain for me the model of academic mentorship. I cannot extend enough gratitude to Andrew Uzendoski, my trusted sounding board and collaborator, and to Sheela Jane Menon, for modeling the warmth and professionalism I aspire to. Thanks, too, to Julie Minich, Emily Lederman, and Charlotte Nunes, and to Kirby Brown, who asked me as a first-year graduate student what we were doing if our scholarship didn't *do* something in the world. I appreciate also the officers and civilian faculty at West Point who eased my way into the strange world of the Army. Thanks to my wonderful neighbors in Austin and in the Hudson Valley, too: friends unconnected to academe who provide support and love and who listen patiently and remind me of life beyond a world defined by semesters.

I would like to acknowledge the larger academic ecologies that generated, transformed, and sharpened the ideas in this book. Some of my peers' most compelling, innovative scholarship will remain unpublished because of precarious academic employment and support, yet those ideas are integral to the work many of us produce. Of course, it's important to acknowledge the privilege not just of gainful academic employment, but formal education more generally, given the profoundly uneven gatekeeping that happens at every step of academic progress. Unlike many, I've been helped at every turn. Thanks to my parents, Patrick and Virginia Gleeson, and my three older brothers, I grew up in a home of learning and curiosity, surrounded by willing teachers. My public school teachers and my professors at Clemson University and the University of Texas at Austin took special interest in me when they didn't have to, and it made all the difference. More recently, I've benefitted from the thorough, generative honesty of anonymous readers of the book manuscript and the journal articles that came from its pages, as well as the support of Ana Jimenez-Moreno and the team at The Ohio State University Press. Thank you all for making this book, then making it better than it was.

I appreciate the Departments of English at the University of Texas at Austin, Willamette University, and the United States Military Academy at West Point for providing me with temporary employment, and especially the West Point Writing Program for offering a lasting and rewarding academic home. Thanks to Jason Hoppe, specifically, for his enduring grace and kindness and for always somehow shouldering more than his share of the load. Thanks to Wynn Klosky for steering our ship to calmer waters.

My sincerest thanks to my students in Austin, Salem, and West Point: I have so very much enjoyed learning together with you.

My partner Dan Eils deserves the greatest thanks of all; I'm fortunate to move through life with such an extraordinary human.

INTRODUCTION

Our present historical moment may seem an inappropriate time for writers of color and indigenous writers to insist on privacy in their fiction: the ongoing fight for equal representation and access to power can hardly be understood as complete as the United States slips into increasingly perilous political times. Ethnic studies programs continue to face bans in several states, news and entertainment media refuse equal representation to people of color and indigenous people in both coverage and talent, and asylum-seekers experience profound violations of human rights on US soil. Only the democratization of video cameras in cell phones and subsequent graphic footage of police violence against (primarily) men of color keeps the specter of state violence and corporate abuse in the mainstream news. Tired stereotypes of marginalized communities still drive campaign rhetoric and elected officials' legislative rationales. Even the publishing industry in which writers make their living remains overwhelmingly white and prone to tokenizing "diversity" rather than soliciting and developing talent. Visibility, more than ever, is one of the most powerful political tools available to those seeking change; privacy is a strange move, indeed, with so much work left to do.

Visibility—and lack thereof—however, has always been political, particularly for people of color and indigenous people, and its conditions often exact a high cost. For every cell phone video of police brutality, for example, a human's bodily privacy is radically and profoundly violated: first by physical violence, then by viral spectacle. For every profile of an asylum-seeker separated from her children, readers gain access to extraordinary trauma. In a visually and narratively saturated world, such viral exposure can be understood as democratic possibility for material change, given stories' and images' broad accessibility. The result, however, is that people of color and indigenous people are, as they have been for centuries, persistently pressured to exchange access to private facets of their lives for (the hope of) recognition of their humanity and attendant protections by those in power.

A generation after the activist writers of civil rights movements and the important fight for visibility and voice in the years leading up to and including the 1960s and 1970s, today's young writers of color and indigenous writers consider, instead, the political and material possibilities of what I term "narrative privacy." Responding both to our present moment of media-saturated hyper-visibility and the multicultural era of depoliticized representations in which they came of age in the 1980s and 1990s, this generation of young writers recalls ways in which colonial and racial ways of looking at indigenous people, people of color, and immigrants inflect the way readers understand fiction.

In the midst of scholarly and popular demands to fill gaps in neglected literary histories, to represent marginalized communities, to correct colonialist accounts, or simply to breach "colonialism's strongest defense: silence," these writers maintain strategic narrative silence in a formal response to the power relations that shape the production of literary representations of people of color and indigenous people as well as the material realities of marginalized communities (Million 57–58). Complementary to rather than antagonistic toward representation, narrative privacy offers an alternative to both absence and compulsory presence by underscoring authorial choice and undermining audiences' expectations about unquestioned racial, ethnic, and indigenous visibility. In making transparent the processes by which authors create, publishers circulate, and readers consume fiction, the stories' metafictional form serves as a "pedagogical example" through which writers self-reflexively comment on their privileges as creators of narratives as well as the political limitations of commercial fiction (Goellnicht 216).

Narrative privacy names both the formal strategies these writers employ across multiple fields of post-9/11 literatures and the theoretical lens offered by those formal strategies through which to examine relationships between readers, authors, and texts. As a formal strategy, narrative privacy manifests itself as moments of deliberate silence, invisibility, or withholding on the part of characters, narrators, or authors that contest readers' expectations of access to narratives. Discrete from the limits of *language*—the impossibility of expressing trauma, emotion, or other inarticulable experiences—narrative privacy is instead a critical response to the limits of *literature* as a politically equitable mode of representation. In crafting spaces of narrative privacy, the writers throughout these pages teach readers to recognize looking as a political act both on the page and in the world around them. As a theoretical lens, narrative privacy imagines the productive possibilities of conceptualizing moments of formal silence or invisibility as acts of agency in response to historical and ongoing demands for representation and privileged access. In its disruption of familiar reading practices and demonstration to readers that how we read—not just what we read—can shape how we view and therefore behave in the world, narrative privacy is also a broadly transportable reading methodology.

As a formal device and reading strategy, narrative privacy has two primary critical interests: affirming the historically political nature of visibility, particularly for people of color and indigenous people, and theorizing privacy as a political assertion of power over representation and material vulnerability. Acknowledging the persistently incomplete and uneven nature of racial, ethnic, and indigenous representation in our present moment, these writers recall histories of compulsory visibility for people of color and indigenous people in North America to contextualize privacy as, often, a luxury only available to the powerful and privileged. The fictions throughout this volume highlight issues of visibility—what can be seen, what must be seen, what is invisible, what is erased—and position reading as an act of looking on the part of the reader.[1] In deliberately and self-consciously evading readers through the form of their fiction, these writers seize upon privacy as a political tool: a tool for claiming and wielding power on both representational and material registers. Given the histories of uneven power relations and compulsory visibility for the disempowered, even a claim to privacy constitutes a political act.

As a literary form, metafiction lends itself to self-critique and the authors at the core of *The Politics of Privacy* do not shield themselves from self-deprecation and criticism. They contend with their own complicity as writers in the political and capitalist processes their narratives contest by highlighting the formal tension between their narratives, which condemn the dissemination of characters' stories for entertainment or profit, and their physical books, which circulate commercially. In crafting characters who accuse them

---

1. More specifically, the authors in this study depict reading as a hierarchical relationship between those with access to privileged gazes and the subjects of those gazes. As the authors make clear in how they rewrite these hierarchal relations, power and visibility are intertwined in complicated—and contradictory—ways. Franz Fanon's articulation of the "white gaze" and Mary Louise Pratt's consideration of "imperial looking" are important theoretical forebears to this critical work on privileged (racialized, imperial) gazes.

of stealing and profiting from their narratives by selling access to their lives to potentially unsympathetic readers, the writers in this book illustrate the worst-case scenario for their published fiction: if stories about deeply personal experiences—even traumas—do nothing but entertain, writers run the risk of simply profiting from others' struggles without returning anything to the communities about which they write, while readers risk naturalizing inequality by uncritically assuming access to the lives of people of color and indigenous people. Publishing fiction, however, is an act of faith that tempers these authors' suspicious treatment of narrative's vexed relationship with privacy, authority, and cultural surveillance. Rather than antirepresentational, narrative privacy seeks an alternative to silence or invisibility.

Discussion of meta-critical projects would be incomplete without acknowledging my own implication in the critiques these texts direct toward not only readers but also specifically literary critics, who often produce scholarly treatments of fiction that, in striving for inclusion and equality, can result in overdetermined readings. Linda Tuhiwai Smith reminds all researchers that "research is not an innocent or distant academic exercise but an activity that has something at stake and that occurs in a set of political and social conditions" (5). Patricia Yeager also expresses concern about academics' responsibilities in studying narratives of trauma: she asks, "If circulating the suffering of others has become the meat and potatoes of our profession, if this circulation evokes a lost history but also runs the danger of commodification, how should we proceed?" (30). Especially given literary studies' long relationship with colonialism and the history of excluding particular voices, responsible critics must, as Dian Million explains, "understand as fully as possible the forms colonialism takes in our own times" (55). In *Culture and Imperialism,* Edward Said tasks his readers with connecting literary texts "with the imperial process of which they were manifestly and unconcealedly a part" (xiv). Updating Said's charge in light of Million's warning, I understand the authors in this book as tasking themselves with illuminating how colonial processes continue to shape critical and public understandings of literature authored by Native American, Latinx, and Asian American writers.

In highlighting writers' work with privacy, *The Politics of Privacy* is thrice-implicated in the critiques of power, visibility, and the access it theorizes. As a reader and literary scholar, I am not always welcome in the novels I read in the following chapters, at least according to characters and their implied authors. Invoking historical contexts of compulsory visibility and uneven power relations, especially with white viewers, these figures view readers like me with a rational and understandable suspicion. My curiosity in these texts' formal maneuvers, in fact, stemmed from their skepticism: committed to reading ethnic and indigenous literatures responsibly, I found a form of relief in narratives that questioned my unearned access as a white reader and scholar. *The Politics of Privacy* is, in many ways, the result of closely parsing these texts for guidance on how to proceed. After all, as a literary scholar, I not only read narratives that may resist my presence, but I expose them to wider audiences, lingering on difficult passages to most clearly explicate the importance of privacy.[2] The irony of this paradox only deepens: with the publication of this book, of course, I am also an author. When Liz, a character in Salvador Plascencia's *The People of Paper* (2005), accuses her author of selling out private information for "fourteen dollars and the vanity of your name on the book cover," she raises real questions about visibility and access to power that implicate this volume and my intentions, as well (138). While my aims are neither fortune nor fame, I am attentive to Liz's accusation and shape my close reading practices accordingly. The result entails staying a bit too close, perhaps, to the page; I go along with the metafictions' formal experiments of positioning their readers as particular forms of viewers, which requires me to believe and attend to characters' concerns.

Of course, characters are figments of writers' imaginations and not human, but that does not necessarily diminish their critiques, to which I remain deliberately vulnerable. Reading vulnerably, or remaining open to critique as an embodied reader with a particular set of expectations and privileges, is—like narrative privacy—a contextual and highly individualized approach rather than a prescriptive practice. Narrative privacy requires that I notice and think through moments that resist my presence, both in fiction and in the world outside of the text, remaining aware of the politics of my gaze and the power structures that condition it. Above all, acknowledging my own implication in these texts' critical projects means foregrounding these writers' work by respecting and thinking deeply about their formal spaces of privacy.

Through narrative privacy and their modeling of vulnerability, the authors in these pages approach fiction and their readers with equal measures of skepticism and optimism. On the one hand, they write persuasively about the myriad reasons they should withhold, hide, forget, or destroy the stories they write, given the weight of historical and contemporary forms of compulsory visibility for people of color and indigenous peoples in the US. On the other,

---

2. Melamed encourages literary scholars to consider our implication in knowledge production: "Literary studies has been a foremost cultural technology for producing, transmitting, and implanting official antiracist knowledges. In this role literary studies has come to play a uniquely powerful part in producing commonsense notions about race in the United States after World War II, for better or worse. It is important to stress that literary texts themselves are not at issue here, rather literary studies as materially produced discourses" (15).

however, they each choose to sell and publish their fiction, albeit with their insistence on narrative privacy intact; in other words, they actively participate in and benefit from the very systems their narratives critique. Narrative privacy articulates through literary form the tension between writers' desires to withhold and to disclose the stories they have to tell. The dissonance between their narratives' insistence on privacy and the texts' evident circulation as commercial fiction refuses any clean resolution to the relationship between fiction, privacy, and surveillance. In a historical moment in which writers are at once exhausted by representational politics and yet acutely aware of the importance of narrative, they formally center their conflicted relationships on privacy and surveillance by taking as their subject the very act of writing the story we—also implicated in their project, as audiences—read.

Of course, neither metafiction nor the literary desire for privacy is new. Drawing on rich engagement with literary antecedents as well as the social and political conditions of our contemporary, post-9/11 moment, however, a generation of young US writers has newly adopted metafictional forms as decidedly political tools. By most accounts, the height of US literary metafiction was in the 1960s and '70s, when the technique was constitutive of high literary postmodernism (Elias 15).[3] Metafiction was at first characterized as the "Literature of Exhaustion"; in the wake of the death of the Author, History, and Authority, John Barth explains that writers exhausted all source material except writing itself, and so they turned their creative and critical focus inward through self-aware writing to take as their subject the process of creating and reading literature (64). Barth later clarified his argument in "Literature of Replenishment," with what is probably a more accurate characterization of metafiction, that it stemmed not from an exhaustion of literary possibilities, but an exhaustion of high modernist projects; metafiction served mid-century writers as a way to explore and recreate literary form. In *Metafiction*, perhaps the most widely cited source on the subject, Patricia Waugh clarifies that while metafiction is primarily a mid-twentieth-century phenomenon, it is not uniquely so: "while the *term* 'metafiction' might be new, the *practice* is as old (if not older) than the novel itself" (5, emphasis in original). Unique to postmodern metafiction, however, is preoccupation with texts' "own condition of artifice" and exploration of "a *theory* of fiction through the *practice* of writing" (21, 2, emphasis in original).[4] As a marker of

---

3. William Gass coined the term "metafiction" in an essay, "Philosophy and Form of Fiction" (1979).

4. Amy J. Elias explains further: "When people talk about metafiction, they often refer to fiction whose themes and narrations focus on the death of fiction; that presents overtly fictional story elements, motifs, and archetypes as reality or realistic actors and existents; and that employs techniques . . . to break the 'fourth wall' and insert real-life authors directly into the fictional construct as narrators or characters" (18).

high postmodernism, metafiction waned in popularity in the 1980s and '90s, and David Foster Wallace reflected on the passing of the form in his 1990 essay, "E Unibus Pluram."[5] Recent texts, including not only those included in these chapters but also work by, among others, Percival Everett, Ruth Ozeki, Ian McEwan, Valeria Luiselli, Lily Hoang, Alejandro Zambra, Tan Lin, Toni Jensen, Jonathan Safran Foer, and Mark Z. Danielewski, however, testify to a persistent interest in the form, which as Wallace suggests has now rooted itself in other media, including television and film.[6]

In practice, "metafiction" can be a capacious category, widely used to refer to any fiction that thematizes writing, reading, or textuality. In this book, however, I use "metafiction" exclusively to name self-referential fiction, or fiction that considers its own creation, distribution, and/or reception as a literary artifact. This self-referentiality occurs by breaking the fourth wall between the text and reader, by including the author–character in the fiction, by including a text by the same name as the novel or story in the narrative, or sometimes by narrating the creation of the story readers hold in their hands. The following chapters consider writers who turn to metafiction not as a matter of stylistic novelty, but to provide a forum for considering the consumption of ethnic and indigenous literature in literary, rather than sociological, terms; the authors stage strategic investigations into how Native American, Latinx, and Asian American fiction is produced, read, and circulated in our present moment. In taking as their subject the creation of their own fiction, their formal maneuvers are resonant with, but crucially different from, mainstream postmodernists of an earlier historical moment.[7] If the permeability of barriers between fact and fiction was what preoccupied an earlier generation of self-referential

---

5. Andrew Hoberek offers a useful survey of various—and at times conflicting—views of the end of postmodernism in his introduction to a special issue of *Twentieth Century Literature*. Mary K. Holland treats the issue at length in her book-length study *Succeeding Postmodernism: Language and Humanism in Contemporary American Literature* (2013).

6. *Ferris Bueller's Day Off* (1986), for instance, famously breaks the fourth wall when the titular character addresses his audience. The mockumentary genre, popularized by UK and US versions of *The Office*, integrates metafiction into its generic definition. Wheeler Winston Dixon's *It Looks at You: The Returned Gaze of Cinema* (1995) offers a book-length study of this move.

7. Distinguishing between these contemporary projects and those of mid-century postmodern writers challenges critics,' reviewers,' and publishers' tendency to place these formally innovative authors in the literary tradition of Philip K. Dick, John Barth, Jorge Luis Borges, Thomas Pynchon, and Italo Calvino, names I understand as functioning as literary markers, rather than as productive comparisons of the actual authors' work. Interrupting these standard comparisons focuses attention on the social, political, and literary theories these contemporary texts produce rather than the impression that ethnic authors are either delivering ethnographic artifacts or finally catching up to poststructuralist aesthetics a decade after Wallace marked the passing of those same aesthetics in literature.

authors, ethnic and indigenous literary visibility in the context of legacies of oppression and exploitation drive the authors in this study.

In contrast to realist texts which naturalize and depoliticize invisible reader–text relationships, these self-referential metafictions draw attention to readers' access to the texts they read. Their self-referential maneuvers are powerful literary theorizations that aim to shape the way readers understand visibility on the page and in the world and, as a consequence, learn to critically and deliberately examine their reading practices. In disrupting conventional literary presumptions—of whiteness, of access, of relationships between character, text, author, and reader—they illuminate the pervasive racial, ethnic, and legal inequalities that continue to condition the processes by which ethnic and indigenous fiction is created, circulated, and read in our contemporary "postracial," post-9/11 moment. These authors challenge reading practices that continue to see and hear cultures in particular ways while also continuing to reject the political, physical, and social needs of the people who originate it.[8] They adopt and transform literary forms most often associated with postmodernism even as postmodernism, in many ways, resists the very critiques they make.

Narrative privacy's emergence, in fact, can be understood as the result not only of 9/11 and contemporary discourses of privacy and visibility, but through a series of historical and political confluences over the last several decades. The rise of postmodernism in the United States corresponded with the rise of progressive social and political movements, including the Chicana/o Movement, Civil Rights, Red Power, and Asian American Civil Rights Movement, as well as the feminism and Gay Rights movements in the 1960s and '70s. As Henry Louis Gates, among others, has noted, it is not without irony that postmodernism evacuated Authority, killed the Author and History, and abstracted meaning from texts just as people of color began publishing in increased numbers.[9] Such theoretical measures might be understood as, at

---

8. Here I adapt Coco Fusco's consideration of cultural appropriation, in which she explains, "the simultaneous embrace of a culture and rejection of the people who originate it [is] a contradictory behavior with a colonial history" (66).

9. Henry Louis Gates similarly considers the timing of the "death of the subject." He writes, "Consider the irony: precisely when we (and other Third World peoples) obtain the complex wherewithal to define our black subjectivity in the republic of Western letters, our theoretical colleagues declare that there ain't no such thing as a subject, so why should we be bothered with that?" (36). Also, I do want to underscore my understanding that Latinx, indigenous, and Asian American (as well as African American, feminist, and Queer) literatures existed before this period of activism. As a result of these social movements, however, these literatures became more accessible and visible.

least in part, defensive against social change. Jodi Melamed characterizes the social movements' demands on universities as radical:

> The insurgencies that took place on college campuses in the late 1960s and 1970s can be viewed as profoundly materialist antiracist activism. Demands for third-world colleges, black and ethnic studies departments, La Raza studies, Asian American studies, and Native American studies were attempts to seize the authorizing power of massive racializing institutions and the material power to produce, validate, and bind knowledge to multiracial, democratized power. (29)

Newly equipped with institutional homes in academe and access to material and intellectual resources, ethnic and indigenous studies enjoyed unprecedented visibility for newly formed academic fields, the capacity to produce scholarship on literary and cultural renaissances across fields of ethnic and indigenous literatures, and courses in which to teach those texts. In writers such as Maxine Hong Kingston, Leslie Marmon Silko, N. Scott Momaday, James Welch, Rudofo Anaya, Toni Morrison, Alice Walker, and other now-anthologized authors, students and readers of color and in indigenous communities could see familiar representations in mainstream cultural productions and on classroom syllabi.

Importantly, as a result of this activism, increased interest in what Anne Cheng terms "submerged" histories and fiction, and institutional support, scholars have been able to recover and to make visible the cultural work people of color and indigenous people in North America had been producing under white supremacy for centuries (143). Recovery efforts have brought previously forgotten, obscured, or marginalized figures and writings to readers' and scholars' attention. Interrogating critical and archival absences, scholars have demanded that these texts and voices be seen and heard.[10] Scholars have done and continue to do important work to demonstrate that women, LGBTQ+ individuals, American Indians, and people of color have continuously contributed intellectually and creatively for the duration of US history, as well as before Europeans entered the Western hemisphere. Committed and principled work during the activist decades and the subsequent institutionalization of ethnic studies and ethnic literatures expanded opportunities for

---

10. A famous example is Alice Walker's resuscitation of Zora Neale Hurston's literary prominence in the 1970s. Other now-canonical examples of literary recovery include works by John M. Oskison, Lynn Riggs, Todd Downing, William Apess, Samson Occom, Jane Johnston Schoolcraft, Jovita González, Josefina Niggli, María Ruiz de Burton, Jane Edna Hunter, John Okada, Younghill Kang, and Winnifred and Edith Eaton, to name only a few.

visibility and voice for indigenous writers and critics and writers and critics of color.

Just as the heyday of postmodernism in the US coincided with the rise of civil rights activism, the decline of postmodernism in the 1980s and '90s was accompanied by the mainstreaming of US liberal multiculturalism, which in celebrating diversity effected a "flattening of otherness into otherness-as-the-same" (Chuh 18). David Palumbo-Liu acknowledges the reasoning, espoused by Michael Omi and Howard Winant, that "multiculturalism was engendered as a reaction to and an accommodation of social activism in the 1960s and 1970s," but also ties the movement to "significant changes in material life in the post-Fordist age," which translated cultural difference into marketable commodities, or what Sylvia Rodríguez names the "commodification of subjectivity" (Palumbo-Liu "Introduction" 7, 5; Rodríguez 105). The same chronology that saw the rise and fall of "high postmodernism," in other words, also saw the rise of social movements and their attendant cultural and institutional changes, which brought increased attention, access, and rights to marginalized Americans before sliding into a multiculturalism in which, since everyone is an "other," political and social demands are muted while particular forms of Otherness are desired and commodified.

I map these two trajectories—civil rights and literary histories—onto one another as a partial explanation for the position of contemporary ethnic and indigenous American fiction, threatened by postmodernism's challenge to literary authority but celebrated by multiculturalism as commodified artifacts of cultural difference.[11] The institutionalization of ethnic studies enabled urgent and still-incomplete projects of literary, intellectual, and critical representations of marginalized US populations, making possible the sustainment and expansion of cultural and intellectual production by groups historically excluded from the academy. However, as the nation moved into a period of what Melamed terms "liberal multiculturalism" in the 1980s and 1990s, universities contributed to national projects of producing "sanctioned knowledges" about race, ethnicity, and indigeneity that flattened difference and spawned depoliticized, mainstreamed forms of visibility for marginalized populations (33). "Liberal multiculturalism," Melamed writes, "socialized whites to see themselves as good antiracists by virtue of their antiracist feeling

---

11. Elias also points to this simultaneity. Ramón Saldívar goes one step further to suggest, "Rather than seeing the rise of postmodernism and ethnic literature in the postwar era as two distinct and unrelated phenomena, viewing both within the domain of a shared aesthetic matrix allows us to see how postmodern and ethnic fiction were shaped by the same institutional histories and practices of creativity" ("The Second Elevation" 4). See also Norma Alarcón and Min Hyoung Song.

and desire for diversity, even as whites continued to accrue unearned benefits from material and social arrangements that favored them" (37). At the same time, "It instituted upon racialized students the capacity to get representation as hyphenated Americans (African-American, Asian-American, and so on) under terms requiring the acceptance of literary multiculturalism as authentic and representative of racialized communities" (Melamed 38). So long as the US contends with its racial diversity on a representational register through official narratives of antiracism, according to the logic of liberal multiculturalism, the material conditions of ongoing white supremacist policies can be overlooked.

The lasting effects of multiculturalism's representational contract continue to influence readers and scholars of ethnic and indigenous literatures. As Cheng explains, despite modernism's and postmodernism's "assault on ideological narratives and the certitude of historical narration," ethnic literature remains mired in popular discussions of representation and authenticity; ethnic literatures are understood as "seemingly transparent vehicles of authentic otherness" (Cheng 150, Chuh 19). The result, as scholars have argued, is that fiction by nonwhite authors is often reviewed in popular media in terms of "authenticity," subject to ethnographic imperatives, routinely held to higher standards of truthfulness, and understood as a way to "know and see the 'other' through reading" (Cheng 150).[12] The disconnect between representation and material reality was not a flaw in liberal multiculturalism's ideology, Melamed argues, but a feature:

> Because multicultural literature was presumed to be authentic, intimate, and representative, white students with minimal knowledge of or contact with racialized communities could nonetheless presume enough familiarity to legitimate their managerial-class position. The capacity of books (and other cultural commodities) to stand in for people was useful considering the gap between the commitment of colleges and universities to diversity and the general decline in African American enrollment. (37)[13]

---

12. "Ethnographic imperative" is Yoonmee Chang's term (7). To be clear, responsible scholarly engagement with literary production by writers of color, black writers, and indigenous writers has jettisoned discourses of authenticity as a distraction from more pressing political concerns; the preoccupation remains, however, elsewhere in publishing economies.

13. Melamed's characterization of liberal multicultural treatment of literature is instructive: "The protocols that liberal-multicultural antiracism defined for multicultural literature can be summarized as follows: (1) As with race novels, liberal multiculturalism identified literature as a means for information retrieval. However, whereas the identity of the author of race novels was secondary for racial liberalism, for liberal multiculturalism the author's racialized identity was of utmost importance because information retrieval for liberal multiculturalism was tied to

Access to multicultural texts, then, rendered contact with the material existence of living people of color and indigenous people unnecessary for white audiences.

Well-meaning academic audiences sensitive to the importance of historical context are not blameless in tasking ethnic fiction with cultural representation, either. David Eng explains: "Since the establishment of ethnic studies in the late 1960s as a political movement as well as a scholarly endeavor, the ethnic literary text in the US has often been said to function as a proxy for history. This has placed particular pressure and urgency on the literary to perform what is 'missing' in history and to represent otherwise unrepresentable communities" (64–65). Faced with gaps in historical and literary records for a variety of reasons—colonial violence, administrative indifference, systemic racism, theft, boarding schools, physical trauma, and language eradication, to name only a few—ethnic studies scholars and scholars working with literature by authors from historically marginalized populations understandably look to literature as a potential avenue for imagining more comprehensive historical and cultural records. However, certain responses to demands for visibility and representation can foreclose other approaches to historical, critical, and literary gaps. Recovery projects share in what Cheng terms a "documentary desire," which assumes inclusion into the historical record or canon to be beneficial and reparative (226n8). Though it comes from a different place, academic documentary desire shares with multiculturalism the desire for texts to represent, and to make whole, fragmented histories.

Unlike earlier generations of indigenous writers and writers of color for whom the struggle for civil rights are memory rather than history,[14] younger writers such as the authors in the following chapters came of age in, or in the wake of, multiculturalism's very different relationship to racial, ethnic, and indigenous visibility. Amy Tang contextualizes her study of form in Asian American literature in "the paradoxical conditions of ethnic literary production at the turn of the twenty-first century" (1). In a characterization worth

---

ideologemes of *representativeness, authenticity,* and *gaining voice*. (2) Literature was to testify to and teach about the race-differentiated history and present of the American experience, multiculturally developed. The story was to stay within the bounds of a master narrative about the civil rights movement that described the triumph of formerly oppressed minorities (symbolically African Americans) in defeating racism and gaining individual fulfillment and group dignity through full inclusion in American democracy. (3) A work of multicultural literature was understood to be an example of the value of different racialized cultures and a commodified form of racialized cultural property. The idea of culture as property owned by people of color functioned within a consumer economy in which antiracism could be expressed by a desire for diversity, which consuming racialized cultural property presumptively fulfilled" (36–37).

14. Here I draw on Saldívar's language, which I discuss further below ("Historical Fantasy" 596n1).

quoting at length, Tang describes the fraught representational environment into which contemporary writers of color enter. We are in, she writes:

> a historical moment in which the widespread institutionalization of multiculturalism means that ethnic voices are now solicited and celebrated in unprecedented ways, even as these new articulations have become the site of their commodification and biopolitical management. If earlier forms of ethnic writing once focused on the promise of visibility and inclusion, today's ethnic writer confronts a scene in which visibility and inclusion form the very modes through which racial minorities in the United States are institutionally managed; a scene in which ethnic literature is now used to legitimate, as much as challenge, dominant institutions; and a scene in which racial protest itself, far from contesting hegemonic forms of power, must be understood as already firmly inscribed within them. (1)

This paradox—the representational contract drawn up by multiculturalism—is one of several interrelated binds contemporary writers face. Desired and sought after, but only in permissible, palatable representations, US writers of color and indigenous writers produce art in a nation in which "everyone is antiracist, and yet oppression is banal and ubiquitous" (Melamed 49). In an ecosystem of paradoxes, the turn to narrative privacy—stories about the stories authors don't tell—in the face of the incomplete project of representation is less of a surprise. The formal imagining of privacy should not be understood as antirepresentational—these writers publish their texts, after all—but rather as a move away from the false representational opportunities afforded by the multicultural environment in which this generation of writers came of age.

Because of these dramatic shifts in visibility for people of color and indigenous people over the last half century, and because I understand narrative privacy as increasingly widespread among young writers writing post-9/11, the focal authors in this study share a generational bond. In what I understand as an emerging trend in the field, Ramón Saldívar uses a similar methodology in his recent publications by focusing on post-civil rights authors. He explains, "For this generation of writers, born for the most part in the 1960s and 1970s, the heroic era of the fight for civil rights is not a memory but a matter of history" ("Historical Fantasy" 596n1). Min Hyoung Song similarly organizes his study on contemporary Asian American literature along generational lines, focusing on "a generation of writers who have largely been born since the mid-1960s and are in the process of making a substantial mark on American literature" (8). Song marks generation not only by civil rights movements, but also by the specific context of the 1965 Immigration and Nationality Act, which opened the US border to Asian immigrants after nearly a century of racialized exclusion (31). My aim in focusing on a younger generation of writers, born since the mid-1960s, is twofold: I hope to increase critical attention devoted to newer, often understudied writers, and I wish to highlight the specific contributions—political and formal—of writers who have matured in a different era of racialized visibility than their predecessors who contributed to the important work of civil rights. This generation's historical and social position in a newly transformed global order that normalizes the erosion of privacy uniquely positions them to produce theoretical tools that help illuminate their literary antecedents and contemporaries as well as our present political moment.

In turning their attention to the political potential of privacy in narrative, these young writers theorize reading strategies through literary form. Extending Cheng's understanding of Asian American literature as theory to ethnic and indigenous literatures, I argue over the course of this volume that narrative privacy is at once a specific formal pattern across fields of literature uniquely prevalent in post-9/11 fiction and—more importantly—a broadly transportable theoretical lens for deliberately examining silence, invisibility, and refusal across literary genres and periods (19). As a theoretical lens, narrative privacy is contextual and subjective rather than prescriptive; readers and scholars experience varied and uneven relationships to visibility, privacy, power, and access as a result of their positionalities, experiences, and life circumstances. Necessarily, then, examining textual silences and resistance to readerly access is an equally varied and uneven process. The writers I examine throughout this volume explicitly and self-referentially draw attention to readers' relationships to their characters and narratives, their metanarratives serving as pedagogical stages for examining the limits of fictive readers' access to characters' lives, even as they extend narrative privacy's critique beyond the page. For instance, in an interview, David Treuer describes his decision not to translate Ojibwe dialogue in his novels as a means of making non-Ojibwe speakers work harder to earn access to his characters (Kirwan 17). Plascencia's explicit implication of whiteness in the colonial processes he critiques indicts white US readers in the social and economic inequalities that self-referentially structure his novel. Viet Thanh Nguyen explicitly frames *The Sympathizer* (2015) as a dialogue between two Vietnamese men, a framing he emphasizes in speaking engagements and interviews as deliberately privileging diasporic Vietnamese audiences (Gross). While the articulations and realizations of narrative privacy throughout these metafictions are necessarily context-, experience-, and subject-specific, as well as contingent on readers' relationships to the communities that animate the narrative, their critical investments remain constant: how might we more closely and deliberately examine the uneven power dynamics of visibility, privacy, and access in literature, literary studies, and the world in which we live? In confining my readings in this volume to post-9/11, self-referential, pedagogical models of narrative privacy, I hope to more fully illuminate and characterize the theoretical lens these writers, read collectively, produce. As a transportable theoretical lens, however, narrative privacy works as a reading methodology through which we might understand earlier texts and those bodies and genres of literature that fall outside the scope of this book.

For instance, a canonical and haunting example of silence familiar to many scholars takes the form of the young, unnamed Chinese girl Kingston's first person narrator abuses in "A Song for a Barbarian Reed Pipe," the final section of *The Woman Warrior* (1976). Capable of speech, as she reads aloud in class when compelled, the young girl nevertheless moves through school and the playground without speaking. The small glimpse readers have of the girl's voice, filtered as it is through the narrator who rejects her schoolmate's insistence on silence, does not reveal duress; in describing the girl's voice as she "whisper-read" aloud in class, the narrator observes, "I heard no anger or tension" (173). Not obviously rendered mute for physical or traumatic reasons, the girl has the capacity to speak, but chooses not to. The narrator's own growing anger focuses less on the girl's silence than her choice not to talk, an anger that manifests violently one day after school when the girls are alone in the bathroom. Through physical intimidation, the narrator tries to force the girl to speak: "'You're going to talk,' I said, my voice steady and normal, as it is when talking to the familiar, the weak, and the small. 'I am going to make you talk, you sissy-girl'" (175). Violently squeezing and pulling on the girl until she was afraid she would pull off her delicate skin, the narrator describes the physical and emotional toll of her efforts. "I was getting dizzy from the air I was gulping," she recounts, "Her sobs and my sobs were bouncing wildly off the tile, sometimes together, sometimes alternating. 'I don't understand why you won't say just one word,' I cried, clenching my teeth. My knees were shaking, and I hung on to her hair to stand up" (181). The narrator's violent attempt to violate her peer's silence ends in failure and takes a lasting toll on her body, as she spends the following year and a half in bed with a "mysterious illness" (182).

In a book that opens with an imperative to silence—"You must not tell anyone"—only to immediately elaborate the very secret the narrator was supposed to keep,[15] the violent assault on silence in the bathroom interrupts the narrative's general progression "from silence to voice" (Kingston 1, Cheung 79). Unlike the imposed, powerfully coded forms of silence the narrator inherits from her mother's stories,[16] the classmate's assertion of silence exists in the text as a presence, rather than an absence, and persists despite the narrator's fervent efforts. Reading the scene through a lens of narrative privacy privileges the classmate's "opaqueness" as an assertion of agency and disrupts narratives that normalize voice as inherently progressive for women of color (Minh-ha 48). Literalizing the at-times violent struggle between speech and silence within contexts of historical erasure, feminine policing, and the complicated power relations between two young Chinese American schoolgirls in a white supremacist, patriarchal community, the bathroom scene illuminates the manner in which demands for representation and voice can be, at times, violent and coercive rather than progressive and liberating.[17] Narrative privacy asks why the narrator insists on penetrating her classmate's silence and highlights the aggression and frustration that accompanies refusal of access, layering important contexts of silence onto *The Woman Warrior*'s canonical—and therefore highly visible—treatment of silence and secrecy.

Linking contemporary discourses about privacy and surveillance with their scholarly antecedents and much longer colonial histories in the US, *The Politics of Privacy* explores how threads of privacy, surveillance, and repre-

---

15. In an interview with Shelley Fisher Fishkin, Kingston explains her evolution on publishing family secrets: "My mother says, 'Don't tell what I am about to tell you,' and I think, 'Well, I'm not going to "tell," I'm just going to write.' . . . But more seriously, what I have told myself was that I will write those stories because I have to, and there's no real way of stopping that, but I won't publish. And that freed me. It made me feel all right to write whatever way I pleased. And then as the years went by and I wrote more and more perfectly, and I wrote with more and more understanding, then I saw that I really needed to publish, and it was all right to publish" (785).

16. An obvious foil to the silent girl is the silenced aunt whose story opens *The Woman Warrior*. King-Kok Cheung writes, "Since the narrator's father explicitly forbids any mention of the aunt and the mother furnishes only the bare facts, Maxine [the narrator] is free to construct variant versions of the aunt's story. Critics have credited Kingston with giving the aunt subjectivity through these versions. But in fact, her aunt—who could not possibly inhabit all these versions—remains inescapably silent" (84–85). Stella Bolaki similarly contends with the epistemically violent silencing of the narrator's aunt, arguing that despite the book's revisioning of the aunt's story, "the aunt is left mute; she is the 'subaltern' who cannot represent herself and therefore has to be represented by the narrator, who becomes the privileged interpreter of her story" (44). The silent girl, on the other hand, chooses speechlessness of her own volition, protecting her story from audiences and the interpretation of the narrator's representation.

17. Jill M. Parrott makes a similar observation: "This power differential emphasizes that important difference between that which is purposefully silent and that which is maliciously silenced; further, this incident shows how sometimes the taking of silence (as Maxine attempts) can also be aggressively enacted" (383).

sentation entangle the literary texts at its core in growing interdisciplinary fields of visibility studies, surveillance studies, and post-9/11 studies. As the following chapters demonstrate, these fields overlap considerably when considering race, ethnicity, and indigeneity since visibility for people of color and indigenous people very often entails surveillance, particularly post-9/11: by the state, by ethnographers, by audiences, or, as borne out in current events, by bystanders with cell phones who either record violence or summon law enforcement.[18] While the political and social background has shifted dramatically in the past two decades, scholars working on silence and invisibility have long theorized the political costs of representation, visibility, and historical recovery.[19] Despite the richness and urgency of post-9/11 literary studies, however, connections between existing scholarship and literary treatments of privacy in post-9/11 contexts remain undertheorized. In linking narrative form with visibility and surveillance studies, *The Politics of Privacy* joins a small but growing body of literary criticism on how the political and social aftershocks of 9/11 have shaped knowledge production in form and content.[20]

---

18. In the past few years, for example, several book-length studies have considered racial visibility and its critical connections to the present through surveillance. *Feminist Surveillance Studies* (2015), edited by Rachel E. Dubrofsky and Shoshana Amielle Magnet, offers multidisciplinary critical approaches to the effect of surveillance on women and people of color, specifically. Simone Browne's *Dark Matters: On the Surveillance of Blackness* (2015) tracks the visibility of African American bodies through US history, an approach similar to Kimberly Juanita Brown's *The Repeating Body: Slavery's Visual Resonance in the Contemporary* (2015), a study of visual and literary texts. Both texts focus exclusively on African American visibility across disciplines. Kumarini Silva's *Brown Threat: Identification in the Security State* (2016), explores political surveillance of "brown" subjects, a population defined by post-9/11 ideologies and politics of deviance. Eleanor Ty's *The Politics of the Visible in Asian American Narratives* (2004) and Monica Chiu's *Scrutinized! Surveillance in Asian North American Fiction* (2014) bridge Asian North American fiction and visibility studies.

19. For example, Lisa Lowe, David Eng, Anne Anlin Cheng, King-Kok Cheung, Laura Mulvey, RosaMaria Chacon, Gerald Vizenor, Naomi Rand, and Vicente Mora consider myriad ways into literary silences and invisibility. Nicholas Mirzoeff, perhaps the most widely read visibility studies scholar, offers several tomes such as *How to See the World* (2016) and *The Right to Look: A Counterhistory of Visuality* (2011), theorizing (in)visibility across media. Relatedly, literary secrecy enjoys a history of critical attention in, for example, Frank Kermode's *The Genesis of Secrecy: On the Interpretation of Narrative* (1979), Wendy Brown's essay "Freedom's Silences" in *Edgework* (2005), Margaret Reid's *Cultural Secrets as Narrative Form: Storytelling in Nineteenth-Century America* (2004) and, especially, Leslie Lewis's *Telling Narratives: Secrets in African American Literature* (2008). D. A. Miller's *The Novel and the Police* (1988) offers an early approach to surveillance in Victorian literature, which, as he observes, is frequently saturated with police presence.

20. In addition to texts explicitly responding to 9/11 and, in recent years, book-length critical treatments of 9/11 literatures, writers and critics have turned their attention to the world *after* 9/11 and the subsequent Global War on Terror. Anthologies of fiction such as *Watchlist: 32 Stories by Persons of Interest* (2016), edited by Bryan Hurt, suggest an explicit move by writ-

In other disciplines, such as political science and law, as well as in popular discourse and public policy, however, privacy is an increasingly urgent locus of study. The twenty-first century rise of the internet, compounded by the expansion of post-9/11 surveillance states, has increased historical concerns over privacy, not only for people of color. Legal rulings in Europe have established individuals' "Right to be Forgotten," or right to have their records expunged from internet search engines, a privilege that may soon extend to the US ("Factsheet"; Toobin). As of spring 2018, when the European Union General Data Protection Regulation (GDPR) went into effect, EU members—as well as patrons of international businesses who comply with EU standards—enjoy more control over their personally identifiable data than previously required. GDPR baseline standards require consent for individual data processing, safer transfers of data, individual rights to privacy, and means of official recourse, among other provisions (Lord).[21]

Even when documentation is democratized and disseminated, involving only information publicly provided by individuals on a social media platform rather than exclusively controlled by the state, privacy is a primary concern. When Twitter published and indexed their entire cache of public tweets in 2014, for example, the media immediately identified the company's actions as a breach of privacy and offered users instructions for deleting their earlier—and potentially embarrassing or outdated—tweets (Zhuang). Privacy concerns about social media are only compounded, as evidenced by the 2016 US presidential election and its aftermath, when political organs access and manipulate social media metadata. As Viktor Mayer-Schönberger, "one of the intellectual godfathers of the right to be forgotten," argues in his aptly titled study of society's changing relationship to documentation in the twenty-first

---

ers toward issues of visibility and surveillance in a post-9/11 world. Georgiana Banita's *Plotting Justice: Narrative Ethics and Literary Culture After 9/11* (2012) takes up such work critically by connecting post-9/11 politics to contemporary British and American ethics and, to a lesser degree, literary form. Similarly, *Narrating 9/11: Fantasies of State, Security, and Terrorism* (2015), edited by John N. Duvall and Robert Marzec, collects essays on literary treatments of the lasting effects of national trauma after 9/11.

21. According to the official EU GDPR website, individuals have the rights to "**information** about the processing of your personal data; **obtain access to** the personal data held about you; ask for incorrect, inaccurate or incomplete personal data to be **corrected**; request that personal **data be erased** when it's no longer needed or if processing it is unlawful; **object** to the processing of your personal data for marketing purposes or on grounds relating to your particular situation; request the **restriction** of the processing of your personal data in specific cases; receive your personal data in a machine-readable format and send it to another controller ('**data portability**'); request that decisions based on **automated processing** concerning you or significantly affecting you and based on your personal data are made by natural persons, not only by computers. You also have the right in this case to express your point of view and to contest the decision" (European Commission).

century, *Delete: The Virtue of Forgetting in the Digital Age* (2009), the potential misuse by a surveillance state or totalitarian government of any comprehensive, permanently recorded cache of information on the internet is clear (Toobin). Old arrest records, misguided tweets, unflattering pictures: an overwhelming anxiety of our present historical moment is that these traces of ourselves we (and others) leave online—decontextualized and manipulable—will come to stand in for who we are. The writers under consideration in this book engage with these contemporary issues of privacy, but they do so with an eye on a much longer history of the perils of documentation.

In joining scholarly initiatives on privacy, *The Politics of Privacy* also draws on recent conversations in critical race narratology that help articulate how race, ethnicity, and indigeneity vitally shape narratological tools. In the introduction to *Narrative, Race, and Ethnicity in the United States* (2017), the first edited anthology of critical race narratology, James J. Donahue outlines the historical whiteness of narrative theory: "only recently have there been attempts not merely to discuss issues of race and ethnicity *in* narratives (print, film, and television), but to explore how race and ethnicity might force us to reconsider what we know about the *nature of* narrative" (3).[22] The collection, edited by Donahue, Jennifer Ann Ho, and Shaun Morgan, joins a small body of recent scholarship aiming to reimagine narrative theory with race and ethnicity at its core.[23]

The historical relationship between narrative studies and ethnic studies—one Sue Kim characterizes as "fitful, even contentious"—has been defined by the fields' different objectives and politics (13). Speaking specifically of Asian American literary studies' relationship with narratology, Kim explains, "The concerns of these two fields have often been opposed, implicitly and explicitly. Asian American literary criticism is interpretive, contextualist, extrinsic, and praxis-oriented; narrative theory is concerned with articulating a formal poetics and is formalist, intrinsic, and abstract" (15).[24] Formalist attention to

22. Donahue makes clear, however, that some of the most influential scholars in the field, including James Phelan and Frederick Luis Aldama, work to include narratives by people of color in their studies.

23. "A critical race narratology," clarifies Donahue, "must be more than the application of existing tools to the study of race and ethnicity" (3–4). Two recent examples of critical narratology are Sue Kim's special issue of *JNT: Journal of Narrative Theory* (2012) and Amy Tang's *Repetition and Race: Asian American Literature After Multiculturalism* (2016).

24. Kim offers a useful, if lengthier, characterization of the fields' distinctions: "While classical narratology has been charged with universalizing insights derived from narratives by a handful of canonical, mostly European and/or American, writers (Austen, Proust, Fielding, James), Asian Americanist literary criticism emphasizes the specificity and historicity of every subject, community, and narrative, focusing particularly on texts by Asian American writers" (13–14). She continues, "Narratology, despite the emergence of contextualist narrative theories

narrative structure, when contrasted with the contextualist approaches central to the study of ethnic literatures, appears depoliticized and therefore of a kind with the flattening scholarship emerging from liberal multiculturalist schools of thought. Ethnic literary studies affirm that "race, history, and politics are inextricable from literature," and that such contextualization forms the backbone of responsible, progressive scholarship (13).

This volume joins scholars such as Kim, Tang, and the writers included in *Narrative, Race, and Ethnicity in the United States,* as well as the numerous scholars pursuing nation-specific readings of American Indian literatures,[25] to illuminate the ways in which writers of color and indigenous writers inject politics, race, ethnicity, and indigeneity into the very form of their narratives. As Ho makes clear in the conclusion to *Narrative, Race, and Ethnicity in the United States,* "Narratives are constructions, fabrications that develop from their authors' imaginations. Race is a construction, a fabrication of society based on the societal will to believe that the human body can be catalogued and differentiated by phenotypic markers" (208). She continues, "these various fabrications both reflect and shape our sense of reality; thus it matters who creates these fabrications, who reads and interprets, and the ethical judgments that are made" (209). In reading for the politics of form—specifically the political utility of evasive forms, or formal assertions of privacy—my hope is in the following chapters to not only demonstrate, as Ho asserts, "There is much that critical race theory and narratology can do together," but also that sustained critical attention to the worldmaking at the center of narrative studies can be a powerful tool for our understanding of the worlds we make outside of literary texts (217).

To highlight specific narrative features of this worldmaking and contend with my own vulnerability to the texts' critiques of readers, scholars, and authors, my close readings in the following chapters tend toward the literal. That is, even as I recognize that characters are fictional and not real people, I take the narrative bait and participate in these fictions' formal projects. As Ho reminds scholars, narrative studies can be politically and socially productive because, after all, "Narratives, especially fictional narratives, exist because authors (implied and flesh-and-blood) construct these worlds and populate

---

as well as the actual heteroegeneity of its pioneers, has historically been seen as a structuralist enterprise seeking to map out the elements of narratives across historical contexts; narratology seeks a poetics or grammar of narrative functions. In contrast, Asian American literary studies has always maintained that race, history, and politics are inextricable from literature" (13).

25. Although not explicitly in conversation with narratologists, I understand scholars of American Indian literature who prioritize nation- or tribal-specific readings of texts as very much engaged with the connections that have always existed between specific indigenous knowledges and narrative form.

them with characters who are imaginative creations" (209). Participation in such constructions means embodying the perspective the narrative formally ascribes to the reader, which in turn entails reading vulnerably by opening myself up to the texts' critiques. I recognize that the fictions' audiences experience the narratives—and attendant critiques—variously, depending on multiple factors including their roles as readers, scholars, and authors, but especially their relationships to citizenship, race, ethnicity, and indigeneity. As a formal lens rather than prescriptive reading, however, narrative privacy accounts for—even relies on—the varying refractions of individuals' diverse perspectives.

In reading the formal structures of the metafictions in these chapters as political projects, I hope, in some measure, to highlight the political efficacy of some narrative studies tools for scholars and readers of ethnic and indigenous literatures. Enmeshing analyses of form in thick historical and political contexts helps center race, ethnicity, indigeneity, nationality, and anticolonialism as not just the subject but also the means of literary production and study. The highly complex formal structures of the novels throughout these pages self-consciously invite close critical attention to the consequences narrative structures—not unlike the real-world structures of inequality and power they critique—have for characters, narrators, and implied authors in addition to their living authors and audiences. While I am principally committed to the political attention to form critical race narratology outlines rather than the adoption of specialized terminology, some narratological terms help provide practical distinctions for describing elements of multilayered texts investigating their own form. For example, diegesis names the "storyworld, the world created by the narration," which might be distinguished from the extradiegetic (the "real world" outside of the text, in which authors and readers live) and the metadiegetic, or stories embedded within the diegetic, or fictional, narrative (Abbott 231).[26] I define my use of narratological terms throughout my analyses, as relevant, and note more thorough sources on scholarly conversation surrounding the terminology. While not as explicitly narratological in nature as the chapters in *Narrative, Race, and Ethnicity in the United States*, *The Politics of Privacy* nevertheless aims to facilitate mutually beneficial dialogue between narrative studies and ethnic and indigenous literary studies,

26. In addition to Abbott, James Phelan's *Living to Tell About It: A Rhetoric and Ethic of Character Narration* (2005) and Mieke Bal's *Narratology: Introduction to the Theory of Narrative* (1985) provide excellent introductions to narrative studies, including the terminology I use here and throughout this volume. Catherine Belsey's *Critical Practice* (1980), Linda Hutcheon's *Poetics of Postmodernism* (1988), and Elizabeth Dipple's *The Unresolvable Plot* (1988) are also foundational texts. Jan Alber's *Unnatural Narratives* (2013) offers a more recent and specific entry into the formal gymnastics the novels throughout this volume undertake.

particularly in demonstrating the urgency of recognizing the politics of form in literature by writers of color and indigenous writers in the US.

From the start, *The Politics of Privacy* has been committed to working across fields of literature, including Native American, Latinx, and Asian American literatures, even as I acknowledge the risks associated with such breadth. Cross-field conversations can offer new insights and productive ways of thinking about the pressures and conditions common to various groups without presuming that those pressures and conditions are experienced uniformly between or even within communities. José Aranda identifies a "need for a more integrated literary history of literatures that historically developed in North America," and suggests scholars "can make transhistorical, transcultural comparative analysis as long as it is not reductive in formal and historical matters or politically naive about the power relations transacted between the dominant and marginal members of society" (73).[27] In other words, careful comparative scholarship is attentive to specific contexts and sensitive to the power differentials scholars have worked to identify as missing in multiculturalist—and many narrative studies—approaches to literature.

Indeed, working across fields of literature runs the risk of distracting—or even detracting—from the specific political, aesthetic, and historical investments that sustained, field-specific scholarship generates. For example, while I foreground Native US writers' political identities by distinguishing their indigeneity[28] from racial or ethnic classifications, the nature of this project makes difficult any sustained attention to indigenous sovereignty, a central focus of Native and Indigenous literary studies. In drawing attention to critical investments that thread through discrete fields, I aim to complement—not shift focus away from—the robust field-specific scholarship on which my project relies. Of course, such threading can only hope to be logical in its path, not comprehensive in scope, requiring enough overlap in texts' contexts to suitably situate and introduce texts' specific political projects. Working across fields of scholarship also poses interesting dilemmas in terms of audience; some of the scholarly and historical contexts I offer in the following chapters will be rehearsals of established conversations for specialists in some fields, while fresher for scholars in others. My hope in outlining the contexts I do,

---

27. I also heed Aranda's concern that following a comparative model "requires a degree of specialization, as well as intellectual breadth, largely unavailable in American universities today [and that] . . . for a viable comparative approach to thrive, scholars need synthesizing models of analysis that simultaneously call attention to differences in form, literary tradition, and political production" (73).

28. I use the terms indigenous, Native, and American Indian interchangeably throughout the text.

however, is to illuminate the interesting and productive resonances between fields' critical investments, even if terminologies or emphases differ.

Those critical resonances are the genesis and driving force of this project, which considers worthy of attention the ideas and relationships that weave a generation of writers from different racial, ethnic, and political backgrounds into conversation. The writers in the following chapters inhabit overlapping literary—and sometimes social—circles, blurb each other's forthcoming books, teach in the same MFA programs, read at the same events, and engage with one another publicly on social media. While the contexts and communities that inform their works vary widely, they often navigate and respond to the same historical and political moment in fascinatingly resonant, though certainly not identical, manners. In other words, they are in conversation in ways conventional academic fields sometimes obscure. *The Politics of Privacy* lends critical attention to the lived realities of today's literary ecologies.

One of the primary costs of working in multiple fields of literature is that the formal and historical criteria for inclusion in this volume are necessarily narrow; while the fiction in the following chapters respond to and stem from diverse contexts, they all emerge from the same historical and political moment in formally similar ways. All of the texts in this study are self-referential, allowing authors to engage with reading practices by writing readers—the readers of their texts, even—into their fiction. Self-referential fiction allows these authors to theorize how readers engage with their texts in what Donald C. Goellnicht terms a "pedagogical," rather than reactionary, way that contends with specific histories and circumstances, and in some cases, particular types of readers. By depicting specific readers and reading practices, the authors offer "pedagogical example[s] of the way a reader should approach and respond to ethnic literature/subjects: with a respect that does not demand knowledge, but rather keeps the reader open to other possibilities" (216). In doing so, they promote vulnerable reading practices in which readers do more than seek to extract readily available knowledge from willing informants. In her study of twentieth-century texts that resist interpretation, Doris Sommer explains that readers "who mistake a privileged center for the universe . . . need obstacles to notice the circumstances of conversation" (xii).[29] Greg Sarris

---

29. Sommer's *Proceed with Caution, When Engaged by Minority Writing in the Americas* (1999) is a case study of myriad ways writers of color resist or alienate readers through narrative. Sommer offers productive theorization of reading practices that include "the anticipation of strategic refusals," but she positions writers as reacting—often aggressively—to presumably white, educated, privileged readers by limiting or thwarting their access to narrative (xv). I understand the writers in this project not as reactionary, but as exploring through literary form ways of engaging with readers in more nuanced, self-conscious ways than Sommer's "rhetoric of particularism" allows.

writes of "cross-cultural" textual encounters: "the task is not to assimilate the text or any element of it to ourselves nor to assimilate ourselves to the text. It is not to reduce difference to sameness nor to exoticize or fetishize it. Rather, the task is to become aware of our tendencies to do any of these things" (92). The authors in this book decline to 'inform' but instead illuminate the political processes of visibility at work in ethnic and indigenous literatures and open a dialogue about reading strategies "that work to validate and respect the subjectivities of text and reader" (Sarris 92). The formal play of self-referential metafictions provides a pedagogical stage for these dialogues that is at once theoretical and deeply personal in its implication of reading audiences.

Written in the years after 9/11, the fictions in the following chapters are all products of a very specific political moment not only in terms of global order and surveillance states, but also with regard to the dramatic expansion of the internet in the twenty-first century. To facilitate responsibly contextualized discussion of specific historical contexts of racialized visibility in our contemporary moment, I have opted not to treat black or Arab American fiction in *The Politics of Privacy,* despite the rich potential of critical attention to privacy in each field. Wanting to extend critical inquiry across literary fields, but not so far that the scholarly conversation stalls, I measure the book's scope according to relative histories of visibility in the US. Black communities and individuals have experienced racial hyper-visibility for the duration black presence in North America. In contrast, Latinxs and Asian Americans, who have been in North America for centuries, and Native Americans, on the continent since time immemorial, have inhabited unstable and historically variable racialized positions outside the black/white binary (Ty 13). In the last several decades, however, Latinxs and Asian Americans have grown in population and visibility, becoming for many the face of an increasingly less-white America, while Native American political activism, including recent work at Standing Rock to resist the Dakota Access pipeline construction, has firmly asserted that Natives are not, as popular narratives contend, "safely dead and historically past" (Berkhofer 67). Furthermore, Native American, Latinx, and Asian American literatures all achieved mainstream visibility for the first time during the political activism of the 1960s and '70s and have continued to grow in number and variety.[30] Nevertheless, contemporary black literature provides rich material examples of narrative privacy; a broader version of this project would include, for example, Percival Everett and Kiese Laymon, both of whom consider racialized privacy and visibility in their metafictions, building on

---

30. Of course, Natives, Latinxs, and Asian Americans have been writing in America for much of the nation's history. My point here is to note the beginning of mainstream readerships for these literatures.

earlier works by Toni Morrison and, of course, Ralph Ellison's *Invisible Man* (1952), among others.

Inclusion of Arab American fiction faces a different challenge from that of black US literature: though the political and social aftermaths of 9/11 render the texts perhaps most suitable for analysis of visibility and privacy, the terrorist attacks and subsequent US invasions abroad have in many ways overdetermined discussions of visibility for Arab Americans in the twenty-first century relative to Natives, Latinxs, and Asian Americans.[31] In tracking the US's post-9/11 shift from understanding what she terms the "brown threat" narrative in terms of Latinx populations to Arab American, Muslim American, and South Asian American populations, among other groups, Kumarini Silva theorizes popular perceptions of "brownness" "both deeply historical and newly established" (19). She explains, "The 'new' brown shifted, groaned, expanded, and settled to include a metaphorical and somatic identity beyond Latino/as to an unidentifiable and amalgamated Global South/Middle Eastern brown that was rooted in discourses of terror. These browns were not, and are not, viewed as 'sleeping giants' or mass hordes washing up in 'tides'; instead, they are seen as carefully organized, disruptive networks that are a threat to American security, especially following the events of 2001" (7). While Arab American—and South Asian American, Muslim American, Iranian-American, and other "brown" US writers—are producing literatures[32] that richly reward reading through a lens of narrative privacy, responsibly analyzing the dynamic political, social, and literary terrains Silva describes would require a different historical scope from that which I offer in this volume, one that allows for higher resolution on the shifting paradigms of the last two decades, specifically. The texts that populate the following chapters, then, are certainly not the only or even the most fitting fictions for contending with visibility, privacy, and power in our post-9/11 world; my hope, however, is that they cohere enough in their political projects and historical scope to articulate concisely the potential of narrative privacy as a critical reading strategy broadly transportable to other eras and genres of literature and, among other fields, to black and Arab American literatures.

To demonstrate the historical and social breadth of the politics of visibility and the potential utility of reading through narrative privacy, the following chapters are organized by forms of institutional visibility. Following Mary Louise Pratt, the chapters might also be understood as organized according

---

31. Carol Fadda-Conrey's *Contemporary Arab-American Literature: Transnational Reconfigurations of Citizenship and Belonging* (2014) theorizes contemporary Arab American literary politics, opening an urgent and important conversation.

32. George Abraham's metapoetic "Against Consolidation," for instance, exemplifies the utility of narrative privacy for reading across not just fields but genres of literature.

to forms of institutional curiosity, ranging from the widely critiqued (ethnography, state surveillance) to the fraught but more frequently bilateral (commodity exchange) and potentially virtuous or at least educational (historical and literary). Put differently, *The Politics of Privacy* moves from immediately understandable assertions of privacy to the more unexpected, from the often-maligned to reading—the one act of curiosity that links all audiences. As a result, the chapters become increasingly more invested in vulnerable reading practices as the fictions at their core call into question our positions as readers and critics and, in the end, the critical viability of *The Politics of Privacy* altogether.

Chapter 1 opens *The Politics of Privacy*'s textual journey with one of the most widely critiqued forms of institutional visibility in ethnic literary studies: ethnography. Treuer, Nam Le, and Rigoberto González contend with expectations of authenticity and transparency in ethnic and American Indian literature by crafting spaces of narrative privacy in their fiction. Recalling historical legacies of compulsory ethnographic visibility, Treuer's *The Translation of Dr. Apelles* (2006) invites comparisons between ethnographic voyeurism and the gaze implicit in reading practices. In the final pages of the novel, the protagonist, Apelles, looks up at the reader, not only drawing attention to his audience's presence but also reversing the gaze implicit in the act of reading. Apelles is not a character–narrator who transparently relates the intimacies of his life or a "native informant" translating his culture, but a calculating storyteller who confronts his audience with his own fictionality. González's *Crossing Vines* (2003) and Le's "The Boat" (2008) similarly limit readers' access to characters to contest ethnographic imperatives in contemporary literature that position ethnic and American Indian authors in the role of native informants expected to offer readers intimate, privileged access to their personal spaces and community secrets. Treuer, González, and Le use narrative privacy to theorize reading practices that emphasize invention and politics—rather than transparency and authenticity—in fiction. In drawing attention to their stories' formal narrative structures, the authors critically consider their positions as fiction writers of color in a nation still deeply influenced by ethnographic legacies of access while newly interested in post-9/11 experiences of surveillance and privacy.

Chapter 2 takes up political surveillance after 9/11 as its organizing principle by attending to the formal relationships between narrative and the political surveillance of people of color and indigenous people in the US by bringing Plascencia's *The People of Paper* (2005) into conversation with Le's "Love and Honor and Pity and Pride and Compassion and Sacrifice," (2008) and Stephen Graham Jones's *The Bird Is Gone: A ~~Monograph~~ Manifesto* (2003). The three fictions consider various facets of state surveillance, ranging from surveillance on the US–Mexico border, in wartime Vietnam by the US Army, and on the Great Plains by the FBI. Plascencia and Le replicate political surveillance through literary form by crafting author–characters who exercise their privilege as mediators of stories, offering readers almost total access to their characters. For instance, in *The People of Paper*, Plascencia's characters decide that their author–narrator, Sal, has too much control over their lives. Sensing Saturn as an oppressive force looking down from the sky at the US–Mexico border, the characters wage a "war on omniscient narration (a.k.a. the war against the commodification of sadness)," elsewhere in the novel named a "war for volition" (218, 53). Le's author–character, named Nam, struggles with writing stories about the Vietnamese diaspora in the aftermaths of wartime surveillance by the US Army and Department of Defense. Both Plascencia's and Le's characters imagine unsympathetic audiences, going to great lengths to destroy their stories before they circulate as entertainment and expose their lives to readers. The chapter then turns to Jones's *The Bird Is Gone: A Monograph Manifesto*, a speculative history in which Native characters attempt to escape the scrutiny not only of anthropologists and the novel's readers, but also federal agents and the FBI. Jones articulates similar frustrations through literary form, but unlike Le and Plascencia, exercises authorial privilege to accommodate characters' various desires for privacy or representation. All three authors implicate fiction writers and audiences in the vexed relationships between commercial fiction, recognizable forms of colonialism, and political surveillance to question how commercial literature can contribute to political and economic equality for diasporic Asian, Latinx, and Native American communities.

If ethnography and state surveillance represent institutional forms of visibility almost universally critiqued in literary, indigenous, and ethnic studies, chapter 3's focus on commodified representations marks a shift to perhaps more difficult questions for readers and critics of commercial literature. The chapter comprises two parts. Part one reads Plascencia's *The People of Paper* and Le's short story, "Love and Honor," examined at length in chapter two, as metafictional meditations on works of fiction as ethnic commodities. In each story, characters identify and, to varying degrees, contest their authors' plans to sell their stories for profit. The frequent tension between characters' explicit desires to end their narratives and authors' decisions to publish their fiction for profit illuminates the difficult negotiations writers must make to responsibly narrate sensitive—even traumatic—stories in commercial fiction while respecting the privacy of lived experiences. Using the analyses of Plascencia and Le as a critical framework to theorize narrative privacy as a response to commodification of racial and ethnic difference, part two looks specifically at how contemporary writers assert narrative privacy in their engagement with the politics of Hollywood's optics and hyper-commercialization. Nguyen's take on *Apocalypse Now* in *The Sympathizer* interrogates Hollywood's treatment of race as spectacle. It does so by extending Plascencia's and Le's critiques of commodified exposure, suggesting that the formal technique of narrative privacy works to diminish the appropriative power of commodification.

Chapter 4 closes the volume with attention to forms of institutional visibility most defensible to readers and critics: textual and literary documentation. The chapter considers authors who employ narrative privacy to write responsibly about characters for whom textual inclusion may have been undesirable. Monique Truong crafts Bình, the protagonist and narrator of *The Book of Salt* (2003), from a marginal account in historical archives—the brief mention of Gertrude Stein and Alice Toklas's "Indochinese cook" in *The Alice B. Toklas Cook Book* (1984)—then assigns agency to Bình's almost complete absence from historical and literary records. Using *The Book of Salt* as a lens through which to reflect on texts analyzed in earlier chapters, chapter 4 considers how contemporary writers complement conventional recovery scholarship that seeks to identify and fill gaps in textual records by using narrative privacy to entertain the possibility of reading such gaps as spaces of historical and literary agency. Retrospectively threading together the previous chapters, chapter 4 considers how narrative privacy formally exposes the limits of literary studies' ability to read particular stories without reinforcing the historical authority of written narrative and the marginality of other forms of knowledge. The conclusion pivots away from written texts to test the utility of narrative privacy for lived experiences outside of fiction.

The authors I consider in this book do not abandon fiction as an artistic tool for crossing social boundaries and achieving political goals, but express anxiety over the way authors create, publishers circulate, and readers consume fiction without attendant progress toward political and economic equality. They link historical patterns of ethnic visibility with newly mainstreamed discourses of personal and communal privacy circulating in the US after 9/11 to respond to the racial and economic politics of our contemporary historical moment, particularly as it informs their responsibilities as fiction writers and our roles as reading audiences.

CHAPTER 1

Ethnographic Surveillance and the Limits of Looking

As a method of anthropological inquiry predicated on observing and describing foreign cultures to institutional authorities, ethnography is a historically fraught form of compulsory and often highly influential visibility for people of color in the United States.[1] From the early amateur and semiprofessional forms produced by colonial explorers, missionaries, and traders to the later scientific, academically disciplined incarnations and today's more self-reflexive, politically aware studies, ethnographic accounts have long shaped public knowledge and policies about people of color and indigenous peoples in the United States.[2] If, as Linda Tuhiwai Smith argues, "Imperialism and colonialism are

---

1. My close readings of *The Translation of Dr. Apelles* in the context of ethnographic inquiry were first published in "The Politics of Make-Believe: Dissimulation and Reciprocity in David Treuer's The Translation of Dr. Apelles," *Studies in American Indian Literatures*, vol. 26, no. 4, 2014, published by the University of Nebraska Press. My articulation of "narrative privacy" and close readings of *Crossing Vines* and "The Boat" were first published in "Narrative Privacy: Evading Ethnographic Surveillance in Fiction by Sherman Alexie, Rigoberto González, and Nam Le," *Multi-Ethnic Literatures of the United States*, vol. 42, no. 2, 2017.

2. George Marcus and Michael Fischer provide a conventional definition of ethnographic practice: "Ethnography is a research process in which the anthropologist closely observes, records, and engages in the daily life of another culture—an experience labeled as the fieldwork method—and then writes accounts of this culture, emphasizing descriptive detail. These accounts are the primary form in which fieldwork procedures, the other culture, and the ethnographer's personal and theoretical reflections are accessible to professionals and other readerships" (18).

the specific formations through which the West came to 'see,' to 'name,' and to 'know' indigenous communities," ethnography has been an authoritative meaning-making mechanism that has enabled this colonial seeing, naming, and knowing (63).[3] Moreover, classical anthropology long insisted on unilateral visibility by dividing the world "in the form of us and them, of viewing subject and viewed object" (Chow 180). Objectified and assumed to be knowable and available to researchers, peoples subjected to ethnographic study have historically experienced a form of compulsory visibility that compromises personal and communal understandings of privacy and makes them more vulnerable to dramatic social and political change. Contemporary practices of looking for differences between groups of people, objectifying Otherness, and assuming the privilege of observing other cultures are learned behaviors with colonial, ethnographic genealogies. The continued perpetuation of these practices reinforces uneven power relations between powerful institutions, such as governments, universities, and publishing houses, and the nation's marginalized populations.

Ethnographic inquiry continues to inform the way authors and publishers produce and audiences—including reviewers and literary critics—consume contemporary US literatures. Under ethnographic surveillance, people of color and indigenous people have historically had little choice about their own visibility to, for example, dominant governmental, academic, and religious institutions. In her analysis of imperial travel writing, Mary Louise Pratt argues that an "ideology that construes seeing as inherently passive and curiosity as innocent cannot be sustained" (67). Similarly to Pratt, the authors under consideration in this chapter direct readers' attention to how views of and curiosity about ethnic and indigenous characters are implicated in colonial ways of knowing and seeing the Other; they question, in other words, the innocence of reading. The texts in this chapter explore how storytelling by Native, Asian American, and Latinx authors for reading audiences—in the context of published fiction—still contends with a legacy of colonial power relations between "native informants" and their audiences.[4] By explicitly drawing attention to the ways they limit readers' access to characters' lives, the authors in this chap-

---

3. Audra Simpson writes, "To speak of indigeneity is to speak of colonialism and anthropology, as these are means through which indigenous people have been known and sometimes are still known" ("On Ethnographic Refusal" 67). Colonial ethnographies in North America have focused largely on indigenous populations, but not exclusively. Ethnographic portraits and folklore studies are similarly the means through which Asian Americans, African Americans, and Latinxs have been known and sometimes are still known.

4. The legacy deeply inflects relations between writers, audiences, and texts. For example, Paula Gunn Allen rather famously censured Leslie Marmon Silko for revealing too much about Pueblo traditions in *Ceremony*.

ter challenge the role of native informant so often expected of indigenous and nonwhite authors by US audiences, instead carving spaces of narrative privacy in acts akin to what Audra Simpson terms "staking limits" ("On Ethnographic Refusal" 70). In doing so, David Treuer, Rigoberto González, and Nam Le theorize issues of access and visibility. They also critically consider their positions as fiction writers of color in a nation still deeply influenced by ethnographic legacies of visibility, surveillance, and privacy while newly interested in post-9/11 anxieties about surveillance and compromised privacy for broader swaths of its citizenry.

Treuer's *The Translation of Dr. Apelles* (2006) anchors the chapter and raises questions of privilege and access by considering the direct correlation between the hierarchy of power implicit in ethnographic inquiry between social scientists and Native informants as well as in relationships among readers and texts, authors and characters. Treuer positions readers as ethnographic voyeurs as he questions the privileges and responsibilities of vision and visibility in fiction in a settler–colonial context, a line of inquiry González extends through an ethnographer character, whose conventional interrogation procedures involve the unilateral taking of stories and information. Containing explicit references neither to ethnographies nor to anthropology, Le's short story tests the capacity of narrative privacy to contend with implicit and systemic ethnographic imperatives that run throughout contemporary ethnic and indigenous literatures.

In the historical context of compulsory ethnographic visibility, narrative privacy names those spaces in narratives by ethnic and indigenous writers that are deliberately and explicitly inaccessible to readers. All narratives are necessarily selective, as writers are ultimately restricted in scope and perspective if not by their publishers, then certainly by the demands of narrative coherency; writers must choose what stories are valuable and which parts of stories get told. Narrative privacy, however, specifically names those instances in which writers use literary form to draw attention to what they willingly leave out of their story. For example, narrative privacy in *Crossing Vines* affords González an opportunity to metafictionally and self-consciously reflect on his own position as a writer who—not unlike ethnographers—decides what stories are valuable and worth recording. Similarly, Treuer metafictionally reflects on his novel's fictionality, highlighting for readers the absence of a "true" story and his unwillingness to play the role of native informant. Treuer responds to historical ethnographic practices, namely the historical acceptance of anthropologists and ethnographic fieldworkers as arbiters of cultural value equipped to speak on behalf of the peoples they studied, by reversing historical power relations; his Native narrator explicitly retains control over his story by declining to share it with readers, whom Treuer positions as ethnographic voyeurs.[5] For Treuer, narrative privacy affords a space in which to insist on reading Native literature for its political and formal contributions rather than merely as an artifact of ethnographic inquiry. Le carves out spaces of narrative privacy in "The Boat" by deflecting readers' gazes from the central traumas of the story as a means of protecting his characters, who—because of the abjection of their situation—do not share the privileges of curiosity or desire for memorialization readers enjoy. By creating spaces of narrative privacy, Treuer, González, and Le each respond in nuanced ways to histories of ethnographers speaking on behalf of nonwhite and indigenous peoples while also critically engaging with their own authorial privilege of controlling and mediating stories about Native, Asian Diasporic, and Latinx communities.[6]

THE ANTHROPOLOGIST AND THE LONE ETHNOGRAPHER AS CULTURAL FIGURES

The archetypical figure of the anthropologist inhabits a special place of derision in writing by scholars of color, perhaps particularly in writing by American Indians. In a statement that enjoys many afterlives as an epigraph, Vine Deloria Jr. famously declares: "Indians have been cursed above all other people in history. Indians have anthropologists" (78). He explains, "behind each policy and program with which Indians are plagued, if traced completely back to its origin, stands the anthropologist" (81). Deloria characterizes the anthropologist as an out-of-touch academic in an intellectually incestuous

---

5. Treuer's resistance to ethnographic readings of Native American literature informed his contentious *Native American Fiction: A User's Manual* (2006), published the same year as *Translation*. His argument that Native literatures should be read for formal, rather than cultural elements, however, ignores or mischaracterizes decades of tribally-specific, deliberate scholarly work in Native and Indigenous literary studies that explicitly engages in such work. For more considered accounts of academic resistance to *User's Manual*, see Daniel Heath Justice, James H. Cox, Karl Kroeber, Lisa Tatonetti, Scott Richard Lyons, and Christopher Taylor. I argue here that Treuer's fiction allows for a more nuanced and productive critique of ethnographic reading practices.

6. Trinh T. Minh-ha describes a similar contradiction of authorial privilege: "In a sense, committed writers are the ones who write both to awaken to the consciousness of their guilt and to give their readers a guilty conscience. Bound to one another by an awareness of their guilt, writer and reader may thus assess their positions, engaging themselves wholly in their situations and carrying their weight into the weight of their communities, the weight of the world. Such a definition naturally places the committed writers on the side of Power. For every discourse that breeds fault and guilt is a discourse of authority and arrogance. To say this, however, is not to say that all power discourses produce equal oppression or that those established are necessary" (10–11).

academic system more interested in confirming his own authority than actually listening to or engaging with the peoples he purports to study. Each year, he writes, anthropologists embark on "the great summer adventure," travelling to "Indian reservations to make OBSERVATIONS. During the winter these observations will become books by which future anthropologists will be trained, so that they can come out to reservations years from now and verify the observations they have studied" (78, 79). Deloria caricatures anthropologists' presumed intellectual authority over the Natives they study, explaining that writing implements are not among the various useless tools they carry with them on their trips to reservations (79). He continues: "You may be curious as to why the anthropologist never carries a writing instrument. He never makes a mark because he ALREADY KNOWS what he is going to find. . . . The anthropologist is only out on the reservations to VERIFY what he has suspected all along—Indians are a very quaint people who bear watching" (80).[7] Deloria characterizes anthropologists by their disengagement with their objects of study; they observe Natives not in the spirit of dialogue, but to seek evidence for what they believe they already know. As Deloria explains, however, anthropological disengagement with the realities of Natives' lived experiences manifests itself in disastrous social and political policies that have deleterious material effects on Native nations.

Deloria is far from alone in identifying the archetypical anthropologist as antagonist, an activity that is certainly not exclusive to American Indians.[8] For instance, Renato Rosaldo, a Chicano who is himself an anthropologist, similarly caricaturizes "the Lone Ethnographer" by casting his yearly summer adventure in the form of a quest narrative: "Once upon a time, the Lone Ethnographer rode off into the sunset in search of 'his native.' After undergoing a series of trials, he encountered the object of his quest in a distant land. There, he underwent his rite of passage by enduring the ultimate ordeal of 'fieldwork.' After collecting 'the data,' the Lone Ethnographer returned home and wrote a 'true' account of 'the culture'" (30). Like Deloria, Rosaldo draws into relief the difference between the fieldworker's "home" in the academy and the "adventure" and "trials" of fieldwork. He ridicules the ethnographer's

---

7. In reviewing the ethnographic body of work on the Mohawk, Simpson confirms this frequent sentiment that fieldworkers seek to confirm what they already knew: "the anthropological and historical project it embodies may be characterised as one that seeks to authenticate cultural forms rather than analyse them" ("On Ethnographic Refusal" 71).

8. Nor is the practice limited to North America. Maori scholar Linda Tuhiwai Smith expresses a similar sentiment: "The ethnographic 'gaze' of anthropology has collected, classified, and represented other cultures to the extent that anthropologists are often the academics popularly perceived by the indigenous world as all that is bad with academics" (70).

presumed authority to determine truth based on these adventures and underscores the tangential nature of objectified "natives" to the entire process.

Deloria's and Rosaldo's witty portraits of anthropologists are part of their larger, sincere critiques of the way ethnographic representations are directly implicated in imperial projects, critiques shared across Native, Latinx, and Asian American Studies.[9] From its amorphous beginnings in the US during imperial "discovery" and expansion but especially since its codification as a discipline in the late nineteenth and early twentieth century,[10] cultural anthropology "accorded with the imperatives of Empire," Audra Simpson writes, by developing "specific technologies of rule that sought to obtain space and resources, to define and know the difference that it constructed in those spaces and then govern those within" ("On Ethnographic Refusal" 67). The process of defining constructed difference involved assuming the power to speak for or to translate the cultures under study.[11] Seeing subjugated groups in terms of difference and through a lens of European and American superiority, early ethnographers aimed to describe and represent colonized peoples, or "fragments of societies . . . on the verge of extinction," before they disappeared through extermination, assimilation, or merely by their presumed incompatibility with Western modernity (Behar 20).[12] Ironically, as Rey Chow explains, "In spite of the grandiose salvational motives of his profession, the very presence of the Western anthropologist means, effectively, that these 'other' cultures are changed and displaced forever from their 'origins'" (176). According to fieldworkers consumed with the pursuit of authenticity, living communities became tainted with influences of modernism by coming into contact and engaging in exchanges with Westerners; "authoritative" knowledge about

---

9. Writing in 1989, Renato Rosaldo divides the history of anthropology into three eras, the pre-1921 era of his Lone Ethnographer, the "classic period" from 1921–1971 driven by Boas's "doctrine of objectivism," and the post-1960s' "reworking" of the discipline in response to the radical social upheavals in the US during the 1960s and 1970s (34–35). Rosaldo's chronology is representative of most overviews of anthropology; the two primary turning points are the start of the Boasian/scientific era (early 1920s) and Clifford Geertz's *The Interpretation of Cultures* (1973), which called for self-reflexive, first-person ethnographies.

10. Robert E. Bieder offers a thorough overview of popular scientific conceptions of Native Americans from European contact, especially the mid-nineteenth century, in *Science Encounters the Indian, 1820–1880: The Early Years of American Ethnology* (1986).

11. Trinh T. Minh-ha writes, "What I resent most, however, is not [the ethnographer's] inheritance of a power he so often disclaims, disengaging himself from a system he carries with him, but his ear, eye, and pen, which record in his language while pretending to speak through mine, on my behalf" (48).

12. Behar explains, "The practice of ethnography originates in the desire to salvage the fragments of societies that were seen as being on the verge of extinction. Ethnography engaged in a language of loss, of preventing loss, of mourning loss, of arriving there just in time to save the old books of culture from a total and permanent loss" (20).

these groups was thus concentrated in ethnographic accounts, and the rights and claims of groups "compromised" by contact with outsiders were more easily ignored. As a consequence, ethnographers' accounts influenced disastrous social and political policies that divested Native peoples in North America of their land and property and excluded people of color from the protections of citizenship and from discourses of civilized modernity.[13]

The early twentieth century saw what scholars term the "classic period" of anthropology, as the discipline became institutionalized in universities and scholars, most notably Franz Boas, sought to align the practice with the scientific method. Though its relationship to the "imperatives of Empire" changed from the accounts produced by early explorers, traders, and missionaries, ethnography remained a powerful tool for colonial processes of objectifying and subordinating Otherness. Boas and Ruth Benedict, among other anthropologists working in the 1920s, argued against biological explanations of race, instead attributing difference to the emerging concept of "culture." Their progressive and ideologically necessary move away from biology, however, had the effect of transforming the communities they studied "from colonized Others (to be assimilated, controlled, or eliminated) into objects of knowledge that could be circulated via institutionalized discourses centered on cultural difference" (Cotera 27). María Eugenia Cotera explains how this process, by virtue of its ostensibly neutral, scientific optic, "often erased or ignored the asymmetrical power relations that enabled this objectification" and that "Although these new relations of domination represented a bloodless form of appropriation—as opposed to the expropriation of land and human resources of the previous century—they nevertheless supported the changing exigencies of American imperialism by enabling a revisioning of the colonial subject within modern power relations" (28, 27–28). Pursuing ethnographic study through the optic of science produced a set of practices that again shaped the way the US saw, named, and knew Others: as "'natural objects' of research" (Smith 122).

Objectifying people is a process of containment that relies on the authority of the researcher and that presumes the knowability of a group of people. Such relations establish a hierarchy of authority and intellect between researcher and researched that conditions ethnography's ostensibly objective observations in favor of the allegedly neutral observer; as Smith makes clear, "Research has not been neutral in its objectification of the Other" (41). Until

---

13. Voicing a sentiment articulated throughout scholarship on the effects of ethnography, Chow concludes, "the methods and practices of anthropology and ethnography have simply served to reinforce and empower colonial administration, and thus to bring about the systematic destruction of these 'other' cultures" (177).

recent renovations of the discipline challenged the hierarchal relationship between researcher and researched, ethnographies conventionally depicted sophisticated, heterogeneous communities as simplified caricatures frozen in time, a process that excludes the possibility of individuality and intellectualism. Smith explains the logic of exclusion in research: "The objects of research do not have a voice and do not contribute to research or science. In fact, the logic of the argument would suggest that it is simply impossible, ridiculous even, to suggest that the object of research can contribute to anything. An object has no life force, no humanity, no spirit of its own, so therefore 'it' cannot make an active contribution" (64). Smith characterizes researchers' practice of extracting knowledge from the people they studied, only to claim it as their own intellectual property to advance their careers and reputation, as "unrelenting" and "of a profoundly exploitative nature" (44).

In addition to the dehumanizing, depoliticizing effects of objectification, those naturalized as objects of research also experience compromised privacy, as researchers assume the right of access and conduct research in the name of universal knowledge. Gerald Vizenor explains that "the institutive sanctions of social science" have attempted "a contravention of native worldviews, tricky origin stories, privacy, and a sense of presence, by surveillance, transcription, translation, and elaborate transmission" (*Fugitive Poses* 58).[14] Enabled by ideologies and practices that understand researched peoples as objects—therefore with "no life force, no humanity, no spirit of [their] own," and so no right to privacy—researchers exercise their privilege to look into the lives of the people they study and manipulate what they see, compromising privacy by surveilling their objects of study (Smith 64). Trinh T. Minh-ha writes, "On the lookout for 'messages' that might be wrested from the object of study, in spite of its opacity or its reticence in sharing its intimacy with a stranger, this knowledgeable man [the "anthropologist-nativist"] spends his time spying on the natives, in fear of missing any of those precious moments where the latter would be caught unaware, therefore still living" (68). Connecting what she terms the "fundamental disparity in the classical anthropological and ethnographic situation" to issues of ethnographic visibility of colonized peoples, Chow draws on Laura Mulvey's theories of visuality to explain how the ethnographic gaze objectifies its subject, who—like women in Mulvey's

---

14. Like Gerald Vizenor, Smith underscores the pervasiveness of colonial invasions of indigenous privacy "in our history under the gaze of Western imperialism and Western science." She explains that research is a site of struggle "framed by our attempts to escape the penetration and surveillance of that gaze" (41).

work—experience "to-be-looked-at-ness" (180).[15] A primary legacy of ethnographic research on indigenous or otherwise differentiated peoples, beyond the specific optics of biological or cultural difference, objectification, or nostalgia, is the presumption that Western—European and US—audiences have access into the lives of Others.

Colonial access to "native" populations in North America—including American Indians but also other populations of study, such as Mexicans and Mexican Americans on the US–Mexico border, African Americans in the US South, and Asian Americans in urban enclaves, to name only a few—have been conventionally enabled by "native informants." Informants are members of a community able and willing, albeit with varying degrees of volition, to translate for researchers and to otherwise explain the inner workings of their community to outsiders. Much as Deloria and Rosaldo caricature established archetypes of Anthropologists and Ethnographers, the role of native informant similarly exists in an archetypical form that obscures the complex negotiations specific historical actors made in engaging with explorers, traders, colonial agents, and fieldworkers. The archetypical native informant provides access to a community for an outsider and stands as an object of research, not as an intellectual or an individual subject. As an object of research, the native informant is subject to surveillance by the "ethnographic 'gaze' of anthropology" and supplements researchers' knowledge not through intellectual contribution but by being self-evident and available for study by experts (Smith 70). Informants ostensibly transparently "translate" their culture for researchers, who claim intellectual authority over informants and their communities. Without an expectation of privacy or intellectual agency, native informants were long considered by researchers as available conduits of cultural knowledge and artifacts.

---

15. Building on Laura Mulvey's argument that to-be-looked-at-ness is "built into the way we look," Rey Chow continues: "What this means is that in the vision of the formerly ethnographized, the subjective origins of ethnography are displayed in amplified form but at the same time significantly redefined: what are 'subjective' origins now include a memory of past *objecthood*—the experience of being looked at—which lives on in the subjective act of ethnographizing like an other, an optical unconscious. If ethnography is indeed autoethnography—ethnography of the self and the subject—then the perspective of the formerly ethnographized supplements it irrevocably with the understanding that being-looked-at-ness, rather than the act of looking, constitutes the primary event in cross-cultural representation" (180). While I agree with many of Chow's premises, I read the authors in this chapter as engaging with ethnographic legacies of visibility in more nuanced ways than simply assuming or refuting to-be-looked-at-ness.

Native informants in the US imaginary are of course not only Native American.[16] While the brief history offered above focuses largely on indigenous encounters with ethnographers, in part because indigenous North Americans have borne the brunt of US anthropologists' interest, and so anthropology and ethnography play a central role in Native histories and intellectual projects,[17] anthropologists, including ethnographers and folklorists, have studied and continue to study myriad groups in the US. For instance, starting in the nineteenth and into the twentieth century, scholars paid particular attention to regional African American folklore in the South and Mexican and Mexican American folklore along the US–Mexico border. Ethnographic reports also played substantial roles in the exclusion acts that restricted the movement and liberties of Asians and Asian Americans in the US and that cut off immigration from Asian countries for parts of the nineteenth and twentieth centuries.[18] Ostensibly authoritative ethnographic works on racial differences in the nineteenth century influenced US racial politics and law, including *Plessy v. Ferguson* (1896) and *Ozawa v. United States* (1922), which shaped race relations well into the twentieth century.[19] Most important for this chapter, ethnography as a way of seeing and knowing groups of people, particularly those differentiated from the assumed white, Euro-American "norm," shapes the way US Americans continue to view "cultural difference" as a natural object of study and consider nonwhite and indigenous fiction writers as native informants. Arguably, it also enabled the conflations of text and human Jodi Melamed critiques in her analysis of neoliberal multiculturalism (37).

Like all other academic disciplines, anthropology has transformed politically, methodologically, and ethically over the last half century. Often critiqued because of their historical practices, anthropologists and the ethnographies they produce are more varied and self-aware than the caricatures Deloria and

---

16. For example, Chang-Rae Lee's *Native Speaker* (1996) famously positions its protagonist, Henry Park, as a spy who commits espionage as a means of gaining access to an elusive sense of belonging in the US.

17. Krupat writes, "from Jefferson forward, America will stand as one of the world's foremost laboratories for anthropological science, a science Americans proceed to establish upon the basis of first-hand study of the Indian" (63).

18. In one example, Colleen Lye explains, "In 1903 the Immigration Bureau adopted the Bertillon system for the inspection of Chinese immigrants. Developed by criminal anthropology, the system was a 'scientific method of identifying criminals by the accurate measurement and inspection of the naked body'" (270n43).

19. Lisa Lowe writes extensively about the influences behind the exclusion acts and *Plessy v. Ferguson*, among other cases, in *Immigrant Acts* (1996). Lye explains, "in *Ozawa vs. United States* the Supreme Court would conclude that Japanese immigrants were not eligible for citizenship on the authority of anthropological science that they were Mongolian and not white" (127).

Rosaldo construct.[20] Increasingly, ethnographers seek "Identification and connection rather than distance, difference, and otherness" (Behar 23). "Unlike anthropologies of the past," Simpson writes, "accounting for Empire and colonialism ... is now becoming more acceptable. This is owing to political currents, critiques and philosophical trends outside of and within anthropology that have embedded the discipline within the history of colonialism" ("On Ethnographic Refusal" 68–69). Acknowledging anthropology's implication in colonialism—a disciplinary "history of shame"—has allowed for more self-reflexive, politically aware ethnographic work (Behar 16).[21] In contrast to Deloria's anthropologist who already knew what he was going to find, Ruth Behar characterizes contemporary ethnography in its many forms as "an edgy form of knowing that dares to surprise the knower too. Curiously, in these situations, you yourself, the knower, don't know fully what you knew until you wrote it down, until you told the story with you yourself included in it" (24). Since Clifford Geertz's *The Interpretation of Cultures* (1973) encouraged researchers to consider their own positionality in relation to the peoples they researched, the discipline has self-consciously distanced itself from both Deloria's archetypical anthropologist and Boasian anthropologists who imagined themselves as objective, neutral observers.

Ethnographies have also transformed as anthropology has expanded to include women and more native researchers, who bring with them not only new forms of knowledge but also particular relationships with and responsibilities to the groups they study.[22] Inclusion of more diverse voices, however, does not entail equal intellectual footing in academic institutions. "No situation is 'innocent' of a violence of form, if not content, in narrating a history," Simpson explains, and there is not "a level playing field of interpretation

---

20. Not all critics view anthropology's disciplinary transformation as redemptive. Minh-ha, for example, argues that the ethnographer "belongs to that fraction of humanity which for centuries has made other fractions the objects of contempt and exploitation, then, when it saw the handwriting on the wall, set about to give them back their humanity" (47).

21. It has also spurred unconventional ethnographies outside of the disciplinary home of Anthropology, such as those produced by artists, activists, and community members. Behar applauds these alternative ethnographic explorations: "Ethnography is not the property of anthropology, sociology, the social sciences, or the academy" (34).

22. Cotera studies the early twentieth-century ethnographic careers of Zora Neale Hurston, who worked with African American folkways in the US South; Jovita González, who worked with J. Frank Dobie on borderlands ethnography; and Ella Deloria (Yankton Sioux), who studied Sioux stories and languages while working informally with Boas. Cotera argues that Hurston, González, and Deloria helped move ethnography toward a "'native ethnographic' model," as "their collaborations with mainstream scholars were of a different nature than those of 'native informants' of an earlier generation. They were, instead, *informed natives*" (28).

within which to assert . . . different translations [of events]" (*Mohawk Interruptus* 99–100). Smith similarly highlights the power relations inherent in academic forms: "Another problem is that academic writing is a form of selecting, arranging and presenting knowledge. It privileges sets of texts, views about the history of an idea, what issues count as significant" (37). While native anthropologists offer and practice a variety of responses to this epistemological inequality,[23] for the purposes of this chapter I am most interested in how some researchers decide to preserve the privacy of the communities they study by limiting what they ask and what they say or publish.

In describing her experience as a Mohawk woman doing anthropological fieldwork in Kahnawà:ke Mohawk communities, for instance, Simpson acknowledges that she withholds portions of her research from her academic audience. Describing her research as "an ethnography of refusal," Simpson terms this practice of withholding as "staking limits" ("On Ethnographic Refusal" 70). Simpson chooses to stake limits, or delineate what information should be shared, "for the express purposes of protecting the concerns of the community" (*Mohawk Interruptus* 105).[24] Limiting access allows her to acknowledge and account for "the asymmetrical power relations that inform the research and writing about native lives and politics" (*Mohawk Interruptus* 105). Women of color anthropologists explain similar methodologies; Behar, for instance, admits that in her research of her own Jewish-Cuban community, "There were provocative topics I chose not to address" (32). Smith (Ngāti Awa and Ngāti Porou) warns indigenous researchers that "Writing can be dangerous because sometimes we reveal ourselves in ways which get misappropriated and used against us" (37).[25] Staking limits allows anthropologists like Simpson, Behar, and Smith to protect themselves and the communities they study, to

---

23. For example, Behar describes how she was able to co-opt and adapt academic tools to further her understanding of her personal (Jewish/Cuban) diasporas (21). In addition to staking limits, Simpson's recent work also aims to "consider what analysis will look like, or sound like, when the goals and aspirations of those we talk to inform the methods and the shape of our theorising and analysis" ("On Ethnographic Refusal" 68).

24. She explains, "I asked questions about the questions that mattered to the community and I had to write in certain ways, as these matters belonged to Kahnawà:ke and yet were being used to vilify the community in the mainstream press" (*Mohawk Interruptus* 98).

25. Ella Deloria offers an early example of staking limits. In a letter to her mentor Ruth Benedict, she explains the ways her place as a perpetual virgin, a specific role in her community, required that she limit her ethnography: "I found I can't possibly say everything frankly, knowing it could get out to Dakota country. I know it must sound silly; but it won't to you. Ruth, I am a virgin; as such, I am not supposed to talk frankly on things I must, to be really helpful. The place I have with the Dakotas is important to me; I can not afford to jeopardize it by what would certainly leave me open to suspicion and you can't know what that would mean" (qtd. in Cotera 11).

create space in the academy for alternative methodologies, to refuse depoliticized transparency, and to contest pervasive understandings of Otherness as available for study—even as it also means they become arbiters of what is valuable or private to the peoples they study.

Despite the radical methodological and political changes in anthropology over the last half century, and despite the increasing inclusion of native researchers in the discipline, Deloria's archetypical Anthropologist and Rosaldo's Lone Ethnographer continue to persist as figures in contemporary imaginations, including in literature.[26] The legacy of their "unrelenting," "profoundly exploitative" research continues to shape accepted and authorized ways of knowing in the US, as well as lived experiences of inequality. Yet, Behar observes, "There is a strange hunger for ethnography in the contemporary world, which is shaped by concepts of the 'really real' and the desire for stories based on the truth and immediacy of witnessing. Ethnography, rather than becoming extinct, has become a necessary way of knowing" (16). This chapter argues that US audiences of commercial fiction, accustomed to the privilege of access to differences naturalized as (depoliticized) objects of study, extend colonial ethnographic imperatives into the literary, where they seek representations of "the 'really real.'" That is, the legacy of the ethnographic imagination in the US positions "ethnic" authors in the role of native informants, offering readers access to transparent translations of cultural difference. In refusing this role by insisting on narrative privacy, these writers affirm that visibility is political, in that it has and always has had material consequences.

THE ETHNOGRAPHIC IMPERATIVE IN CONTEMPORARY LITERATURE

Recent scholarship traces the paired intellectual histories of anthropology and literary studies since the mid-nineteenth century, focusing on the role of difference and "culture" in the two disciplines. In *Before Cultures* (2005), Brad Evans explores the ways anthropologists and writers grappled with describing and analyzing different groups of people before the modern concept of "culture" emerged after 1910. He traces an intellectual history of treating literary texts as ethnographic objects of study back to Hippolyte Taine, a French philosopher writing in the 1860s, who himself traces it back even further (12).

---

26. Quoting Robert Warrior, Lisa Brooks writes, "'Everyone . . . who takes up the task of researching and writing about the indigenous world comes into an arena of inquiry already left in ruins by generations of bad faith.' Undoing this legacy is a burden we all share" (245, ellipses in original).

Evans's study, ranging from 1865 to 1920, dovetails with Michael A. Elliot's *The Culture Concept* (2002), which describes at length the confluence of literary realism and ethnography in the early twentieth century. Other scholars have also paired early histories of anthropology and literature, including Pratt's study of travel narratives and Simpson's attention to captivity narratives. Others have traced the relationship between literature and anthropology through the twentieth century; Arnold Krupat, for instance, devotes several chapters of *Ethnocriticism: Ethnography, History, Literature* (1992) to mapping the way ethnography and literature have come into contact and how they have respectively negotiated the various theoretical and political trends of the late nineteenth and twentieth centuries. Still others trouble the boundary between the disciplines; Alvina Quintana asserts that "Once we admit that these cultural representations [in ethnography] should also be viewed as a mixture of descriptive and interpretive modes of discourse, the gap between imaginary and ethnographic writing shrinks before our eyes as both forms of writing are reduced to a particular way of seeing the world" (76). For the purposes of this chapter, however, I am less interested in the pairing of the histories of the fields than I am in the way ethnographic legacies inflect contemporary literary criticism and reading practices, as well as the ethnographic imperative writers must negotiate to publish their fiction. That is, I am most interested in those instances in which publishers and readers conflate ethnography and literature in ways that tokenize and depoliticize representation.

While literary scholars, particularly those who work in fields such as Native, Asian American, and Latinx literatures, have long since traded explicitly ethnographic indices of cultural authenticity and representational accuracy for formal and political literary criticism,[27] traces of ethnographic practices linger in popular and some academic readings, as well as in the well-meaning desire for representation by academic and popular readers alike. Concern over such problematic relationships between literature and ethnography is not new in literary criticism. Min Hyoung Song broadly describes this anxiety as stemming from "the tendency to make ethnic writers merely, or only, spokespersons of their respective groups, turning what they write into simply the raw material for an anthropological or sociological form of investigation," a move Yoonmee Chang names the "ethnographic imperative" facing contemporary writers (Song 77, Chang 7). Understanding ethnic literature as cultural translation that can be mined for cultural truths undermines its status as an intellectual, artistic, often political creation, which reinforces the culture/intellect

---

27. Christopher Teuton offers a history of how these shifts occurred in Native literary studies (200–201).

divide, a key tenet of colonialism in which people of color produce culture but lack the capacity for intellectual engagement. Song and other critics who share his concerns argue that reading ethnic literature as cultural artifacts places an unwarranted pressure on authors to represent their communities accurately and blunts their political and aesthetic interventions.[28]

Popular demands that literature somehow represent culture in authentic ways reinforce ethnographic assumptions dating to the era of the Lone Ethnographer, who expected native informants to translate their cultures transparently from an inside perspective for an outside audience.[29] Expecting an author to only authentically—a term problematic in its own right—represent his or her culture divests the author of his or her humanity by taking away the capacity for choice or invention. Kandice Chuh argues that failure "to allow for the complexity of 'ethnic literatures,' which are effectively coded as transparent, self-evident expressions . . . obviously makes difficult an engagement with minoritized literatures as anything other than ('authentic') artifacts of an ethnography of the Other" (18). As "self-evident expressions," texts are objectified and their authors denied full credit for their intellectual and creative production. Even when demands for referentiality emerge from well-meaning academics and readers frustrated with the dearth of nonwhite representation in popular and academic discourses, expectations of authenticity in ethnic fiction carry damaging colonial legacies.[30]

Similarly, ethnographic imperatives encourage non-threatening, depoliticized cultural portraits in fiction. Derived from colonialist ethnographic practices that assume unidirectional flows of information, these expectations aim to avoid implicating audiences in texts or the uncomfortable issues texts often raise. Chang identifies this requirement of the ethnographic imperative in her discussion of the types of fictions Asian Americans were able to get published in the early twentieth century: "They caricaturize and decontextualize Asian

---

28. Other critics who take up these concerns include Elaine Kim, Yoonmee Chang, Kandice Chuh, David Eng, Anne Anlin Cheng, Linda Smith, Charles Ramírez Berg, and Paul Lai. To offer an alternate view, Alvina Quintana and Tey Diana Rebolledo explore the ways writers can inhabit the role of ethnographer productively.

29. Elliot proposes a similar timeline for what he calls the burden of "mimetic accuracy": "For over one hundred years (at least), our vocabulary for discussing the presence of cultural difference in written texts has presumed a mimetic referentiality, a relationship to truth that can be apprehended through methodical observation. The burden of this mimetic accuracy weighs more heavily on those literary texts that attempt to represent groups outside of the dominant culture than those that do not" (186).

30. Christopher Lee describes "literary and cultural studies in the North American academy" as "a context in which the demand for referential knowledge from writings by minority authors is part of an imperialist legacy that implicates ethnography, the humanistic disciplines, and the social sciences" (21).

culture, omitting attention to the historical contexts that created that culture, both in Asia and America, as well as to historical contexts more generally, especially of the racial discrimination and social inequity that immigrants experienced in the United States. It is for these omissions that ethnographic texts are praised, not to mention published and widely read" (60). These depoliticized, "authentic" portraits do not make demands on audiences or otherwise implicate audiences in dialogues about race, gender, sexuality, or other inequalities in the US, allowing audiences to experience difference passively while avoiding engaging actual people and the pressing issues emerging from lived experiences.[31]

Instead, audiences are able to peer into characters' lives from the abstracted, depoliticized position of a reader looking down on a page. The authors in this chapter compare the practice of looking into a text with the forms of ethnography conducted by Deloria's Anthropologist or Rosaldo's Lone Ethnographer. Engaging questions of visibility raised by living under "the penetration and surveillance of that [Western imperialist] gaze"—who gets to see, who must see; who gets to be seen, who must be seen—the authors challenge the hierarchy implicit in readers' ethnographic voyeurism (Smith 41).[32] Ethnographic voyeurism, or unidirectional gaze at Otherness, involves issues of privilege, access, and visibility stemming from ethnographic legacies in the US. The authors in this chapter engage with ethnographic voyeurism through their play with narrative form. Crafting characters who return—or of their own volition explicitly decline to return—readers' gazes, the authors in this chapter refute assumptions that readers are neutral observers, unimplicated in the texts they read.

---

31. Jace Weaver makes this point: "Too often, non-Native critics have no real knowledge of, let alone commitment to, Native communities. They simply want to read Native texts without ever engaging, let alone encountering, Native peoples. In this they are little different than early anthropologists who exploited their indigenous 'informants,' and saw themselves as adding the value for increase in the 'universal' body of knowledge, even as they burnished the luster of their own careers" (12). Palumbo-Liu similarly explains, "The deployment of ethnic texts as proxies for ethnic peoples can be related to the general function of 'diversity' in contemporary US society" (*The Ethnic Canon* 13).

32. Drawing on Victor Turner, Rosaldo raises the issue of ethnographic voyeurism: "'Cartesian dualism,' he [Turner] says, 'has insisted on separating subject from object, us from them. It has, indeed, made voyeurs of Western man, exaggerating sight by macro- and micro-instrumentation, the better to learn the structures of the world with an 'eye' to its exploitation.' Turner thus connects the 'eye' of ethnography with the 'I' of imperialism" (41).

STAKING LIMITS: *THE TRANSLATION OF DR. APELLES*

In *The Translation of Dr. Apelles,* Treuer disrupts ethnographic assumptions by underscoring the novel's fictionality and explicitly curtailing readers' access to his characters. He depicts Native storytellers as sophisticated intellectuals capable of displacing existing centers of knowledge rather than simply objects of study or willing native informants. In the final scenes of the book, Treuer has his protagonist, Apelles, acknowledge his readers to implicate the audience in the novel, turning the critical lens long pointed at Natives back on his readers. Read against a legacy of appropriation and exploitation of Native informants, the novel points to a tradition of dissimulation as resistance to show the political potential of narrative privacy.

The novel begins with a "Translator's Note," in which the narrator—the novel's apparent translator—describes finding "a very particular book in a vast and wonderful library," from which loose sheets, "covered with a text in a language [he] did not understand" fell (1). While the translator focuses his efforts on translating the story on those loose pages—to do so he must find someone who reads the language to dictate the story to him—the form of the novel suggests the composite text he first opens: two separate narratives alternate by chapter for the length of the novel, as if pages of one were inserted into a bound copy of the other. The first narrative—which begins with the last sentence of the Translator's Note—is a retelling of the Greek pastoral *Daphnis and Chloe,* in which two naïve orphans find love and sexual fulfillment in each other through a series of coincidences. In the novel's retelling, however, the Greek youths are written as Native characters Bimaadiz and Eta, and the story unfolds on Ojibwe lands in the nineteenth century.[33] The other narrative in the novel centers on Apelles, a 43-year-old Ojibwe man living in a major US city in the twenty-first century. Apelles works at RECAP, a library of retired books, and in his free time he translates obscure Native texts for publication in academic journals. In part because of his overwhelming fear of being reduced by stereotypes to a character "in a story like all other stories about his people," Apelles has lived a solitary, private life (203). Faced with increasing loneliness he likens to the feeling of a book without a reader, however, Apelles risks becoming a character and undertakes the project of translating himself "into a language that someone, somewhere, will want to read" by writing the story of his life and his love for his white coworker, Campaspe (39).

---

33. The novel provides some textual evidence for this date (76), but as Treuer points out in his interview with Kennedy, many stereotyped stories about Natives exist outside of time (51). The same might be said of the pastoral.

The two narratives exist next to each other but do not explicitly intersect until the final pages of the novel when Campaspe steals the translation Apelles is working on—a story about their love—and loses it while at work at RECAP. Jealous coworkers then hide the manuscript pages in a copy of *Daphnis and Chloe,* where it is presumably lost forever, stored away with other "unknown, unloved" books (304). Just as the story seems to come full circle and solve the puzzle of the novel's form by suggesting that the composite text, lost as it is in "a vast and wonderful library," is the source material from which the translator creates *Translation,* the narrative ruptures: Apelles becomes omniscient and, as he reveals himself to be the story's narrator, divulges that the story he tells from the Translator's Note forward is "make-believe," not an actual account of his life or, in the novel's vocabulary, a faithful translation (312). At the same moment, Apelles acknowledges his readers by looking upward from the page, noting "they [the readers] know me best of all" (313).[34] In breaking narrative distance, Apelles not only draws attention to his audience's presence, but also reverses the gaze implicit in the act of reading to implicate readers in the story he tells. Apelles is not a character-narrator who transparently relates the intimacies of his life or a native informant translating his culture, but a calculating storyteller who confronts his audience with his own fictionality to foreclose any possibility that his story might be mined for cultural truths.

Apelles's insistence on the fictionality of his story and his recognition of readers' participation[35] in the novel becomes political when read within a history of exploitation and appropriation of Native informants' work. In the United States, literature canonized the representations of Natives produced by irresponsible ethnographic fieldwork through stories of Native absence and cultural authenticity, both of which portray Natives as static characters of the past, incapable of change, survival, or contributing intellectually to the present. These manifest manners, to use Vizenor's term for "the racialist notions and misnomers sustained in archives and lexicons as 'authentic' representations of *indian* cultures" did not strip Natives of their intellectualism or agency, but they did—and continue to—require Natives to develop creative forms of survivance, or an "active sense of presence" ("Preface" vii, italics in original). Treuer points to this history of theft, appropriation, and manifest manners in several ways, not only by crafting *Translation*'s narrator as a Native translator and focusing the novel on questions of personal and cultural translation, but

---

34. Apelles's reference to his readers here bears comparison to the moment in Thomas King's *Green Grass, Running Water* (1993) when the narrator asks readers whether we remember the story he is telling (432).

35. Espen J. Aarseth terms literature that requires extraordinary participation by readers "ergodic literature" (1).

also by embedding Apelles's story within a pastoral story that capitalizes on stereotyped tropes informed by irresponsible, exploitative ethnographic fieldwork. In disrupting conventional reading practices and drawing attention to Treuer's agency as a Native storyteller, narrative privacy models a form of the active presence Vizenor describes.

The legacy of such history manifests itself in Apelles's daily life, where expectations and stereotypes circumscribe his personal relationships. Apelles's overwhelming anxiety in the novel stems from the demands he faces from other characters to act as a cultural translator, or native informant, for a society in which familiar representations of Natives predetermine his story, regardless of the translation he offers. Inevitably, when people learn he is Native, they ask "what was it like?" and Apelles "felt he was at a disadvantage because he, and all those like him, were measured against the stories that were told about Indians by those who did not know Indians. Not at all like the way men were measured against the stories about men because, for most people, men existed in life not just in stories. And how could he overcome that?" (204, 205). Apelles overcomes this disadvantage by substituting fiction for the story of his life; he maintains control over "that sovereign part of himself" and shifts critical attention from a Native man as an object of study to a Native story as a site of Native intellectual production (204). In refusing to play native informant, Apelles stakes limits around the intimate details of his life, offering readers a fictional story rather than personal testimony to delineate the limits of readers' access to characters' lives and to ensure the personal remains private.

Despite Apelles's fierce desire for privacy, Treuer offers readers access to Apelles's life and desires through an explicitly voyeuristic narration. The narrator draws attention to his and readers' violation of Apelles's privacy by pausing and rationalizing the intimate views he offers. For example, after offering important narrative background on how Apelles came to work at RECAP, the narrator pauses and invites readers to peer with him into Apelles's domestic life as well, seemingly on a whim: "Not forgetting for a moment that it is Dr. Apelles' working life we are here interested in exploring, we will, in any event, step into his apartment" (49). The narrator shows the reader the contents of Dr. Apelles's closets—down to his eight pairs of underwear—pausing to assure the reader, "It is important to know all of this. It truly is, for reasons that are not at all obvious yet" (51). Similarly, after describing Dr. Apelles's daily habits, the narrator again addresses the reader, noting, "the importance of the order of Dr. Apelles' day will become clear when certain things happen to him later on" (52). The contents of Apelles's underwear drawer and the order of his daily routines are not crucial to the novel's plot and are superfluous for his character development. Their importance, instead, is in how they underscore the degree of access readers have to a private character who harbors deep anxieties about being read.

Apelles's anxieties about being read, in fact, are further intimate details Treuer invites readers to examine. In trying to work through his relationship with Campaspe, Apelles acknowledges that her feelings are more complex than they seem in the story he tells himself about her. He then observes, "He has thought of himself as a simple man, too, but he is not a simple man. And there is nothing simple about his feelings. Simple feelings only occur in stories" (194). Apelles seems unaware that his fears are actually realized, for as readers know, his feelings are already part of a story. Watching Apelles negotiate his anxieties about becoming a character is deeply intimate not only because for much of the novel he appears apparently ignorant of readers' access to his thoughts, but also because his anxieties are tied to his sense of self. In a moment of vulnerability, Apelles considers why he declines to let people access his story:

> His life was real to him, and if he told it in the wrong way or for the wrong reasons it would cease to be real, it would no longer be his life because it would become a story like all other stories about his people, and if he told it he would only become a character in that story and would be the only Indian they knew and the Indian they told their friends about. His life would cease to be his and he would not even recognize himself anymore. (203)

Apelles's anxiety over being read—over becoming a character in a story—is not an irrational desire for privacy or an exclusionary impulse, but protection against objectification and decontextualization. Apelles draws limits around his story to prevent the flattening caricature and stereotyping can effect. Treuer's narrator implicates readers in Apelles's anxieties by drawing attention to the access to Apelles's life we enjoy, apparently against his explicit wishes.

The final scenes of the novel, however, emphatically underscore the novel's fictionality and therefore its limitations as a source of "authentic" ethnographic information. Maintaining control over the narrative he offers, Apelles strategically manipulates his narrative by displacing authenticity with deliberate narrative falsehoods, or "make-believe" (312). After losing Apelles's manuscript and visiting him in his apartment to confess and apologize, Campaspe confronts Apelles about his omniscience and her own fictionality as a character in his translation:

you didn't really find anything in the archive, did you?
I found myself, he says with a twinkle in his eye.
but where's the original, then? *what* is the original?
you should know that by now.
this all feels make-believe, she says after a while. even my heart—it feels like make-believe. but it isn't. is it? my heart is filled with something. so there is something to it after all, something you can weigh and measure. it is real. but everyone is going to think you made all this up. I can't believe it's actually happening. (312)

Apelles confirms her suspicions: "it is happening, he says, his eyes wild. it *is* happening and what's wrong with make-believe? isn't that how it works: we make belief? besides, happiness is more real than any illusion" (312). Apelles clearly separates his story from conventional understandings of authenticity, which require belief in and fidelity to an essentialized identity. Rather, as in the Translator's Note that characterizes the novel as a "gift of beauty," Apelles underscores his story's aesthetic nature, both through its complex narrative structure and its shifting syntactical experiments. He reminds readers that the novel is a fictional creation rather than the exposé of self-discovery it first seems; Apelles is performing, rather than divulging, intimate insights into what it means to be Native. In other words, Apelles shows he is capable of dissimulation and that he rejects authenticity or realism.

Treuer embeds Apelles's narrative in Bimaadiz and Eta's pastoral romance, a story that locates the political potential of dissimulation and narrative privacy in a specifically Ojibwe historical context. Replete with stereotypes and canonical tropes about Natives, the pastoral illustrates the Euro-American fantasies that threaten to overwrite Apelles's translation.[36] By alternating the two stories for the length of the novel, Treuer links their projects and contextualizes them in a longer history of survivance stories by Native storytellers and translators.

---

36. David Yost suggests that the pastoral is a projection of Euro-American fantasies as cultivated and made familiar by canonical American texts. For example, he compares a scene in which a jealous suitor disguises himself as a bear in an attempt to rape Eta—an effort so successful even Eta's dogs are fooled—to a scene in James Fenimore Cooper's *The Last of the Mohicans* in which Hawkeye and Uncas, disguised as bears, "walk unrevealed through a hostile band of Hurons" (64). Looking to the familiar tropes the pastoral adopts, Yost concludes, "By putting this Cooper-esque story—and implicitly, the destructive stereotypes authors like Cooper helped to shape—in conversation with the more realistic narrative of Dr. Apelles, the novel again suggests that these stories have nothing to do with the lived experiences of Anishinaabe individuals and everything to do with Euroamerican fantasies of Indians" (64).

The diegetic or "storyworld" world of Bimaadiz and Eta's love focuses on a year in their adolescence in which they transition from friendly playmates to married lovers (Abbott 231). As several of the novel's early reviewers note, the pastoral closely mirrors the Greek story *Daphnis and Chloe*. David Yost tracks the similarities in detail, concluding, "Though he infuses the story with fresh language and detail, Treuer has done little else beyond changing Greek names to Anishinaabemowin ones and adjusting the setting accordingly" (65). Indeed, the plot sequence and even specific scenes can be traced to the Greek myth, from the youths' early abandonment to their unlikely reunion with their birth parents in the story's serendipitous conclusion.[37] Perhaps most notably, the fantastic innocence Bimaadiz and Eta display is directly linked to the "famous innocence of Daphnis and Chloe—who, despite their careers in animal husbandry, manage to lack the slightest knowledge of sex—[which] also suggests the Rousseauan noble savage, a patronizing stereotype long used to portray the 'Indian' as 'safely dead and historically past'" (Yost 8, quoting Robert Berkhofer). Treuer's adaptation of *Daphnis and Chloe* so successfully adopts the tropes about Natives made familiar to US audiences by American literature that many reviewers lauded the pastoral as "lush," "sensuous," and "real and affecting," without noting the parodic quality of the narrative.[38] Despite nation-specific and politically centered emphases in indigenous literary studies, the novel's popular reception suggests the degree to which readers read for evidence to affirm social fantasies of Natives as noble innocents and willing cultural translators.

Treuer frames his depiction of the Native youths as noble innocents in touch with nature but not with their own sexuality as a form of voyeurism involving complicity between readers and a knowing narrator. Ironically positioning his story as ethnography rather than literature, the narrator asserts, "They are humans after all, not characters in a story," a move similar to his justification for taking readers into Apelles's underwear drawer in the other narrative (160). The voyeuristic quality of the narrative is reminiscent of what Linda Tuhiwai Smith characterizes as the intrusive and assuming "ethnographic 'gaze' of anthropology" (41). In this iteration, however, the pastoral's ethnographic voyeurism specifically implicates readers' gazes, which are directed by the omniscient narrator playing the part of native informant. For instance, in key moments in the couple's relationship, the narrator addresses the reader to comment on the story, and in doing so disrupts narrative distance and reminds the reader that she and the narrator are peering in on

---

37. See William Freiert, a classicist who outlines in detail Treuer's use of *Daphnis and Chloe* and the story of Apelles.

38. See Emily Roiphe and Donna Seaman, for example.

unsuspecting characters. In the moments following the youths' first kiss, for instance, the narrator interrupts his description of the proceedings with a parenthetical caveat to his characterization of Bimaadiz: "when he blinked it was a lazy, hooded gesture (if we can call blinking a gesture, and most certainly we can when describing lovers and how they look at each other)" (162). The narrator further underscores the voyeurism he invokes by explicitly linking the story to the couple's pursuit of sexual satisfaction: Bimaadiz and Eta's sexual frustration and eventual consummation is not incidental to the story, but rather its purpose. He explains the connection as he describes the couple's discovery of handholding in a deliberately lengthy, detailed passage:

> And so they walked along hand in hand with no idea where they were going—experiencing a quiet pleasure lost on adults, who, because they have experienced it all, because they have climbed the peak of life, look down on everything. They have forgotten how beautiful the view is from the valley floor. But how soon we search for the higher trail! Because, if Bimaadiz and Eta had reached the end of their efforts we could end ours and stop the story here—with the two impossibly beautiful children, walking hand in hand down the wooded trail. But since their satisfaction *did* end, and much sooner than they expected, our story must continue. And so, even though holding hands was a big step for the two, and even though it brought them pleasure that they themselves would have been hard-pressed to describe, it can't be imagined that it brought them total happiness. (160)

Mimicking the language of *Daphnis and Chloe*, the omniscient narrator slows down the reader not to develop the narrative or build suspense, but to contextualize why he offers readers access to Bimaadiz and Eta. The point of the passage, of lingering on the youths' sexual inexperience, is to draw into focus readerly expectations about what sort of story we are consuming and what would constitute satisfaction for the story's audience—in other words, under what conditions he might "stop the story here." Treuer parodies what Yost terms "Euroamerican fantasies" of complete access to Native lives, fantasies driven by expectations of access cultivated by ethnography and ethnographic narratives canonized through literature.

Translation's conspicuous reliance on a classic European pastoral nods toward a tradition of Native informants identifying and capitalizing on the blindness that social fantasies cultivate. Jace Weaver offers Herbert Schwarz's *Tales from the Smokehouse* (1974) as an example of an informant subverting expectations by explicitly catering to stereotypes. One of the stories in Schwarz's collection is about a young Native woman naïvely seduced by a priest who capitalizes on her ignorance and sexual innocence, reportedly related to Schwarz from "the real 'gentle Indian girl' involved in the incident" (51). Finding the recent convert lying "naked on the stone floor," a missionary removes his clothes to lie next to her to share in her suffering (51). Weaver summarizes the story:

> Seeing the man's erection, the young girl inquires, "What is that pointed stick that stands out from your belly?" His Pauline response is: "My child . . . this stick is a thorn in my side, which causes me great pain and misery." The naïve catechist replies, "It grieves me to see you so. Although I am cold and hungry, my suffering is but small compared to yours. . . . I want you to torture me with that thorn of yours, and put it where it will hurt me most!" The story then progresses to its obvious, gruesome conclusion, made all the more disgusting because it implicitly says that Native women do not know their own bodies. (50–51)

The story, as Weaver explains, is the "put the devil in hell tale" from Giovanni Boccaccio's *The Decameron* (51). He surmises, "I believe that Schwarz's 'informant' was having a bit of fun at the expense of the amateur ethnographer, a not uncommon practice (though Italian Renaissance literature is not normally involved in the jape)" (51). The Native woman clearly recognized the degree to which the ethnographer desired evidence of familiar narratives, so she obliged, at his expense; in doing so, she used the political tools available to her to assert privacy by withholding her own story. *Daphnis and Chloe* serves Treuer's pastoral narrator much as *The Decameron* provided source material for Schwarz's informant: the narrator thinly veils an old European story as Native by changing the names and setting but keeping intact the stereotypes through which canonical American literature renders Natives legible. In other words, the pastoral offers evidence for what readers already "know" about Natives through legacies of Eurocentric scholarship and representation.

In perhaps less obvious ways, Apelles's diegesis can be read in the same tradition of Native dissimulation. Apelles and Campaspe, as critics point out, are historical figures from Alexander the Great's court, and their love story resonates with the characters' romance in the novel: an artist, Apelles, paints such a beautiful likeness of Campaspe, one of Alexander's concubines, that Alexander gifts Campaspe to Apelles in exchange for the portrait.[39] The novel's Apelles, likewise, crafts a beautiful likeness of Campaspe through prose, writ-

---

39. John Lyly's *Campaspe* (1584) reprises an account of the story first recorded by Pliny the Elder. For more complete consideration of Apelles's and Campaspe's relationship to the historical figures, see Freiert, Robinson, and Yost.

ing their relationship into existence. More importantly, Treuer's Apelles—like the Native woman in Weaver's anecdote—gives his audience the impression that we have access to his life by appearing to transparently translate his memories and intimate experiences for our consumption. Whereas Schwarz's informant leaves the ironic tension in her story intact, Treuer tips his hand in the final scenes. In both cases, the storyteller maintains control over access and rewrites conventional power relations between Native informants and their audiences; the storytellers carve out—and then draw attention to—spaces of narrative privacy by substituting "classic" stories for their own. Instead of accessing authentic testimony, readers are returned to the Western canon.

Apelles's disclosure that he has fabricated the self he translates for his audience underscores the limits of readers' access to the novel's characters. Like the young Native woman in Weaver's anecdote, Apelles declines to provide readers with transparent insight into his life; he tells a story that is "meant to be read" but refuses the role of cultural translator historically demanded of Native individuals (24). By insisting on the novel's fictionality, Treuer shifts focus from cultural artifacts to storytelling, from amateur ethnography to literary study.[40] In other words, he asserts his ability—and prerogative—to dissimulate and to exercise narrative privacy by translating on his own terms.

Indeed, in a novel centered on acts of translation, Treuer conspicuously declines to translate some Ojibwe dialogue. In an interview, Treuer explains his decision to leave some Ojibwe phrases in his novels untranslated:

> We novelists have inherited an ethnographic impulse—there's an equation in ethnography where you have the ethnographer and you have the informant, and novelists have inherited that, so that the world is the ethnographer, we feel compelled to explain ourselves out to the world, and why should we? Why shouldn't the world reach a little closer and push a little harder, dig a little deeper, towards us? And that's why I won't translate. (Kirwan 17)

Treuer privileges authorial—and in this case, specifically Ojibwe—knowledge by declining to translate private Ojibwe conversations and thoughts for his audience.[41] While Treuer has on occasion translated phrases from his novels, in an interview about his second novel, *The Hiawatha* (1999), he explains his reluctance to render a character's thoughts into English for scholars as an alle-

---

40. Currently on the Literature and Creative Writing faculty at the University of Southern California, Treuer earned his Ph.D. in Anthropology.

41. Most Ojibwe phrases in the pastoral can be understood through context. In Apelles's narrative, however, such is not the case. When a character in the story translates Ojibwe dialogue into English, the meaning changes dramatically (Yost 63).

giance he shares with his character: "Betty's life is terrible, for the most part. And when she remembers her early life with her husband it is the one precious and beautiful and unsullied part of it. So she protects it in her mind from the rest of her life by remembering it in Ojibwe. To translate it in the book would be, in a way, to violate Betty's memory" (Kennedy 53–54). He explains further, "of course, Ojibwe speakers will understand it, but that understanding must be earned by the reader. The chance to look into Betty's life completely is a chance that is earned" (54). While untranslated Ojibwe is less critical to understanding Apelles's stories than Betty's, *Translation* similarly underscores the limits of some readers' access to the characters. As Treuer's interview indicates, formal assertions of privacy affect audiences unevenly; a critical lens rather than prescriptive reading strategy, narrative privacy accounts for reading audiences' range of positionalities and access to linguistic and cultural knowledges. Moments that remain opaque to some readers, in other words, are accessible to others.

Through Apelles, Treuer invites the novel's audience to read vulnerably and to engage with *Translation* literarily, even as he forecloses the possibility of ethnographic voyeurism. Treuer's insistence on Apelles's fictionality disrupts historical power relations between informants and ethnographers, texts and readers by rendering visible Apelles's refusal to translate, or to make accessible, anything other than make-believe.

WITHHOLDING STORIES: *CROSSING VINES*

In *Crossing Vines*, González takes up similar concerns about visibility and literary access to historically marginalized communities by paying particular attention to characters' desires for privacy. Like Treuer, González invokes a long history of uneven power relations in conditions of visibility for people of color and indigenous people by crafting a character engaged in an ethnographic project against his subjects' wishes. González's researcher, however, is a member of the community he studies, or a participant observer. In one plotline of the novel, a Chicana protagonist, Doña Ramona, records stories and her conversations with her friends for her son's college Chicano studies project. Her son, Leonardo, disrupts family relations by asking his mother to record her stories, an action that angers his father and puts his mother's employment as a farm worker at risk. Leonardo plans to incorporate his mother's stories "as footnoted and cross-referenced material in the folklore/oral culture section of the project. *Crossing Vines: A Field Study of the Culture of Work (Grape Pickers Are People, Too!)*" (204). González's play with

Leonardo's school project title invites critical comparison between the ethnographic taking that the character performs and the borrowing that González does in writing fiction about contemporary Mexican American farm workers from California, where he was born. He thus implicates his role as author as he literarily explores the types of ethnic stories—ethnographic and fictional stories of determined struggle—that continue to matter most in academe and to commercial audiences. González also narrates the ways Leonardo's informants, particularly Doña Ramona, limit his access to their stories. In metafictionally attending to the limits of the stories he includes in his novel, González uses narrative privacy to engage with ethnographic imperatives in ethnic literature by negotiating the tension between choosing to remain silent and telling the intrusive and extrusive narratives Leonardo—and by extension, potential publishers and readers—desires.

Doña Ramona is fully aware that her son has positioned her as an informant; as long as she can tell stories on her own terms, however, she is a willing participant. She learns to take pleasure in recording her stories and in her ability to adapt to new technology despite her initial suspicion of the microcassette recorder Leonardo lends her. She explains: "Leonardo got his reward, and she got hers: listening to her own voice embedded in the static had the effect of someone else talking to her. Hearing the stories through a different voice made them sound so fresh and new" (5). Similarly, when Leonardo asks her to bring a camera into the grape fields to document the working conditions of contemporary farm workers, an action that her husband, Don Manuel, feels compromises their jobs because the "foreman's going to think we're playing around instead of working," Doña Ramona enjoys the novelty of photography with her girlfriends, who snap pictures of each other working and playing (8). She understands that Leonardo uses her as a native informant and accepts the role willingly, albeit fully aware of her son's naiveté and the contradictions of his academic project.

Although he belongs to the community of farm workers in Southern California that he purports to study, Leonardo views his family through an academic lens that distances him from their daily lives. Entering his fourth year of college, Leonardo is fully indoctrinated in academic worldviews:

> In college he learned fast and adapted swiftly to the tenets of the culture. Books were knowledge. History was subjective. The past informed the future. Identity was political. Anything was susceptible to challenge, analysis, or deconstruction. He now searched for deeper meanings and more difficult truths in that vocation of his father's that had once caused him such anxiety. Farm worker. (201)

For Leonardo, "farm worker" is a discursive concept rather than a lived reality, despite the fact that both of his parents and most of the community in which he was raised still earn their living in the fields. González draws particular attention to the way "Leonardo's skin glowed with an unblemished smoothness because he never had to work in the sun," and Leonardo's father observes that "Leonardo's hands were smooth as book covers, his face tight and unscarred by the hardships of the fields. Leonardo didn't know horsepower from horseshit but that didn't keep his mouth shut" (5, 60). In the mornings while home on break, Leonardo lounges in bed, calling out for his mother to remember to bring a camera to work as she and Don Manuel leave the apartment in the early hours for a long day in the fields.

González highlights the tension between Leonardo's academic epistemologies and the worldview of Leonardo's family by having characters contemplate the relative value of various forms of knowledge. Interested in ethnographic data, Leonardo instructs Doña Ramona to record only true stories:

> "You can tell me about your childhood in México. Or about the first time you crossed over to the United States. About your friends, your lovers."
> "Leonardo!"
> "Or tell me stories."
> Stories. Not fairy tales, not legends, Leonardo made it clear. People stories.
> "You mean, like chisme?"
> Leonardo laughed. "Why not? But stories about people you know. Like the ones you tell me all the time." (5)

Doña Ramona, while delighted to have her youngest son home from college for a time, is fully aware of the contradictory nature of his sudden interest in family and community history:

> He came to take things from the family album, to make photocopies of birth certificates, church records, old postcards and letters. He even took her palm prints by pressing her blistered hands into a dish with blue paint. Now he wanted to take the stories she had been telling him all along. Now he wanted to pay attention, but through the little black box. As usual, documents held the only truths, the only valid facts. No matter. (5)

Doña Ramona understands that her "people stories" gain value in her son's eyes once they are required for his academic study and recorded on tape so he can transcribe them into his records as "footnoted and cross-referenced material" in his project (204). The intimacy that interests Leonardo is not in relation to his mother but to her private stories.

Despite the pleasure she finds in recording her stories, Doña Ramona ultimately experiences Leonardo's fieldwork as extractive: he "came to take" pictures, palm prints, and family artifacts, as well as her stories. She understands Leonardo as pursuing a particular construction of authenticity, despite his supposedly precise academic methodologies, and recognizes his emotional disregard for his subjects:

> She was sure Leonardo had selected that one [photograph] in particular because it was the only one she owned in sepia, cracked and faded with age. Its removal bothered her because it was the only picture she had left of her mother, Cleotilde. The white backing of the pictureless picture frame appeared to glow almost obscenely, as if her mother's dress had been removed, leaving her to hide behind the embarrassed undergarments. At best the pristine pillow of her mother's casket came to mind. In either case the missing body of her mother hinted at a sacrilegious act. (212)

Doña Ramona interprets her son's theft of the sepia-toned picture as sacrilegious and an invasion of her mother's—and her own household's—privacy. She values the picture because of her relationship to its contents whereas Leonardo takes it for his project because its appearance adheres to his assessment of authenticity. For Doña Ramona, Leonardo's reasons for taking the photograph—so different from her own reasons for wanting to keep it—add insult to the theft. In describing Leonardo's taking as "sacrilegious," González, like Treuer, invokes historical contexts of ethnographic interest in and invasion of sacred institutions, practices, and objects, as well as the institutional theft of human remains.

Although she humors Leonardo's project for two weeks despite her misgivings, Doña Ramona ultimately stakes limits to her son's access the night Don Manuel returns home after a shooting at the grape warehouse. Hearing his father's excited talk about violence during a labor dispute, Leonardo emerges from his bedroom to record his father's account. Frustrated with his son and unnerved by the evening's events, Don Manuel cuts his story short and Leonardo retreats to his bedroom, allowing his parents space to talk quietly.[42] Once Don Manuel goes to bed, however, Leonardo overwhelms his mother with

---

42. Leonardo's decision not to eavesdrop on his parents' conversation might be read as his staking limits to his project. Watching from a crack in the door as his "mother stroked his father's balding hair lovingly, in a tender gesture he had not witnessed in a long time . . . shamed him enough to make him withdraw from the door and shut it" (208).

questions, pumping her for information: "'So what happened, Ma? What did my father say?' he asked. Doña Ramona took a step back towards the recliner. 'Who got shot? Anyone die? What are the police saying? Has the UFW been contacted? Are the farm workers organizing? Do you think I can go to the field tomorrow and conduct some interviews? What's the boss like? Here, speak into this'" (210). Reaching the limits of her patience, Doña Ramona reacts in anger: "'Enough, Leonardo!' Doña Ramona yelled and accidentally slapped the beloved little black box out of Leonardo's hand. The tape recorder bounced off the carpet and struck the wall. Leonardo, taken aback, stared at her with surprise as he knelt down to pick the recorder up. 'What?' he said. 'I'm just asking'" (210). Leonardo's insistence on the innocence of his curiosity and his insensitivity to his mother's emotions shuts down Doña Ramona. Willing to humor her son when she can, she turns down his insistent demands for information when she feels she needs quiet and privacy.

The final scene of the novel demarcates the limits of Doña Ramona's willingness to share herself with her son, illustrating her desire to be distanced from the academic narrative he is producing. After Leonardo once again retreats to his bedroom, leaving his recorder with his mother in case she changes her mind, Doña Ramona is alone in the living room, when she realizes that Leonardo forgot to put a tape in the machine. As she considers the empty recorder, "speechless as a tiny black coffin," the electricity goes out, turning off the fans and swamp coolers and bringing the men out of their bedrooms (211). For entertainment, Doña Ramona tells her husband and son a story, allowing Leonardo to believe he is recording the tale with his tapeless machine. When she finishes, Doña Ramona asserts the privacy she feels her son has violated through his extractive ethnographic project:

> "I have another story if you want to hear it," she said, stomping her feet and she stood upright. "I can tell you a dozen stories and then a dozen more. My head is filled with them. What good am I if not to entertain you with these senseless little tales? How else will you know I once lived? And what will you remember of me when the last word has been spoken, Leonardo? Even now I'm simply a ghost of a voice to you, aren't I? Well, you know what? Forget about the next chingada story, you ingrate. Forget about me entirely. I have nothing more to say. Chingado." (215–16)

Mimicking her son's patronizing view of her "little tales," Doña Ramona confronts Leonardo with the distance between her experiences and his. Instead of listening to and valuing his parents, Leonardo extracts information that fits his agenda. Discarding the stories his mother has always told him, he now listens only to her recordings, to her "ghost of a voice." The epistemologies Leonardo values exclude his parents even as he imagines himself as speaking for them in academic writing.

González invites comparison between his character's ethnographic pursuits and his own literary project. In titling the ethnographic study at the center of Leonardo's relationship with his parents *Crossing Vines,* the same title he uses for the novel, González widens the critical lens the narrative focuses on Leonardo as a native ethnographer to include his own position as an author writing about Mexican and Mexican American characters in fiction. In a moment of frustration with his parents, "Leonardo rolled his eyes and shook his head. Why hadn't he stayed enrolled in that fiction writing class? He would have learned to invent his family history. Too late, he concluded as he shuffled the papers strewn across the bed" (204). Despite Leonardo's suggestion that writing fiction would solve his dilemma, González questions the difference between mining family experiences for fiction and the extractive ethnographic methods Leonardo practices. Through his characters' insistence on privacy, González illustrates the ways in which ethnographic and narrative accounts can be invasive, even when written by members of the community. As if acknowledging his own implication in the processes the novel critiques, González grants his characters privacy by ending the novel almost immediately after Doña Ramona's outburst.

Notably, González positions a woman of color, historically a demographic particularly vulnerable to ethnographic exploitation, as a potential cultural and literary informant. Doña Ramona's attitude toward Leonardo's report—by turns amused, reproachful, and frustrated—acknowledges the historical ethnographic traditions in which she participates and challenges Leonardo's assumption that inclusion in academic records is honorific or important. She also understands that her interlocutor, like his literary audiences, covet more than the stories she is willing to share; Leonardo pursues access to the sacred and the private with the explicit aim of sharing his access with academic, reading audiences. Le, in his short story about Vietnamese refugees, expands González's critical project to consider more directly what it means to narrate the private, the sacred, and the traumatic for reading audiences.

LOOKING AWAY: "THE BOAT"

Like Treuer and González, Le positions readers as curious voyeurs into his characters' experiences and similarly shields his characters through narrative privacy. Le invokes ethnographic imperatives in US ethnic and indigenous literary markets, however, without including an ethnographer character or otherwise explicit reference to ethnographic practices. Rather, Le confronts readers' curiosity and presumed access to his characters, questioning the politics of readers' desire to comprehend characters' trauma. Goellnicht similarly understands Le as engaging readers' ethnographic lenses, observing that "Le emphasizes the viewer's incomprehension, but more than this, he insists that the viewer does not have a *right* to comprehension. Too often readers of ethnic literature maintain a voyeuristic gaze that assumes the right of the dominant culture, the viewing subject, to know the viewed as an ethnographic object of study" (216, emphasis in original). Le protects his characters in spaces of narrative privacy and invites introspection on the part of the reader: Do we really think we could understand? What are we looking for in these characters? Why are we looking?[43] In other words, Le focuses on the historical processes and unequal power relations undergirding readers' potential approaches to his story. Building on the connection Goellnicht draws between ethnographic inquiry and "The Boat," I argue that Le not only identifies readers' ethnographic gaze and desire for comprehension, but also that he responds by indicting readers' curiosity and his own position as a fiction writer. Narrative privacy, in other words, affords Le an opportunity to preserve his characters' privacy while also working through the implications of writing fiction that necessarily discloses stories to reading audiences.

"The Boat" follows a group of refugees who have left Vietnam hoping to escape the trauma and deprivation of colonial wars and their aftermath in the late 1970s. Escaping by boat, the group meets adversity almost immediately and drifts at sea for more than a week. Mai, a sixteen-year-old girl traveling alone, focalizes the narrator's perspective. She befriends Quyen and Quyen's six-year-old son, Truong, the two of whom become something of a surrogate family for Mai over the course of the journey. Le offers readers extensive access to the physical, visible abjection the characters experience, while limiting readers' access to the psychic, emotional level of characters' experiences on the boat, including hunger, overcrowding, and Truong's death on the same day they sight land. Even Mai's internal narrative that helps guide the story remains largely superficial in its treatment of her emotional experiences. Like González, Le stymies readers' access to his characters to deny the possibility

---

43. As works on visual representations on trauma, Susan Sontag's *Regarding the Pain of Others* (2003) and Frances Guerin and Roger Hallas's *The Image and the Witness: Trauma, Memory, and Visual Culture* (2007) ask similar questions about witness and spectatorship. Sontag, for example, asks how and why we view images of trauma as she considers how viewing photographs of lynchings implicates audiences as co-spectators (91–92).

of comprehension and to resist contained, extractable narratives that can be studied, circulated, and commodified.

Through Truong's story, Le raises questions about the politics of representing, or expressing, traumatic experiences. "In facing a genuine historical trauma," Michael Roth explains, "only silence appears, at least to some, an honorable response because it does not trivialize the event. On the other hand, silence always raises the problem of forgetting, for the event seems to demand representation, commemoration" (84). Le negotiates this representational bind through narrative privacy, revealing to readers the precise limits of what he is willing and able to narrate. Le reflects these limits even in his characterizations; the colonial wars, subsequent reeducation camps, and a volatile political atmosphere taught Vietnamese faces "how to be expressionless" (240). As a young child, Truong has only known war, which manifests itself physically in his expressionless exterior. Le describes the boy as "like an old man crushed into the rude shape of a boy" (235) with "preternaturally calm" eyes and a "face as smooth and impassive as that of a ceramic toy soldier" (231). Truong's inexpressive countenance, however, belies his emotional turmoil:

> When Mai first met him they'd been gliding—silently, under cover of night—through a port full of enemies. Even then his demeanor had been improbably blank. The war had that to answer for too, she'd thought—the stone-hard face of a child barely six years old. Only when the boat shifted and his body leaned into hers had she felt, astonishingly, his heartbeat through his trunk—an electric flurry racing through the concavities of his back, stomach and chest. His body furious with life. He was engaged in some inward working out, she realized, and in that instant she'd grasped that nothing—nothing—was more important than her trying to see whatever it was he was seeing behind his dark, flat eyes. (235)

"Furious with life," a characterization that points to not only his racing heartbeat but also the gross injustices of his short existence, Truong contains worlds of emotion. Le does not depict in Truong a child evacuated of life by war, but rather he illuminates through Mai's focalization the limits he stakes around readers' access. Even as an insider sharing Truong's experiences, Mai is unable to translate for readers. Goellnicht observes: "Truong never has his story told; it remains a complete, unreachable mystery, his trauma shut off from narrative, without even the possibility of attempted retrieval" (218–19). Importantly, trauma studies scholars theorize the inscrutability and inexpressibility of traumatic experiences and memories. Truong could be understood, therefore, as Goellnicht suggests, as embodying the limits of language to express the inarticulable. Reading his inscrutability through the lens of narrative privacy suggests another interpretation, however: he illuminates not the limits of language but of literature. Le is uninterested in retrieving Truong's trauma—or even attempting such a retrieval—but rather, is invested in protecting it from readers' curiosity. In doing so, Le draws attention to the nature of readers' curiosity; Le affords his characters narrative privacy to underscore the often superlative nature of narrating trauma, abjection, and the unseemly details of life.[44] Because readers do not need to know, Truong's story remains secret.

In addition to considering how characters' lives are rendered visible, "The Boat" also turns explicit attention to characters as seeing agents. Notably, it is characters' frequent refusal or reluctance to look that underscores their agency and their importance to Le's theorization of narrating trauma. On the boat, which endures enemy encounters and a strong storm only to list aimlessly without direction or power for more than a week, Le describes characters who choose to look away from dead bodies being tossed overboard rather than look on in curiosity. The first casualty, a small child, elicits an apparently unanimous reaction from the boat. "To the terrible drawn-out note of a woman's keening the bundle was tossed, a meek splash, into the water" (250), the narrator reports, and, "Like everyone else, Mai looked away" (251). Each of the passengers chooses not to watch the sea burials, perhaps to protect themselves from the emotional trauma of watching babies tossed into the sea or to protect the privacy of mourning families. Their insistent choice to not look becomes a pattern over their listless days and nights at sea: "That night another bundle was thrown overboard. Minutes later they heard a thrashing in the water. It was too dark to see anything, yet, still, everyone averted their gaze" (251). Even when it would not be possible to see, the passengers insist on looking away. Mai's resistance toward looking extends beyond the actual sea burials to include their aftereffects: "As more and more bundles were thrown overboard she taught herself not to look—not to think of the bundles as human—she resisted the impulse to identify which families had been depleted" (257). For Mai, not looking becomes a survival strategy that also affords mourning families privacy. Because she focalizes the narrative and therefore readers' access, we, too, look away. Le uses narrative perspective as a forcing feature, limiting readers' perspectives according to Mai's sense of decorum in the face of trauma.

---

44. In "Love and Honor and Pity and Pride and Compassion and Sacrifice," examined in chapter 2, Le similarly intervenes to protect his characters' stories from readers; the protagonist writes his father's account of surviving the massacre at My Lai only to have his father burn the manuscript before readers have the opportunity to read the narrative. For the father, as for Mai, forgetting is a survival strategy.

The last body the narrator describes being tossed overboard is Truong's. After delivering their own sad bundle to the men tasked with disposing of bodies, Mai and Quyen move to the front of the boat: "They stood together in silence, the spray moistening their faces as they looked forward, focusing all their sight and thought on that blurry peninsula ahead, that impossible place" (272). Mai and Quyen look intently away from Truong's inanimate body and its inevitable encounter with the sharks trailing the ship and toward the blurry color in the distance that the passengers have tentatively identified as land. For the two women, choosing not to look protects their psychic health. In writing a story in which characters choose not to look at the animating trauma of the narrative, Le raises questions about readers' curiosity. The final image of "The Boat," in which Mai and Quyen stand silently at the front of a boat, looking forward toward the hope of reaching land safely, committed to ignoring everything going on behind them—Truong's sea burial, sharks attacking his body—is not a memorializing gesture. Rather than remembering or sating a sense of curiosity, the women choose not to look back. If the players in the traumatic journey away from a homeland devastated by colonial warfare and into an uncertain future choose not to look or to look back, what would it mean for readers to have access to the images of bundles being thrown into water? The characters choose to look away, but readers continue reading, looking in on characters' lives, a curious looking enabled by Le's representation of the events.

Le maintains privacy in his story, however, by diverting his narrative along with his passengers' eyes. Readers have access to the sounds of mothers wailing and small bodies being tossed to the sharks—sensations to which passengers are also subject—but Le's narrator never describes what Mai and her peers choose not to see: what the bodies look like entering the water or when they are attacked. Once again, Mai's respect of others' privacy limits what readers can see and know. The closest readers get to a description is the brief account Mai imagines as she stands with Quyen, adamantly looking forward toward land and away from "the men at the back of the boat peeling the blanket off, swinging the small body once, twice, three times before letting go, tossing him as far behind the boat as possible so he would be out of sight when the sharks attacked" (272). The men who conduct the burials likely have more extensive perspectives than the other passengers with the liberty to avert their gazes, but theirs is a view Le withholds completely.[45]

---

45. Interestingly, artist Matt Huynh adapted "The Boat" into an interactive, digital graphic narrative. The narrative, produced by SBS, offers readers black and white visuals of the moments Le narratively deflects; readers also listen to the story and have the option to manipulate the story's pace.

By tethering readers' access to Mai's decisions about when and whether to look, Le considers how narrative might be experienced as a violation of privacy in which deeply personal traumas are rendered visible for reading audiences. In her theorization of productive forgetting, Y-Dang Troeung raises similar concerns, asking, "What is the effect on traumatized subjects to turn, or who are turned, back to look at their trauma? How can we envision a political project that takes better ethical care of those who bear the burden of remembering?" (91). "The Boat" models one potential approach to this project. Even as Le relates a narrative of trauma, he does not explain what goes on under Truong's surface, in part because it might be a violation of privacy to pin down such an experience in narrative, to render it somehow knowable, even banal, to curious reading audiences, and an act of violence against "those who bear the burden of remembering." The characters show that looking is a choice, and Le chooses not to allow readers to look into particular spaces. By crafting these spaces of narrative privacy, Le offers an alternative to silence and representation of trauma and draws critical attention to his choices as a writer invested in destabilizing ethnographic imperatives in literature.

If Treuer focuses his critique of ethnographic imperatives in fiction on publishers and readers, Le and, especially, González likewise consider difficult questions about the ways in which authors, by virtue of their fictional representations, may also be complicit in colonial processes of looking. González suggests narrative privacy offers one way of negotiating the tension between silence and telling intrusive and extractive narratives by narrating the ways informants organically limit their own spaces of privacy; Le models a more definitive form of narrative privacy by explicitly omitting portions of his narrative.

The questions of representation Treuer, González, and Le raise are compounded in a twenty-first-century context in which the stakes of visibility continue to rise in an era of increasing political surveillance. Discourse around border policing, immigration and travel bans, and the rise of biometric technologies center on the conditions under which individuals might be surveilled, tracked, and otherwise policed by the state. For Native communities and communities of color, the specter of state surveillance is nothing new, but rather part of a longer—and deeply fraught—history. Building on this chapter, which explores why and how writers desire privacy in the face of persistent ethnographic surveillance, chapter 2 considers how writers theorize narrative privacy by considering the possibility of literature as a surveillance technology.

CHAPTER 2

Omniscient Surveillance and the Politics of Visibility After 9/11

In January 2015, PEN America released its conclusions from a survey of 800 authors in a report titled *Global Chilling: The Impact of Mass Surveillance on International Writers,* a follow-up to their 2013 report on the influence of mass surveillance on US writers. The authors of the study report that US surveillance policies have damaged the United States' reputation as a "protector of freedom of expression at home" and as a "champion of freedom of expression around the world" (12, 13). The report calls for US Congressional action on the principle that reasonable protection from mass surveillance is specifically guaranteed to US citizens and, more broadly, constitutes a universal human right (16). In their 2013 study, PEN America found that US writers increasingly assume their research, talks, and writing are under surveillance, and that the "assumption that they are under surveillance is harming freedom of expression by prompting writers to self-censor their work in multiple ways" (*Chilling Effects* 2). Among their recommendations, the study authors ask that the US government cease broad profiling practices to restore "required due process protections, including probable cause and individualized suspicion," and to make "the right to be free of unwarranted surveillance a cornerstone of surveillance policy and practice" (9). The institute's conclusions in the two studies, that people—including writers—ought to be entitled to due process and freedom from unwarranted state surveillance, indicate growing mainstream concern about issues with which Native communities and communities of color (among others, including LGBTQ+ communities) have long contended.

PEN America's anxiety over surveillance and privacy surfaces across contemporary fiction in response to 9/11 and subsequent political shifts around the world, manifesting itself in many ways, including in literary form.[1] Many contemporary writers' literary projects seek new forms to contend with and better understand a century marked by multiple dramatic social and political shifts, including reconceived ideas about privacy, narrative, and surveillance. As Georgiana Banita notes in *Plotting Justice: Narrative Ethics and Literary Culture After 9/11* (2012), her study of the relationship between ethics, surveillance, and literary form in post-9/11 fiction, surveillance "is a recurrent trope in post-9/11 literature" (10). Further, a primary feature of the post-9/11 fiction Banita studies is attention to characters' emerging awareness of their vulnerability to the state and other organizations who might track their behavior and lifestyles. She identifies recognizable formal patterns emerging as a result, arguing "surveillance has influenced character construction and development in the post-9/11 novel, interfering with familiar notions of omniscience, focalization, and readerly experience" (55).[2] As Banita rightly contends, the "panoptic impulse in fiction is by no means a recent development"; rather, as she explores in depth, the impulse has a long history in and beyond US literary traditions (252). What is new, however, about post-9/11 fiction is that authors are crafting fiction in a historical moment of unprecedented expansion of state security and surveillance technologies. As a result, Banita argues, many post-9/11 fictions center on characters who are facing for the first time the specter of state surveillance. For US writers of color and Native writers, however, the sense of being monitored, of being under constant—or apparently constant—state surveillance has a much longer history.

For the writers in this book, particularly those in this chapter—Salvador Plascencia, Nam Le, and Stephen Graham Jones—state surveillance has long been a way of life for their communities and the communities of the char-

---

1. In a contentious editorial published in the *Guardian* in September 2013, Jonathan Franzen characterizes the "panoptical surveillance" of social media and divisive twenty-first-century US politics—in contrast to the simplicity of his childhood in the 1950s and 1960s—as apocalyptic for serious contemporary literature.

2. "The post-9/11 novel builds on Otherness as a fundamental structural principle. I say *structural* to point out that the post-9/11 novels' interest in Otherness exceeds the thematic. As I will show, formal narrative choices contribute as much as the notions of foreignness and distance to the post-9/11 novel's concern with alterity" (Banita 22). Banita explores how post-9/11 literary forms introduce alterity rather than the ways in which constructions of difference have always conditioned the politics of visibility in the US. Further, for most of the characters in the books she examines, alterity is a subject of exploration rather than a lived experience.

acters they craft. As Simone Browne argues in her interdisciplinary study of black surveillance, "rather than seeing surveillance as something inaugurated by new technologies, such as automated facial recognition or unmanned autonomous vehicles (or drones), to see it as ongoing is to insist that we factor in how racism and antiblackness undergird and sustain the intersecting surveillances of our present order" (8–9). Similarly ongoing and historical surveillances—not of blackness but border surveillance, wartime documentation by the Department of Defense, and FBI investigations—permeate and organize the fictions in this chapter. These historical resonances structure the texts' responses to 9/11 and its aftereffects on privacy and surveillance; through narrative privacy, Plascencia, Le, and Jones critically engage with relationships between post-9/11 discourses of surveillance and much older domestic surveillance policies. Each of the texts in chapter 2 positions readers as placing characters of color or indigenous characters under surveillance, a surveillance enabled by the authors who expose characters' stories through fiction. Using form to implicate literature as a surveillance technology positions writers as informants or as otherwise facilitating surveillance, and readers as, in a way, voyeurs or surveyors—and calls into question the politics of literary studies in new and urgent ways. While this chapter's texts emerge from disparate contexts, they share a formal investment in privacy in ways that invoke and reflect both on contemporary discourses of surveillance and privacy and the histories of racialized visibility with which these writers contend.

In his 2005 novel, *The People of Paper*, Plascencia metafictionally explores his position as a Mexican American, an immigrant from Guadalajara, and a fiction writer in the US writing after 9/11. Specifically, he invites critical attention to how his narrative—which exposes the lives of his Mexican and Mexican American farmworker characters for reading audiences—relates to ongoing surveillance of people of color along the US–Mexico border and throughout the United States. Le shares Plascencia's concerns about exposing his characters' lives in "Love and Honor and Pity and Pride and Compassion and Sacrifice," a short story from his 2008 collection, *The Boat*. In "Love and Honor," set not on the border but in Iowa, Le's characters do not experience political surveillance in the same ways that Plascencia's farmworkers in California do, but they still feel the burden of readers' gazes down on the page as well as the afterlives of state surveillance of military actions abroad. Like Jones's Native characters in the Great Plains under surveillance by the FBI in *The Bird Is Gone: A Monograph Manifesto* (2003), Plascencia's and Le's characters experience the burden of explaining their presence as nonwhite men and women in the US, the burden of revealing their histories and lives, and the burden indigenous and nonwhite authors face in contemporary fiction markets to make accessible the intimacies, joys, and traumas of negotiating the twenty-first-century US as indigenous and ethnic subjects. Plascencia, Le, and Jones make connections between recognizable forms of colonialism, political surveillance, and commercial fiction (55). In their work, the literary gaze is a privileged act of dominance and surveillance that mimics oppressive US political processes of targeting marginalized populations.

Plascencia, Le, and Jones narrate anxieties about writers' and audiences' relationships to a publishing environment that enjoys a measure of commercial success through ethnic and indigenous fiction by letting readers into the intimacies of marginalized characters' lives even as living people of color and indigenous people are disproportionately surveilled by the state and corporations. Plascencia and Le do so by crafting metafictions that feature author–characters named Sal and Nam, respectively, who confront vexed decisions about what it means to make visible stories about people of color as entertainment for reading audiences in a post-9/11 US in which people of color are under heightened surveillance. For Plascencia, exposing depictions of fieldworkers in Southern California—including undocumented workers—to curious readers constitutes a form of colonial betrayal. Plascencia further suggests that Sal (and by extension, Plascencia) runs the risk of replicating the unequal power relations driving contemporary US political surveillance on the US–Mexico border by using his omniscience to expose the lives of his Mexican and Mexican American characters. Le, on the other hand, narratively destroys a character's "true" testimony by countering US Army accounts of the My Lai massacre and instead—like David Treuer in chapter 1—offers readers a fictional story full of gaps and speculation. Both Le and Plascencia also write characters who envision their reading audience as unsympathetic and their authors as allowing readers to peer into characters' lives and hardships. The characters imagine their stories as highly invasive surveillance rather than as political representation. For the characters, authors are intrusive and opportunistic, and readers are unwelcome voyeurs, awarded unwarranted access to farmworkers' lives. As a result, neither Sal nor Nam—the author–characters in the two stories—actually follows through with publishing the stories that he writes. Unlike their fictional avatars, Plascencia and Le do publish their fiction, however, and use the relationship between characters and their fictional authors to illustrate the conflicted stakes of offering readers access to vulnerable populations in our present political and historical moment.

Federal agents and the FBI permeate Jones's novel, a narrative structured by layers of federal and colonial surveillance Jones paratextually extends to his role as author. In an interview posted to his author website, conducted by a fictional federal agent from *The Bird Is Gone* years after the novel's publication, Jones denies any involvement with the novel under surveillance. While Jones shares only his last name with the interviewing agent, Chassis Jones, who also serves as the novel's primary narrator, his disassociation from his work under paratextual interrogation resonates with Plascencia's and Le's self-deprecating exploration of the ways in which writers risk replicating the same uneven power structures they critique in their self-aware fictions. In response, all three authors write characters who recognize writers' and narrators' power of manipulation and who actively seek to escape readers' curious gazes, illuminating the power relations behind their visibility.

By formally highlighting characters' compulsory visibility to readers, Plascencia, Le, and Jones work through the implications of narrative exposure. For example, in what ways does fiction work as a surveillance technology? What does it mean for people of color and the working class to be visible in literature and cultural representations while under sustained and punitive surveillance by the state? Further, what does it mean for undocumented workers, refugees, and indigenous people to be subjected to constant state surveillance while their economic and intellectual contributions remain largely invisible? Plascencia's metafictional, self-deprecating war over narration, Le's similarly self-deprecating short story, and Jones's paratextually disowned novel do not abandon fiction as a tool for crossing social boundaries and achieving political goals—their very existence suggests persistent faith in the liberatory power of narrative—but express anxiety over the way they make lives visible despite their acknowledged concerns about exposing stories to reading audiences.

STATE SURVEILLANCE AND NARRATIVES POST-9/11

The US–Mexico border and contemporary immigration politics provide a particularly illustrative example of the pervasive surveillance many people of color in the US experience. Drawing on Laura Mulvey's theories of visibility, Rey Chow argues that people of color often experience "looked-at-ness," or a sense of being on display for privileged audiences (180). This spectacular nature of race and ethnicity in the US, which includes assumptions of criminality and difference, is a primary factor driving a culture of surveillance of nonwhite people: as scholars have argued, black people, people of color, indigenous people, and the formerly colonized are often understood as the objects of colonial surveillance.[3] David Palumbo-Liu asks, in the context of

---

3. See, for instance, Mary Louise Pratt, Eleanor Ty, Linda Smith, bell hooks, Coco Fusco, and Rey Chow.

US history, "why does it surprise these sociologists that racially marked people might have a particular intuition of being watched?" (*Asian/American* 301). His larger point is that surveillance has historically shaped racialized experiences in the US; aggressively asserting the right to look into the lives of people of color in order to observe, to police, to name, and to take ideas and images as one's own is a learned behavior with a colonial history.

For example, using as justification first the "War on Drugs" and then the threat of terrorism post-9/11, the US has steadily increased political and military surveillance of the US–Mexico border over the past half century even as Mexican food, drinks, and iconography dramatically expanded in popularity in the US.[4] It comes as no surprise that members of Donald Trump's administration sought dinner in a Mexican restaurant while, simultaneously, the administration's policies separated migrant children from their parents at the border (Rosner). In addition to a heavily militarized border and strictly regulated border crossing stations, state and local governments have increasingly relied on racially profiling immigrants, residents, and citizens who phenotypically resemble Mexican or Central/South American immigrants, a practice Arizona codified in 2010 by passing SB 1070, which was "introduced and put into effect as the strictest anti-immigration bill in the country" (Silva 64). To protect reactionary nativist beliefs, authorities conduct police actions that compromise the privacy of individuals, asserting the right to monitor their actions "in public shopping areas, on residential streets, and at bus stops," as well as in their own homes (Mize and Swords 181–82). Border surveillance and racial profiling exemplify a broader US culture of surveilling and invading the privacy of indigenous people, black people, and people of color.

Central to this popular culture of surveillance in the US is a presumed right of privileged citizens to monitor marginalized populations, a practice closely related to practices of racial profiling by officers of the law and the assumptions of ethnographic access considered in chapter 1. For instance, the Texas Border Sheriff's Coalition (TBSC) and BlueServo, a private social network, with the support of Texas's then-governor Rick Perry, launched a

---

4. While immigration reform in the 1920s prompted increased attention to the US–Mexico border, attention that "coincide[d] with new techniques of surveillance [and] the creation of the Border Patrol," recent decades, especially after the September 11, 2001 terrorist attacks, have seen renewed attention to border surveillance (Chavez 23). Noting as precedent how the US "War on Drugs" conflated Mexican immigrants with drug dealers, Ronald Mize and Alicia Swords argue "terrorism has been wantonly connected to the calls for increased border militarization. As part of the Homeland Security Act of 2002 that followed the USA Patriot Act, the reorganization and renaming of INS as Immigration and Customs Enforcement (ICE) under the auspices of the DHS [Department of Homeland Security] has meant a change in name but not its mission to enforce immigration law" (98).

"Virtual Community Watch" program along the US–Mexico border in 2007 by live-streaming images recorded by military-grade cameras of known border crossing sites (Magnuson). Anonymous online users could monitor the video stream and report "suspicious activity" electronically, essentially crowdsourcing border surveillance. Perry's press release, announcing that "Texas will use $5 million to begin placing hundreds of surveillance cameras along criminal hotspots and common routes used to enter this country," insisted that cameras will only monitor the border, "not the neighborhoods where families will continue to enjoy their privacy" ("Perry Authorizes"). The program was ended because of cuts to the homeland security budget, but not before illuminating the ideology of twenty-first-century conservatism that insists individual privacy is a right, even as it denies privacy to non-citizens and citizens of color. Even before its cancellation, for example, the program lost popularity among disgruntled users who were alarmed that their accounts were not entirely anonymous, as the website could monitor activity related to individual internet protocol (IP) addresses. The vocal detractors of the website's policy to track users succinctly illustrate users' double standards of privacy. One forum commenter writes, "So, tell me, who the FUCK are they really watching? So it begins" ("WTF!?!"). For citizens not routinely subject to racial surveillance, such monitoring might be understood as the beginning. For many others, however, surveillance has long been a way of life. In a post-9/11 US deeply influenced by discourses of nativism and national security as well as national traditions of personal privacy, determining who can reasonably expect privacy—even, as in the case of Virtual Community Watch participants, total anonymity—is a contemporary means of delineating categories of "us" and "them."

Border surveillance is only one historical instance of a long-standing US culture of surveilling nonwhite and indigenous peoples. Public outcry about concerns over state surveillance after 9/11 and subsequent political action, including the USA PATRIOT Act, the creation of the Department of Homeland Security, and the strengthening of the National Security Agency, has recently mainstreamed concern over the loss of personal privacy. This chapter will demonstrate that for people of color and indigenous people in the US, concerns about surveillance and privacy have always been firmly situated in US racism and white supremacy. For example, Barack Obama's election as president in 2008 heralded, for many commentators, the dawn of a postrace era in US history. During Obama's campaign and early years of his presidency, however, racist "birther" activists, among them current US president Donald Trump, demanded access to Obama's complete birth records to prove he was born in the US and thus eligible for the presidency, demands stemming from his race and the perceived foreignness of his name. Despite Obama's compliance with conspiracy theorists' demands—demands not placed on previous or subsequent (white) presidents—the pervasiveness of these so-called birther claims in conservative media even after Obama circulated his birth certificate illustrates the degree to which expectations of access to nonwhite people has been normalized. Birthers' public demands can be understood as one manifestation of contemporary "spectacles of surveillance," to use Leo Chavez's term for the heightened, politically driven attention to border surveillance, in which the spectacle of access to nonwhite or indigenous lives often matters more than the surveillance itself.[5] Obama's actual birth certificate, in other words, mattered far less than the public spectacle of demanding and achieving access to his private records.[6]

Obama addressed the excessive surveillance of African American men in his response to the 2013 ruling in the trial of the man who killed Trayvon Martin, recalling his own experiences with racial profiling.[7] Veiled in discourses of homeland security and terrorism, recent US wars and surveillance projects (including the expansion of satellite, drone, and balloon technologies over the Middle East and US borders as well as inner-city video surveillance programs and debates over police body and dash cameras) almost exclusively monitor black people, people of color, and indigenous people (Sternstein). The Trump administration continues to expand surveillance technologies and policies, citing the threat of terrorism as the rationale for targeting primarily people of color, including Black Lives Matter and other activist groups, as well as individuals from several majority-Muslim countries entering the US. In his statements issued through Twitter, Trump's response to violence abroad is consistently xenophobic and exclusionary, manifested in part in his insistence on "extreme vetting" of certain groups entering the country. According to the Trump Administration, the right to privacy, just as it is along the US–Mexico border, is an important delineation between in-groups and out-groups in the US.

Contemporary writers of color and Native writers are not only responding, therefore, to a specific historical moment of unprecedented surveillance in the

---

5. Chavez argues that these "media spectacles transform immigrants' lives into virtual lives, which are typically devoid of the nuances and subtleties of real lived lives"; they become spectacles, "the object of the viewer's gaze" (5–6, 5).

6. Notably, Trump refused—and was politically enabled in his refusal—to release even standard tax documents throughout his candidacy and presidency.

7. Listing the various lenses through which African Americans understood the Trayvon Martin murder and court case, Obama explained, "There are very few African-American men in this country who haven't had the experience of being followed when they were shopping in a department store. That includes me" (Obama).

twenty-first century, but are also contending with a much longer pattern of state surveillance of people of color and indigenous peoples. Unlike the experiences of many of the characters Banita analyzes in canonical post-9/11 fiction, breaches of privacy and hyper-visibility are nothing new for Plascencia, Le, and Jones or for the characters they craft. Similarly, as the authors in this chapter make evident in their fiction, the US culture of surveilling nonwhite peoples also shapes their authorial decisions as cultural producers about the literary content they produce. Insofar as fiction about nonwhite and indigenous people offers US audiences insight into the lives of the subjectivities, geographies, and ideas that animate the fiction, the writers in this chapter ask how fiction might be understood, at least in part, as a surveillance technology.

BETTER KEPT HIDDEN: *THE PEOPLE OF PAPER*

The People of Paper comprises two distinct but interpenetrating worlds. On one narrative level of the novel, Mexican and Mexican American farmworkers in El Monte, California work in flower and strawberry fields to support themselves and their families. Most of the characters are affiliated with the gang El Monte Flores, or EMF, and fight the war against omniscience, battling their author–narrator, Saturn. While Saturn makes appearances in EMF's world as a vague presence in the sky, he inhabits another narrative level where he is an author called Sal Plascencia. Sal shares his narrative world with an ex, Liz, a new lover, Cameroon (Cami), and the various minor characters with whom they interact. Sal writes from New York, though he travels to his hometown of El Monte, where he once lived with Liz. Outside of the two narrative worlds is that of Salvador Plascencia, who wrote the novel readers hold in their hands. The author figure, in varying forms, threads through each world: to distinguish between the three, I call the omniscient being EMF perceives Saturn, the fictional author Sal, and *The People of Paper*'s author Plascencia.

The two fictitious worlds can be understood as running parallel to one another, even as EMF's story is also embedded in Sal's. Narratologists such as Gerard Genette and H. Porter Abbott offer language for describing these narrative relations. Sal exists in the diegetic level, or fictional world (Abbott 231). "The 'diegetic level' consists of all those characters, things, and events that are in the storyworld of the primary narrative," meaning that reading EMF's narrative in parallel with Sal's qualifies it as also diegetic (231). However, as a character world within the diegetic novel Sal writes, also titled *The People of Paper*, EMF's narrative can also be considered metadiegetic. The diegetic levels in Plascencia's *The People of Paper*, however, are permeable, as EMF's and Sal's worlds interact, ultimately spilling over into Plascencia's.[8] Crafting a diegetic author who shares his name and basic biographical information, Plascencia critically considers his role as author. By inviting readers to conflate Sal with Plascencia, he implicates himself as an author in a legacy of literary surveillance even as the fictional nature of the story allows him authorial distance from his critique of those same processes. Cami and Liz exist both inside and outside of Sal's fiction as his lovers but also, as they find out, his characters. In both instances, Plascencia narratively imagines how fiction replicates historical and contemporary modes of racial, economic, and social oppression by invading the privacy of individual characters, curtailing their volition, and commodifying their representation for paying audiences.

Even the physical appearance of the novel's pages, ordered into columns and replete with images, blocks of ink, and holes in the page, defying conventional uses of margins and white space, take part in the novel's illumination of literary power dynamics. Arguing that "Plascencia creates a visual representation of social inequality through his use of columns," Anne Mai Yee Jansen characterizes the novel's materiality as political in nature (109). Observing the relative distribution of page space, she explains: "The fact that Saturn gets an entire page to himself illustrates his position of power by privileging his voice: he is allotted more physical space, and his words' position on the verso ensures that they will be read first. Saturn's pages represent a hegemonic narrative about the characters—a grand narrative that attempts to overshadow their voices in an attempt to profit from their pain" (109). Similarly, Sal cuts Liz's new partner's name out of the pages, an exertion of narrative privilege literalized in the materiality of the book.

Plascencia's interest in the politics of narrative form is at once playful and somber. As fictional characters, members of EMF do not have rights, and, until their author animates them, they lack even the capacity to recognize injustice, suffer, or rebel against oppressive forces. At its most basic level, therefore, the novel luxuriates in formal play to pose abstract, if entertaining, literary questions. As Plascencia's formal interest in omniscience and access illustrates, however, writing a novel about Mexicans and Mexican Americans

---

8. A cinematic example of a narrative relying on intersecting diegetic worlds (a narrative technique termed "metalepsis") is Peter Weir's *The Truman Show* (1998), in which Jim Carrey's character, Truman, lives a metadiegetic story under the command of a corporation profiting from his representation, which is itself a diegetic world in a Hollywood film. Other examples range from Warner Bros.'s *The Lego Movie* (2014) to the "mocumentary" genre pioneered by television shows *The Office* (UK and US) and *Parks and Rec*. Thomas King's *Green Grass, Running Water* (1993) and Ruth Ozeki's *A Tale for the Time Being* (2013) are two examples from US ethnic fiction; Laurence Sterne, Italo Calvino, and John Barth (particularly *Lost in the Funhouse*, 1968) are the standard literary touchstones of metaleptic diegesis.

at times too closely allegorizes contemporary racial politics for readers to sit comfortably. Through the novel's metafictional play, Plascencia explores the formal connections between the narrative view he offers readers about Mexicans and Mexican Americans on the US–Mexico border and contemporary US surveillance of the same border region. The government deploys military surveillance technologies to monitor the border, including "helicopters, night-vision equipment, electronic intrusion-detection ground sensors," in addition to border guard stations, drones, guard patrols, and extensive networks of video surveillance, all in hopes of achieving the omniscience EMF and their leader Federico de la Fe battle against (Mize and Swords 181). Local governments monitor people of color through racial profiling, and citizens such as those in the Virtual Community Watch Program monitor the border from the privacy of their homes. As EMF's omniscient and oppressive narrator–author, Sal hovers almost invisibly in the sky, particularly when the narrative takes place on the border, and monitors EMF's every move, requiring neither justification nor outside authorization to conduct his surveillance.[9] As is often the case with many undocumented Mexicans and Latin Americans working in the US, Sal's characters have no real recourse against the shadowy authority that monitors their lives.

De la Fe is first to understand that the characters' lives, scripted by Saturn to include economic and political inequality as well as personal heartbreak and physical trials, are designed for Saturn's profit and the entertainment of readers. He teaches EMF to recognize their position as subjects under surveillance, commodities, and prisoners of the novel. Readers first meet de la Fe in his home of Las Tortugas, Mexico, where he lives on a farm with his bride, Merced, and his daughter, Little Merced. De la Fe believes Saturn inflicts him with nightly incontinence and consequently drives away Merced and replaces her with inconsolable sadness. De la Fe turns to self-harm to alleviate the sadness and repress his incontinence, burning parts of his body covered by clothing when he thinks Little Merced is not watching. He finally decides to move to California with his daughter in hopes of leaving his sadness behind and starting a new life by obtaining a job in a dress factory (19). As the pair near the US–Mexico border, de la Fe begins to feel as if he is being watched: "In Tijuana, Federico de la Fe exited Bus Number 8 and instantly felt a hovering

---

9. Through his loose allegory, Plascencia critiques the ostensibly defensive gaze of US surveillance and outlines the types of Mexican and Mexican American subjectivities the state authorizes: "It was never Saturn's intention to destroy any of them, if only they had not rebelled and just lived their lives without looking up. If they had not listened to Federico de la Fe and his crazed speeches, his claims of dignity through privacy and their right to be unseen—it was he who prompted the unneeded war. Saturn wanted only to watch, to see their story develop and unfold" (46–47).

force pressing down on him. He sensed that he was being constantly watched from above" (26). De la Fe seeks out a mechanic's shop with lead tortoise shells in the yard and, sending Little Merced on an errand, asks permission to hide under a shell where he can escape the abstract surveillance he senses. After some time, he emerges and looks upward. "His black eyes moved a little to the left, toward the direction of Saturn. For years he had sensed something in the sky mocking him as he peed in his bed and dreamed of dress factories and of his lost Merced. And today, as he stood outside a junkyard hundreds of miles from his home, the force upon him felt heavier than ever before" (28). Saturn confirms de la Fe's suspicions, narrating, "Saturn was aligned directly over Federico de la Fe, following him wherever he went, budging a half a space centimeter for every five hundred land miles de la Fe and Little Merced traveled" (30). Now convinced he has located the source of the obstacles in his life, de la Fe focuses his animus on Saturn, whom readers later learn is his author-narrator, Sal Plascencia.

Saturn continues to put obstacles into the narrative as de la Fe enters California. In addition to feeling unfairly observed as he moves throughout his day, de la Fe learns his undocumented status precludes the possibility of obtaining the work he desires. Little Merced explains, "When we reached Los Angeles none of the dress factories wanted my father. They wanted people who carried laminated cards with the stamp of a bald eagle" (33). De la Fe pursues the only option available to him by settling in El Monte, California, "a small town fifteen miles east of Rita Hayworth's Hollywood mansion, a town of furrows and flowers" (33). In proximity to the wealth and glamor associated with Hollywood—and a particular form of commodified Latinx-ness embodied in Hayworth[10]—El Monte relies on a different sort of commodity: cheap labor to fuel the opulence of neighboring towns.[11] In El Monte, de la Fe joins other Mexicans and Mexican Americans in the fields where he is afforded little pay, few legal or human rights, and no opportunity for advancement.

Plascencia situates El Monte as a palimpsest of colonial economic histories, starting with US westward expansion and extending into contemporary labor practices partly responsible for the current militarization of the border. Glossing over the violent European invasions of the North American Southwest, Sal writes that the "original settlers of El Monte" arrived via the Santa Fe Trail and, later, Route 66 (34). Settled in the course of Manifest Destiny, El Monte is shaped from the start by colonial processes of land theft. The

---

10. I consider Plascencia's treatment of Rita Hayworth as a figure of racialized, gendered betrayal in chapter 3.

11. Mize and Swords describe "the central tenet by Marx": "human labor is the ultimate source of commodities" (xxxii).

nature of colonialism in El Monte changes with time, as the area gentrifies and segregates: the "original settlers . . . gradually moved from El Monte to the foothills of Arcadia and Pasadena, towns that did not have the foot traffic of flower pickers or the smell of oregano and lard bubbling from the boiling pots of menudo stands. The only time that the pioneers of El Monte returned was in December, when they bought flowers to decorate the motorized carts that floated down the avenues of their newly adopted towns" (34). In addition to explicit colonial practices of invasion and settlement to gentrification fueled by racism, ongoing processes of isolating and segregating labor along racial and legal citizenship lines shape the region around El Monte. Those with money move to the foothills, while those who fuel wealth with their labor remain in the fields of El Monte. These shifting economic arrangements elicit another migration, not from east to west, but from south to north. Plascencia tracks the northward movement of labor out of Mexico to California: "El Monte was one thousand four hundred forty-eight miles north of Las Tortugas and an even fifteen hundred miles from the city of Guadalajara, and while there were no cockfights or wrestling arenas, the curanderos' botanica shops, the menudo stands, and the bell towers of the Catholic churches had also pushed north, settling among the flowers and sprinkler systems" (34). Highlighting the gulf that exists between producers and consumers in the region, de la Fe labors in El Monte's fields, transforming his undocumented labor into flowers, which serve as ephemeral decorations for the yearly celebrations of the wealthy.

The farmworkers experience their time in the flower fields much differently than do tourists from Pasadena and Arcadia who, secure in their citizenship, visit for the beautiful sights and to collect flowers for their annual Rose Parade. Organized as EMF, the farmworkers bear the burden of tourists' consumption:

> For them there was no softness in petals and no aroma in flowers. They felt only the splinters and calluses from tilling the land and smelled only the stench of fertilizer and horse shit. Their shoes were wet and the cuffs of their work pants crusted with mud. At midday they took off their shirts, wringing the sweat and then tossing them over their shoulders. And always a cutting knife was in hand. It was from these blades and hands that bouquets and potpourri came. (34)

The violence implicit in the gang's knives does not manifest itself in criminal acts, as with the gangs in "pressed zoot suits" from LA (34). EMF "did not loot fruit stores or steal car parts; they just drank mescal and worked in the furrows harvesting flowers," but touring gangs knew better than to call them "a gang of sissy flower pickers," because they recognize that the violence EMF experiences, while understated, is nonetheless real and systemic (34).[12] The banality of capitalist violence against EMF renders it at once as invisible as the political surveillance tourists do not see and as ostentatious as their parade floats and potpourri.

While systemic and self-inflicted violence saturates the novel, the narrative present of Sal's diegetic novel finds EMF's energies focused toward political action rather than physical resistance. De la Fe organizes EMF by turning their political consciousness toward fighting surveillance and desiring volition in a world they experience as subject to Saturn's determination. He encourages them to concentrate on the root of the inequalities they experience by rising up against Saturn, the oppressive being in the sky. EMF member Froggy describes the speech de la Fe delivered to rally EMF to his cause and enlist soldiers in the war against omniscience:

> He said it was a war for volition and against the commodification of sadness. "It is a war against the fate that has been decided for us," he said. I asked who had given us the fate. Federico de la Fe shook his head and said he was not entirely sure. All he could tell us was that it was something or someone in the sky, hidden and looking down on us safely from the orbit of Saturn. And that entity had driven his wife away and cursed him with a perpetual sadness that was alleviated only through fire. And everybody else in El Monte was subject to the temper and whims that emanated from Saturn. "Right now, as I say this, we are part of Saturn's story. Saturn owns it. We are being listened to and watched, our lives sold as entertainment. But if we fight we might be able to gain control, to shield ourselves and live our lives for ourselves," Federico de la Fe said. (53)

Exhausted by Saturn's constant omniscient surveillance, which limits their freedoms and opportunities, EMF join de la Fe in condemning Saturn and turn their energies toward ending or possibly stealing then erasing the novel.

De la Fe structures the war against omniscience around inducing writer's block in Saturn.[13] Writer's block produces two desirable effects: temporary

---

12. I understand the zoot-suiter's respect for EMF as Plascencia's recognition that the city gangs, who the novel suggests may engage in looting and theft, are subject to the same banal violence of capitalism, although it takes different forms in urban areas.

13. Jansen reads the characters' activist resistance as, instead, a strike over their intellectual labor: "Most of Saturn's characters have little agency in the telling of their own stories, and they rebel against Saturn by refusing to operate within the confines of the columns he has provided

privacy from authorial surveillance and, de la Fe hopes, the potential abortion of the narrative project.[14] At the start of the war, de la Fe returns to the mechanic's shop where he once escaped Saturn's gaze by hiding under a tortoise shell. He purchases the lead shells in bulk and cuts them into pieces to hide his war plans:

> Pressed against the two slabs of lead were Federico de la Fe's schematics for a war of eventual emancipation, safely hidden from Saturn's view. Some of the parchment paper stuck out from between the heavy sheets of lead. Parts of Federico de la Fe's home-taught cursive, with uncrossed *x*'s, undotted *i*'s, and unlopped Spanish *q*'s, were exposed, along with what appeared to be a triangle with numerical measurements. But Saturn could not extrapolate any of Federico de la Fe's plan from the protruding scribbles. (86)

De la Fe soon procures enough lead to line the ceilings and walls of all the houses of El Monte, thereby excluding Saturn from the privacy of EMF's homes and their war meetings. De la Fe instructs members of EMF to hide their thoughts in "a loop of irrelevance" when they have to venture out from under the lead shields, thereby giving Saturn nothing to write and impeding the progress of the novel (90). Saturn admits, "Everything they thought of had to do with carnations and farm animals and objects too brown or formless to have any meaning. Unable to see the notes that Federico de la Fe hid underneath the lead, Saturn had not foreseen this type of attack. De la Fe's plan was to stump Saturn in the midst of the story, to hide their lives behind lead walls" (90). By explicitly excluding Saturn from their thoughts and thwarting his surveillance, the characters win a measure of privacy and volition.

EMF ultimately hopes not just to evade Saturn's omniscient surveillance, however, but also to end his narration. They hope that he will retreat to more distant orbits and give up the novel if he experiences writers' block for long enough, though they are prepared for more immediate action, as well. In real narrative time on page 105 of the novel, de la Fe gives EMF specific instructions about what to do if they ever encounter Saturn: "The carnation knife

---

for their words. Essentially, they exercise their agency by going on strike against Saturn, thwarting his desire to profit from the exploitation of their problems. In this way, the characters' self-censorship is a refusal to conform to Saturn's use of their intellectual labor" (111).

14. To fund the war on omniscience, or the commodification of sadness, EMF initiates an alternative economy based on cockfighting and sustenance farming. Burning tires in an unsuccessful attempt to block Saturn's vision, groups of EMF members pool their money and make runs to the border to procure more lead tortoise shells, goats, chickens, and other materiel. Despite Saturn's omniscience and control over their fates, the characters exhibit agency in responding to his authority.

must be pulled out of the waistband and then put to the throat of Saturn, dragging the blade across the skin and stubble of his neck, letting his ink drip. . . . At the very least, if rushed, steal the plot lines and the hundred and five pages that have been written. Leave nothing behind but the title page and table of contents, on which you write, 'You are not so powerful'" (104–5). De la Fe prefers the destruction of his story—and consequently, himself—to circulating narratively as entertainment.

As the story progresses, the characters reveal a variety of positions toward Saturn, as well as a series of techniques for resisting, embracing, or ignoring his surveillance of the most intimate moments of their lives. Like the authors throughout these chapters, Plascencia's characters critically engage with the power relations dictating who has access to their stories. De la Fe, who blames Saturn for the tragic events written into the opening of the novel, represents the staunchest resistance to omniscience; he understands Saturn as the force that predetermines the courses of characters' lives. Baby Nostradamus, an indigenous child with supernatural wisdom adopted by El Monte's curandero, blocks Saturn's thoughts altogether by obscuring text with blocks of black ink. He teaches de la Fe's daughter, Little Merced, to do the same, and over the course of the novel she increases her ability to shield herself and those around her from Saturn's omniscience; she learns to, in Jansen's terms, replace "her passive resistance of *non*-narration with active resistance of *hidden*-narration" (110). In addition to his capability to shield his thoughts from Saturn, "Baby Nostradamus knew how *The People of Paper* ended. It concluded with a plain, nine-word sentence that read, 'And there would be no sequel to the sadness'" (166). He has the capacity to engage in "a terrorism of summation, prematurely bringing everything forward," but instead adheres to the "codes of his profession" by allowing the story to unfold through Saturn's telling (167). Froggy, another EMF member, does not harbor de la Fe's vitriol against Saturn, but still seeks to experience "our story unobstructed, unexploited by Saturn" (212). To varying degrees, most characters tolerate Saturn even as they wish for privacy and an escape from the indignity of having their sadness commodified and circulated while they remain rooted in social and economic inequality.

While other characters decide to resist Saturn's surveillance of their lives, one character, Smiley, rather enjoys the thought of constant attention and pursues his creator out of curiosity. As another member of EMF explains, "Smiley wanted some form of celebrity, even if it came from simply lying naked in his bed" (185). He pulls out of the war effort, and while the rest of EMF "took refuge in inane thoughts and under the weight of lead, Smiley walked outside and gathered goat droppings to scoop into his pots. And after watering his plants and removing his clothes, he lay down on his bed, enjoying the rest and carefree comforts that came with peace. But still he stared up at the sky, hopeful that perhaps Saturn would look down and notice the nude wunderkind of botany and mathematics" (169). Seeking recognition, Smiley learns Saturn's name—"Salvador Plascencia de Gonzalez, to be exact, though he dropped his maternal name long ago"—from a curandero who also provides him a map leading to Saturn's home (102). Smiley follows the curandero's map to a "rough spot" in the sky, where he peels away "the deteriorating glaze of blue, collapsing part of the sky and exposing a layer of papier-mâché" (103). After opening a hole in the sky, Smiley crawls through and emerges into Saturn's bedroom, metaleptically penetrating the divide between character and author. Saturn, however, fails to recognize Smiley because he is preoccupied with his own heartache.

Saturn's heartache constitutes another diegetic layer of *The People of Paper*'s narrative that involves similar confrontations between characters and author, this time explicitly framed in the language of colonialism. When Smiley finds him, Saturn—Sal—is asleep, heartbroken, and "no longer in control" (103). Smiley observes, "He did not have the foresight to see that I was coming, nor did he care" (103). As Sal writes a book about de la Fe, Smiley, and the people of El Monte, his long-term relationship with Liz, to whom the book is dedicated, dissolves, and she leaves him for a white man. Sal reacts in anger, telling Liz, "You weren't supposed to spill out of the dedication page. But then you fucked everything. Made holes in my ceiling, cracks in my ribs, my whole wardrobe to dust. All for a white boy. [. . .] The trajectory of the novel altered because of him. They colonize everything: the Americas, our stories, our novels, our memories" (117).[15] In the emotional turmoil accompanying heartbreak, Sal understands Liz's departure and her subsequent relationship with a white man through the politics of colonialism. He considers her decision to leave an act of betrayal and part of a larger pattern of colonization in which "they"—presumably white people like Liz's new boyfriend—colonize more than the geographic space of "the Americas," but also "our stories, our novels, our memories," or the cultural capital of, presumably, Mexican Americans like Sal (117). While his conflation of his breakup with the colonization of the Americas is hyperbolic, Sal's comparison points to the degree colonialism structures the way he understands the world. He suggests that as a Mexican American man, recognizing colonialism—past and ongoing—is not a choice but a matter of course. In the face of the narrative and romantic colonization

---

15. Sal refuses to include Liz's new lover's name in the book, so cuts out all references in the hardback volume, and scratches out his name in paperback printings of *The People of Paper*.

he experiences, Sal asserts omniscience over his characters, a form of control he understands as political and akin to conquest. Having internalized a worldview that understands power and privilege in terms of colonization, Sal sees his war against de la Fe and EMF as a way "to prove that I too am a colonizer, I too am powerful in those ways . . . I can wipe out whole cultures, whole towns of imaginary flower people" (238). In his heartbroken state, however, Saturn temporarily retreats from his war on EMF and focuses his anger on Liz.

Sal's heartbreak over the dissolution of his relationship with Liz and the discomfort of his present relationship with Cami structure the novel's other diegetic world. Sal accuses Liz of leaving him for a white boy, a decision he characterizes as a form of betrayal in the gendered tradition of la Malinche, Pocahontas, and Rita Hayworth, legacies he invokes in the novel and which I explore fully in chapter 3, where I more directly consider Plascencia's critique of selling the story he writes. As diegetic and occasionally metadiegetic characters when they appear in Sal's novel, Liz and Cami have different concerns from those of EMF. The women are not, generally, subject to Sal's omniscience, but they still recognize the degree to which his fiction invades their privacy by exposing them to outside surveillance by the novel's readers. Liz worries about how her future children will think of her because of Sal's unflattering account of their breakup. She asks Sal to "Start this book over, without me," a request Sal accommodates by interrupting the novel with new title and dedication pages, this time scrubbed of Liz's name (138). Liz, like EMF, is concerned about the effects of her story circulating. She tells Sal, "You need to remember that I exist beyond the pages of this book. One day, I don't know when, I will have children, and I don't want them finding a book in which their mother is faithless and cruel and insults the hero" (138). As Liz understands her inclusion in the novel as codifying a failed relationship and imposing a particular narrative on her future, Cami raises concerns about the novel's implications for her day-to-day life. She expresses disgust at strangers knowing intimate details of her life and physiology by reading scenes depicting her and Sal's sexual relationship. In a letter to Sal reproduced in the novel, she reproaches his decision to include her in his fiction: "In your world of fiction and imagination you may fuck whomever you want; masturbate with your genius. But I'm not of paper. It is not decent, Sal. To fuck and then tell is one thing, but to write about it—to allow the telling to never end . . ." (226–27, ellipsis in original). Implicit in Cami's disparagement of Sal and in Liz's disgust at her depiction in Sal's writing is an indictment—though certainly not equal to the responsibility they place on Sal's position as author—of *The People of Paper*'s readers.

Plascencia's self-awareness becomes increasingly self-deprecating in nature as the novel progresses. In a scene in which Little Merced finds her father in the throes of lead poisoning out on their front yard, Plascencia characterizes Saturn's diegetic omniscience and authorial privilege—not unlike his own—as lacking decency and empathy. Recognizing de la Fe's pain, Little Merced brings her father inside to bathe and comfort him. "If there was ever an instance that Federico de la Fe wanted his privacy, his right to be shielded from the sight of Saturn," Saturn observes, "it was at that moment" (184). Saturn, however, "lacked the decency to look away, the ability to empathize with Federico de la Fe and his daughter and their need to be alone and unseen," continuing to voyeur and narrate the scene for his readers (186). Unlike Le's decision to deflect readers' gazes from the central traumas in "The Boat," or Treuer's decision to substitute fiction for Apelles's story, Saturn's narrative exposes the details de la Fe would rather remain private: "Saturn focused on the vomit on Federico de la Fe's lap, slowly panning upwards to his bare stomach and chest, revealing the dry and ashing skin, the scars, and the still-blistering burns. And then to Little Merced as she tended to her sick father, Saturn listening to everything that they said" (186). Saturn identifies in his role as author the potential to look away from the intimate moment, then refuses. Instead, he draws attention to the invasive, gratuitous access he offers readers by refusing to give his characters privacy in moments of acute emotion, such as the scene in which de la Fe must explain his practices of self-harm to his daughter, an incredibly private and heartbreaking event.[16] As she looks at her father's burn scars, Little Merced extends his critique of Saturn to also indict the reading audience for violating their privacy:

"I'm sorry," Federico de la Fe said to his daughter. "There are some things that are better kept hidden." And Little Merced quietly nodded, sensing Saturn's presence. She began to feel her own resentment, not only toward Saturn, but also against those who stared down at the page, against those who followed sentences into her father's room and into his bed, watching as he pressed matches to his skin, perhaps even laughing and saying to themselves, "Get over it, old man—it is only a woman." Little Merced wanted to protect

---

16. He says simply, "Sometimes I really miss your mother" (184). Saturn's apparent willingness to publish a scene of abjection raises questions for readers about how and whether we read the scene. In his consideration of photographers who "abused the native sense of privacy to capture an image and then either sold or distributed the pictures to various agencies," Gerald Vizenor reflects on the choices surreptitiously commodified images of Natives pose for viewers: "How should we now respond to the photographs that have violated the privacy of the natives? Cover the eyes? Whose eyes should be covered?" (*Fugitive Poses* 163).

her father, hide him from mockery, from the pity of strangers, and to conceal her own rage. (186)

Like Doña Ramona in Rigoberto González's *Crossing Vines,* Little Merced demands privacy in moments of emotional duress. In fact, Little Merced's anger drives the ending of the novel, as it is she who dresses her father and packs their belongings before opening her parasol, "shading her and her father" as they walk off the page and out of Saturn's—and Plascencia's—novel.

Sal finally yields to his characters' demands for privacy not because of the war EMF wages against Saturn, but because he concedes to Liz's accusation that turning stories about his hometown, friends, and family into a commodity is a form of selling out. Sal's concessions allow EMF to win their war against omniscience and the commodification of sadness as they pack their belongings while he muses over a future without Liz. The novel ends with de la Fe in his Pendleton shirt and Little Merced carrying her parasol, walking "south and off the page, leaving no footprints that Saturn could track. There would be no sequel to the sadness" (245). The last page of the novel contains only a black circle, Little Merced's parasol shielding her and her father from Saturn's and readers' surveillance.[17] De la Fe achieves his aim of ending Saturn's omniscience and earning privacy from the novel's audience. The last scene, furthermore, is one of the characters' volition; the novel ends not once Sal surrenders, but after the characters remove themselves from the book. Still, the narrative remains despite their escape, allowed to circulate for the author's profit and made available for scholarly close readings, like this one, that will linger over and find meaning in its most vulnerable moments. The privacy Plascencia affords his characters through his metafictional machinations, in other words, is almost entirely performative.

BETTER TO FORGET: "LOVE AND HONOR AND PITY AND PRIDE AND COMPASSION AND SACRIFICE"

Le derives the title for his metafictional short story from William Faulkner's advice to young writers in his 1950 Nobel speech to write about the universal "verities" the story's title comprises. Le's subject, however, is the gap between Faulknerian expectations of literature in general and the particular demands nonwhite authors in America face. Specifically, "Love and Honor and Pity and

---

17. The characters enjoy the privilege of the last word, yet decline; in fact, the black circle is identical to Little Merced's thought-block, meaning she explicitly blocks her last words from readers.

Pride and Compassion and Sacrifice" considers the afterlife of state surveillance during wartime and the role survivors and writers play in relation to official state narratives. How do state images of war, for instance photographs of the Vietnam War and the ensuing violence, structure subsequent narrative responses? Expose groups of people to visual scrutiny in times of acute distress? Le resists writing within narratives made familiar through wartime surveillance by the US Army by refusing to offer testimony, counternarratives, or other "verities" behind state images of the My Lai massacre. Rather, Le circles around a central testimony in "Love and Honor" while shielding the actual trauma from readers, asserting narrative privacy just as he does in "The Boat," where he deflects readers' gazes from characters' central traumas to protect the privacy of, in both stories, the lived experiences of refugees fleeing a Vietnam torn apart by colonial wars.

The story's first-person protagonist, Nam—as distinct from the author, Le, whose biography he shares—is a Vietnamese Australian writer up against a deadline for a short story submission at the Iowa Writer's Workshop. Nam faces polarized advice from his advisors and colleagues on whether or not to mine his "*background* and *life experience*" for story material, by which they mean his family's history in Vietnam and his own experiences as part of the Vietnamese diaspora (9). Unlike Faulkner's background and life experiences that undoubtedly informed the verities he invoked in his Nobel speech, Nam's knowledge of Vietnam and Vietnamese are treated as niche, rather than universal. His treatment of love, honor, pity, pride, compassion, and sacrifice are received as specifically Vietnamese, as Nam is not afforded the privilege of universality usually available only to white writers like Faulkner. Nam experiences a contradiction facing contemporary nonwhite writers: facing a market with a supposedly "whetted appetite" for ethnic literature, Nam must choose between turning his background and life experience into a depoliticized multicultural representation (rather than a universal verity) or deliberately avoiding Vietnam in his writing (Song 90). In both cases, his "background and life experience" confine and dictate his options. Nam understands that his narrative decisions will be read—as, admittedly, I read Le's here—as negotiations of his position as a member of the Vietnamese diaspora.

To further complicate Nam's decisions about what to write, much of his potential material fits into well-worn historical narratives about Vietnamese people, many of which stem from images made available by the US military and US reporters during the Vietnam War. Nam is writing, in other words, in the heartland of a nation whose cultural understanding of Vietnam is saturated with images from colonial wars and their aftermaths. In a context in which Vietnamese are often portrayed as victims or villains and stripped of privacy even in moments of acute violence, Nam hesitates to explore his family's trauma and his vexed relation with his personal history. Nam's father's generation experienced the brutalities of US military action in Vietnam, reeducation camps, and the diaspora of Vietnamese refugees, or "boat people."[18] Whereas some witnesses, like US Army photographer Ronald Haeberle, choose to disseminate representations of US violence in Vietnam, specifically in the My Lai massacre, Nam hesitates to contribute to the narrative exposure of Vietnamese trauma in the face of state-sanctioned violence. While Nam has written a short "refugee story," it appears he largely avoids drawing on Vietnam in his own work (22). Min Hyoung Song describes Nam's reluctance to write about Vietnam as "a principled, and even a political, stance against turning his and his family's experience into a commodity. It gives expression to his desire to write about what is important to him without at the same time falling into the trap of writing what is merely expected of him because of his ethnicity" (91). Nam's aversion to writing accounts of his own and his family's traumatic past is not a generalized aversion to exploring trauma through literature, however. Readers learn he has written other stories—"Colombian assassins, Hiroshima orphans—and New York painters with hemorrhoids"—that engage with difficult situations and sad histories (10). Le, similarly, includes stories that meet the same descriptions in the same short story collection as "Love and Honor." Rather, Nam's resistance to writing about Vietnam is a resistance to exposing, once again, individuals affected by state-sanctioned violence in Vietnam.

Nam negotiates his relationship to his family's past as he contends with a bout of writer's block that keeps him from finishing his final story of the semester in advance of his estranged father's visit a couple days before his deadline. Nam has resorted to using a Smith Corona typewriter and lubricating his imagination with scotch in hopes of producing a story, but to no avail. His father, whom he has not seen in three years and with whom he has a strained relationship, arrives early, and despite his father's protestations, Nam feels responsible for socializing (4). After a strict childhood and a substantial rupture in their relationship while Nam was in high school, the two are not intimate, and Nam is sensitive to his father's disapproval of his decision to leave his job as a lawyer to become a writer. In the context of Nam's fears about failure and desire for paternal approval, his writer's block takes on added significance.

After desperately casting around for ideas as his deadline approaches, Nam decides to write a story he remembers his father telling once when Nam

---

18. Nam's father claims the identity "boat people" for himself and for Nam; I use the term here to reflect Nam's father's self-identification in the story, even as I recognize the objectifying use of "boat people" as problematic (13).

was young. Acknowledging that he is capitulating to his advisors' expectations, he titles his draft "ETHNIC STORY": "*Fuck it,* I thought. I had two and a half days left. I would write the ethnic story of my Vietnamese father. It was a good story. It was a fucking *great* story" (17). The "ethnic story" Nam writes is his childhood memory of walking in on his father telling a story during a gathering of old Vietnamese friends. Nam remembers his father drunkenly recounting the My Lai massacre: the villagers' impotent cries for mercy, the terrible scale of violence, the murder of his family and friends.[19] After drafting what he remembers of the story, Nam acknowledges that his own version is incomplete, as he never again heard his father talk about his past: "Maybe he didn't tell it exactly that way. Maybe I'm filling in the gaps. But you're not under oath when writing a eulogy, and this is close enough. My father grew up in the province of Quang Ngai, in the village of Son My, in the hamlet of Tu Cung, later known to the Americans as My Lai. He was fourteen years old" (16–17). Working with "close enough," Nam stays up working on the short story until the early hours of the morning.

Nam's father, however, has reservations about both his son's fictional account and the potential repercussions of writing a more accurate story. Having read "ETHNIC STORY" before Nam wakes up the following day, he dismisses the draft as having "mistakes in it" (22). In response, Nam implores his father to recall the events of the massacre so he can write a more accurate account:

> He [Nam's father] was silent for a long time. Then he said, "Only you'll remember. I'll remember. They will read and clap their hands and forget." For once, he was not smiling. "Sometimes it's better to forget, no?" "I'll write it anyway," I said. It came back to me—how I'd felt at the typewriter the previous night. A thought leapt into my mind: "If I write a true story," I told my father, "I'll have a better chance of selling it." He looked at me a while, searchingly, seeing something in my face as though for the first time. (24)

Nam asks his father to recount a traumatic episode from his past for the first time in order to sell it, raising questions about the commodification of trauma, an issue explored more fully in chapter 3. He also asks his father to

---

19. In the version of the massacre included in the short story, Nam does not shy away from graphic details: "They made us turn around. They made us kneel back down in the water. When they started shooting I felt my mother's body jumping on top of mine; it kept jumping for a long time, and then everywhere was the sound of helicopters, louder and louder like they were all coming down to land, and everything was dark and wet and warm and sweet" (16). Notably, the version Nam's father shares with his son is entirely absent from "Love and Honor."

recount for readers a personal testimony of US violence against Vietnamese villagers, to expose his memories of past trauma for a public audience, so that Nam can meet the professional expectations he faces as an author in the Vietnamese diaspora.

Nam's father nevertheless agrees to tell his son about his past; after sitting for hours talking with his father, Nam once again stays up all night, this time producing a draft he feels captures his father's story. The following morning, Nam discovers his typewritten draft missing, replaced by a note from his father that indicates he has taken the draft with him to read on his morning walk. With refreshed confidence in his purpose as a writer, Nam believes the story he has written has the capacity to repair his long-broken relationship with his father. "He would read it, with his book-learned English, and he would recognize himself in a new way. He would recognize me. He would see how powerful was his experience, how valuable his suffering—how I had made it speak for more than itself. He would be pleased with me" (27). Donald Goellnicht argues, "For Nam now, the story is testament to the power of language to validate and, even more, to enhance experience, to make it more valuable in an affective rather than commercial economy, as well as to heal relationships that have deteriorated over time" (201). Nam believes his ability to articulate his father's experience in language—something his father warned was impossible—validates him as a writer and a son, but more importantly, renders his father's childhood trauma into something more valuable: valuable as a tool for repairing their relationship, valuable as a memorial and testimony, valuable perhaps even as an epistemology. While Nam does not dismiss his comments the day before about the salability of a "true story," his account of his father's memories clearly takes on value in extra-monetary terms, as well. In making his father's story "speak for more than itself," Nam understands narrative as a form of witnessing, of rounding out official narratives dictated by the US government; narrative offers Nam's father the opportunity to speak back to the federally authorized accounts. State surveillance, in this case the accounts of US Army soldiers, would have to share space with an account from the local Vietnamese perspective.

For Nam's father, however, the value of telling his son about My Lai rests only in the experience of intimately sharing his story with his son. While his son sleeps, Nam's father takes the typewritten manuscript and burns it in a homeless man's fire, destroying the only copy of the narrative. Rather than displaying his traumatic experience for paying audiences who will "clap their hands and forget," he temporarily joins the homeless man in a space outside of prevailing capital circuits to erase his story irrevocably. Like his son has come to believe, Nam's father understands the value of his story as existing outside of its potential status as an "ETHNIC STORY." Goellnicht, who reads the act of burning the manuscript as a gesture toward the burning of paper money as a Vietnamese tradition of ancestor worship,[20] sums up the destructive act: "For Nam's father, no story will ever suffice, especially one told secondhand and thrust into a marketplace of commodity exchange. Sometimes it is better to forget" (204). Like de la Fe in *The People of Paper*, Nam's father chooses to destroy his story rather than have it circulate for others to consume as entertainment and as part of the archival records of state violence.

Rather than taking a side in the polarized debate raging in Nam's Iowa Writers' Workshop about what ethnic writers should write by sympathizing with either Nam, who wrote the story, or his father, who erased it, Le ends "Love and Honor" with a son's nebulous regret. The story does not include direct description of Nam's reaction to his father's act of destruction, only the lament of a presumably older, more knowledgeable Nam:

> If I had known then what I knew later, I wouldn't have said the things I did. I wouldn't have told him he didn't understand—for clearly, he did. I wouldn't have told him that what he had done was unforgiveable. That I wished he had never come, or that he was no father to me. But I hadn't known, and, as I waited, feeling the wind change, all I saw was a man coming toward me in a ridiculously oversized jacket, rubbing his black-sooted hands, stepping through the smoke with its flecks and flame-tinged eddies, who had destroyed himself, yet again, in my name. (28)

The narrative pans away from the impending confrontation, framed as though Nam's father is stepping out of the past, away from the traumatic memories of war he protects through fire from unsympathetic audiences. The question Le's ending raises—what does Nam know later that helps him make sense of the tension between his impulse to write and his father's to sacrifice and "forget"?—teases an answer the story does not deliver about the role of ethnic authors in contemporary literary marketplaces; instead, Nam points to narrative privacy as a means of negotiating the difficult, personal limits of what writers share in literature and what their responsibilities are in responding to official state narratives. For Nam's father, as for de la Fe, privacy is worth even the high price of destroying himself.

---

20. Goellnicht reads Nam's father's act of destruction as also a way to honor the dead: "This honoring of the dead by burning paper 'money' or 'hell notes'—a traditional Vietnamese and more broadly Asian ritual of ancestor veneration that cuts across all religious affiliations—turns the story away from the realm of capitalist exploitation of the traumatic past (the saleable story Nam claims to be writing) and carries it into the register of spiritual enterprise" (202–3).

Le considers how writers should treat trauma in literature, particularly when it is a trauma experienced by a previous generation rather than personally.[21] For Le, this is not just an academic, literary, or economic question, but a political concern with implications for living populations: what psychic or emotional effect would seeing an account of the My Lai massacre sold for the profit of its author have on survivors and their children? Circulated, once again, without the explicit permission of survivors? Similarly, Y-Dang Troeung interrupts a common impulse in Asian American literary studies toward testimony and remembrance to remind scholars that these are not faceless questions. She asks, "What is the effect on traumatized subjects who turn, or who are turned, back to look at their trauma? How can we envision a political project that takes better ethical care of those who bear the burden of remembering? Going a step further, I ask is there a space left for forgetting in our endeavours to develop a politics of loss?" (91). Le, similarly, asks how writers can care for those like Nam's father, who feel "Sometimes it is better to forget, no?" (24). In part, "Love and Honor" is an experiment in writing with respect for forgetting; Le circles the trauma of My Lai without explicitly recalling the details or how Nam's father coped with the aftermath.[22] The circumstances of how the story works in Nam's relationship with his father and the effects of their private remembering become the story, while Nam's father maintains privacy from readers and is allowed, narratively, to forget.[23]

By including a brief fictional account of the massacre at My Lai while omitting the "real story," Le's story evokes the questions raised in chapter 1 about the ethnographic imperative placed on ethnic writers. Notably, Nam

---

21. Goellnicht identifies this question as one the field of Asian American literature faces: "Nam Le has consciously evoked in this opening story of his collection some of the central debates that have raged in Asian American literary studies for decades: questions of cultural authenticity, authorial ownership and voice appropriation, responsible representation of trauma, the selling out of the community by subsequent generations, what constitutes the content of Asian American literature, and what is marketable as 'ethnic literature'" (199).

22. Though working in a vastly different context of racialized visibility—the spectacular nature of violence in slavery in the US during the nineteenth century—Saidiya V. Hartman asks critical questions about reproducing representations of trauma that resonate with Le's and Troeung's concerns. She asks, "Are we witnesses who confirm the truth of what happened in the face of the world-destroying capacities of pain, the distortions of torture, the sheer unrepresentability of terror, and the repression of the dominant accounts? Or are we voyeurs fascinated with and repelled by exhibitions of terror and sufferance? What does the exposure of the violated body yield? . . . At issue here is the precariousness of empathy and the uncertain line between witness and spectator. Only more obscene than the brutality unleashed at the whipping post is the demand that this suffering be materialized and evidenced by the display of the tortured body or endless recitations of the ghastly and the terrible?" (3–4).

23. The presumed conflict between Nam and his father after the narrative cuts away in the final scenes remains similarly private.

declares it is the "real story" that sells, and readers discover it is the "real story" Le omits from "Love and Honor." Recognizing the literary market's desire for authenticity and testimony, Le undermines his own marketability—as defined by the ethnographic imperative—by omitting Nam's father's account of My Lai. As readers, we can only access the "close enough" fiction Nam creates from his childhood memory by "filling in the gaps"; Le outlines the contours of Nam's scotch-fueled discussion with his father and reveals Nam has taken forty-five pages of notes, but withholds the story Nam's father burns (17, 16, 26). In the case of Nam's first story draft, readers learn what he will write before he stays up to write it; Le could have revealed Nam's second story to readers and still had his father burn the pages, but he decides not to. Like Treuer, Le substitutes "make-believe" for the "true story," offering readers fiction rather than ethnographic testimony, staking limits around readers' access. Readers are left not knowing what Nam will do in the wake of his father's destruction: will he rewrite his story from his extensive notes and submit his story, albeit late, to the Workshop? Or, does the regret that permeates the final passages of "Love and Honor" suggest he ultimately reaches an understanding with his father's decision to prevent his testimony from circulation and exposure? While Nam's diegetic, or fictional, course of action remains hypothetical, Le insists on narrative privacy for his main characters by never offering readers more than a fictional account of My Lai from Nam's father's perspective.

Contextualizing Le's commitment to narrative privacy as a method of contending with issues of state surveillance in the tragedy of the My Lai massacre provokes comparison to Haeberle's photographs of the massacre and their subsequent sale and deployment as propaganda art. Haeberle was an US Army photographer who documented the March 16, 1968 massacre with both an official Army camera and his personal camera. While the photographs he took on his Army camera were state property and subject to government control and censorship, those on his personal device were legally ruled private property. In the fall of 1969, a year and a half after the massacre, Haeberle sold some of his personal images to *Life* magazine; the graphic images quickly became fodder for anti-Vietnam War movements. The Art Workers Coalition, an antiwar artist collective, selected one photograph of dead Vietnamese bodies—most are clearly women and children—piled along a path to create one of the most iconic propaganda art pieces of the Vietnam War era, titled "And babies." The poster, which superimposes red text reading "Q. And babies? / A. And babies." on Haeberle's photograph, quotes an interview between Mike Wallace and former army Private First Class Paul Meadlo in which Meadlo describes his participation in killing women, children, "and babies" at My Lai (Meadlo).[24] The interview was part of the public reckoning of the US Army officers and soldiers who conducted the massacre, a process in which Haeberle participated on an official level. Using his photographs, he identified the fates of his Vietnamese photographic subjects for the Armed Services Investigating Subcommittee; with few exceptions, his subjects were murdered moments after they were photographed (United States 502).

Nam's father's story and Haeberle's photographs represent two disparate approaches to disseminating representations of the same traumatic event. Scholars and activists frequently make the important argument for recovering, remembering, and memorializing traumatic or violent histories for various ends, including political activism to effect change. In deciding to burn his son's version of his story, Nam's father eliminates the possibility that his experience might be used as a counternarrative to the US's persistent diminishment of what is still officially termed "the My Lai Incident." Similarly invoking the critical counterpoint to Nam's father's course of action and Le's deployment of narrative privacy, Goellnicht lists prototypical questions: "Doesn't he have an obligation to remember, to speak out, to refuse the silencing and repression, the 'prescriptive forgetting' by the American authorities and public? Isn't it the ethnic writer's responsibility to remember and record oppression, abuse, colonial exploitation, murder at all costs?" (203). Put differently, doesn't Nam have a responsibility to respond to the official narratives produced by state surveillance? Haeberle's photographs, especially those such as "And babies" which were transformed into propaganda art, appear to fulfill the duties implied by Goellnicht's questions: the photographs were for many Americans the first visual images of the violence committed against Vietnamese civilians by US soldiers, and the "And babies" poster, in particular, was responsible for an upsurge of protests against soldiers, fueling the common epithet "baby killers" (Holsinger 363, MacPherson 497).

At the root of the Haeberle photographs, however, is an abject loss of privacy on the part of the victims. Images of villagers taken just moments before their violent deaths, in the midst of a massacre that included the rape and mutilation of women and children, spread widely from a US Army photographer and representative of the state through the media, notably *Life* maga-

---

24. "[Mike Wallace] Q: And you killed how many? At that time?
    [Paul Meadlo] A: Well, I fired them on automatic, so you can't—you just spray the area on them and so you can't know how many you killed 'cause they were going fast. So I might have killed 10 or 15 of them.
    Q: Men, women and children?
    A: Men, women and children.
    Q: And babies?
    A. And babies." (Meadlo)

zine.[25] Stripped of their lives, My Lai villagers were also denied control over their representation. In the intervening years between the massacre and the photos' publication, the US saw dramatic increases in antiwar sentiment, potentially increasing the market and political value of the photographs, while the passage of time diminished the possibility of immediate political action for the victims, including survivors, of My Lai. Haeberle explained that he sold the photographs because "I just wanted to get it off my chest, let the people see exactly what happened," but he accepted the $17,500 payment for their rights (United States 267).[26] His testimony in front of the Armed Services Investigating Subcommittee offered a measure of political accountability, but in 2009 Haeberle confessed to destroying the most damning of his personal photos of the massacre to protect soldiers he anticipated would be later tried for their actions.[27] Like Le, Haeberle drew lines around the depiction of trauma he was willing to sell, and which he needed to irrevocably destroy, albeit for privacy motivated by reasons different from those driving Nam's father to burn his son's account of the massacre.

In Le's story, Nam's father takes steps to ensure his son's story never reached popular audiences for less-clearly articulated reasons than those that motivated Haeberle, who sought to protect friends from legal action. For Nam's father, more important than potential political activism is protecting the memory from further dissemination and the cheapening effect of being consumed as entertainment. Le's decision to talk about the transfer of testimony between father and son and to point to the effects of the storytelling experience on the two men but to withhold the actual story of the My Lai massacre is a strategic deployment of narrative privacy that imagines a way to respect both the importance of bearing witness and the deep need for privacy and even forgetting that Nam's father represents. Le breaks the silence Nam's father models by showing readers that such stories circulate, but he chooses to not participate in systems that would make intensely private narratives of trauma available to curious audiences.

Le's collection, *The Boat,* comprises seven stories, starting with "Love and Honor," which insists on protecting a story of Vietnamese trauma from read-

---

25. The photographs were broadcast on CBS on Nov. 20, 1969, "one after another, in complete silence" (Oliver 48).

26. While Haeberle explains, "I had no intention of any profit off these [photographs] whatsoever," he and a journalist friend "asked for $125,000" from potential buyers before finally selling the images for $17,500 and other additional smaller fees (United States 261, 270).

27. PBS reports: "Forty years later, in November 2009, Haeberle admitted to destroying his most graphic personal pictures depicting soldiers in the act of killing in an attempt to prevent the identification and persecution of additional soldiers. 'I had actual photos of actual guys who were doing the shooting and stuff like that. I never showed those . . . I was there in the operation, but I'm not gonna point a finger at some soldier out there and have him, you know, put up. We were all guilty'" ("Sergeant Ronald Haeberle").

ers, and ending with "The Boat," which, as I argue in chapter 1, tells a traumatic story yet protects characters by deflecting readers' curious gazes in acts of narrative privacy. The five intervening stories range in setting from Hiroshima, Japan, immediately before the US drops an atomic bomb, to a Colombian barrio, to Tehran, to Australia, to Carnegie Hall. Le's range, often cited by critics as exemplary of his cosmopolitanism, extends to his depictions of trauma: each story details a different form of abjection, delivering for readers the intimacy "Love and Honor" and "The Boat" deny. "Love and Honor" opens the collection by suggesting that readers' desire for trauma is destructive and extraneous to political action or emotional care for victims. After five stories in which he takes readers into the horrors of colorectal cancer, militarized youth, and impending nuclear war, Le delivers his audience to "The Boat," the careful, concluding story. Read as a collection, *The Boat* draws into relief Le's use of narrative privacy in his stories about Vietnamese and diasporic Vietnamese characters. He can—and is willing to—write revealing narratives of others' trauma, but he challenges readers' desires for such brutal, intimate accounts and asserts control over what stories he sells.

Le's collection of published short fiction attests to his faith in the power of narrative, but "Love and Honor" complicates the relationship between representation and surveillance in part by demarcating spaces off limits to readers. Reading "Love and Honor" next to "The Boat," Goellnicht concludes that Le's stories suggest that the "ethical way to pay homage to the dead left behind, those who didn't make it to the boats and those who died at sea, and to the living who may yet survive, is to use the admittedly limited tool of language to convey bodily memory, the sensory experiences of traumatic suffering. Despite its limitations, language may be able to take individuals out of their isolated experience into empathetic identification with others" (216). I would add the important caveat, however, that Le, like Plascencia, uses literary form to intrude on readers' identification with characters to remind us of the limits of our access. Le questions the efficacy of literary witnessing, "resisting the notion of memory as universal or collectively available/accessible for redemption" (Cheng 147). Rather, for Le, looking away—from the bodies in "The Boat" and from Nam's father's account of My Lai—serves as a way to respect the vast differences between lived experience and literary stylizations.

BETTER TO JUST PRETEND: *THE BIRD IS GONE*

Stephen Graham Jones's *The Bird Is Gone: A ~~Monograph~~ Manifesto* (2003) is a novel under multiple forms of surveillance. A speculative fiction set in the

("Indian") Territories several years after the US Congress passed the Conservation Act, "an aggressive bill requiring 'the restoration of all indigenous flora and fauna to the Great Plains,'" an action that required the reintroduction of aboriginal grasses, buffalo, and peoples, the story imagines historically probable responses to an alternative reality (164).[28] The Conservation Act brought Native peoples from across the US to the Great Plains, where they are subject to surveillance not only by each other and by tourists who visit by the busload in pursuit of a more authentic America, but also by the crowds of anthropologists who "massed at the border with their binoculars and their listening devices and their Scalpel-brand pencils, each of them wanting you to confirm their pet theory" (32). Natives in the Territories are also under surveillance by federal agents, including undercover Special Agent Chassis Jones, the novel's primary narrator, and Blue Plume, the federal agent to whom Chassis Jones's undercover report is directed in the second person (151).

Primarily narrated by and to federal agents, the novel is liter(ar)ily framed as an investigation in which readers participate. Like Plascencia's and Le's characters who deliberately break the fourth wall to acknowledge readers' surveillance, Jones's framing and use of the second person reminds readers that, formally at least, we are aligned with agents of state surveillance and that fiction can function as a surveillance technology. Chassis Jones's undercover investigation into the disappearance of thirty-nine tourists to the Territories is complicated by her status as non-indigenous. As she notes at the beginning of each of her chapters, "Pinkeye was all the rage" (43). She explains, "It was the new strain: only Indians could get it. Everyone else was white-eyes, pale face, headlights; not to be trusted. But there are ways. There are always ways" (43). Purchasing red contacts and a wig, Chassis Jones attempts to pass as Seminole and embeds herself in a community of Natives who frequent Fool's Hip, a local bowling alley, where she monitors her primary suspects (45, 43). FBI agents and federal agents not specifically attributed to an agency, in fact, permeate the novel, showing up periodically to investigate or terrorize Natives. An

---

28. According to LP Deal's "Terms": "**Conservation Act**—*n. Hist.* the accidental solution to the 'Indian Problem' (under pressure from Keep America Beautiful, the American Congress signed into law an aggressive bill requiring 'the restoration of all indigenous flora and fauna to the Great Plains.' As wildlife biologists soon pointed out, though, for a disturbance-dependent landscape to regain anything approaching self-sufficiency—to say nothing of momentum—the reintroduced grass (*buchloë dactyloides*) needed buffalo (*bison bison*) to 'disturb' it, and, just as the prairie dog (*cynomys ludovicianus*) needed the disturbance of the blackfooted ferrett (*mustela nigripes*), so did the burgeoning herds of reintroduced buffalo need the INDIAN (*canis latrans*))" (164). Notably, "*canis latrans*," ostensibly the Latin term for "the INDIAN," is actually that for the coyote, a trickster figure in many Native traditions as well as throughout *The Bird Is Gone*.

appendix to *The Bird Is Gone*[29] includes FBI memos and transcriptions, suggesting that federal bureaucracy shapes the novel's form, or its conditions of existence, not unlike the disproportionate influence federal investigators and bureaucrats have had in Native communities throughout US history.

Fool's Hip is not only under surveillance by Chassis Jones and the US government, but also by LP Deal, the alley's janitor and handyman. LP Deal keeps a microphone in his left arm sleeve, "its delicate lead snaking up his arm, embracing his shattered ribcage, plugging into the wafer-thin recording unit tucked into the inner pocket of his overalls" (15). At the end of each workday, he "unwinds himself from the mic, jacks an earphone into the recorder, and transcribes his notes feverishly. That's how manifestos are written: with fever. Anything less would be trivial, not worth slogging through concessions and lane duty by day, guarding the place at night" (15). LP Deal's "manifesto" influences the form of the novel at several points, comprising several chapters, including a series of character profiles, histories, and definitions, as well as several "Artefacts" included at the novel's close and on the author's website. The novel's revised subtitle, "A ~~Monograph~~ Manifesto," underscores LP Deal's influence on the narrative and illuminates the multiple forms of surveillance that permeate the novel.

While LP Deal's commitment to monitoring Fool's Hip may be unmatched—he has not left the building in seven months—he and Chassis Jones are not alone in their respective surveillance projects (15). The narrative carefully notes characters' various acts of looking. For example, Mary Boy, an "old Winnebego with a greystreaked ponytail," and a regular at Fool's Hip, wears a pair of sunglasses that shields his eyes—and therefore his identification as Native through pinkeye—in a "shady habit he picked up from the FBI," ostensibly from an encounter with federal agents who coerced him into an informal drug trial that permanently dilated his eyes (17, 21). Chassis Jones, in her own observations of the bowling alley, notes that she feels "like Mary Boy, watching Fool's Hip under glass, from a distance" (122). Denim Horse and Back Iron, twin brothers known as the Twin Towers from their high-school basketball days in a nod to the novel's post-9/11 context, Cat Stand, and Courtney Peltdowne, all Fool's Hip regulars, keep constant track of who is in the

---

29. The title comes from a definition of the passenger pigeon included in LP Deal's "Terms," after the end of the novel: "**passenger pigeon**—1. a large bird with red eyes, of the family Columbidae (*ectopistes migratorius*), which once 'roamed the virgin forests of North America in unbelievable numbers'—*n.*, *Cryptozoo.*, *Hist.* 2. according to Audubon, a bird 'steered by a long well-plumed tail, and propelled by well-set wings, the muscles of which are very large and powerful for the size of the bird. When an individual is seen gliding through the woods and close to the observer, it passes like a thought, and on trying to see it again, the eye searches in vain. The bird is gone.'—*n.*, *Lit. see also: VANISHING INDIANS*" (169, underlining mine).

building, what their bowling scores are and should be, and what is going on between other individuals. Eddie Dial, another regular at Fool's Hip, is known for his acute perception and is, according to Chassis Jones, "the one person in the place who could tell Denim Horse from Back Iron if they didn't want you to" (148). Even Nickel Eye, Chassis Jones's primary suspect in her investigation, known for monitoring Fool's Hip from his regular place at the bar, is known specifically for "His acquired ability to tell how many pins a bowler's knocked down, going solely by the sound they make, crashing up the alley, into the kitchen, over the counter, washing over him" (24). Every character, it seems, is engaged both in the act of surveillance and of being watched.

Seemingly unbeknownst to Chassis Jones, who believes herself to be successfully undercover, the Natives in the novel all appear to be fully aware of their status as subjects under federal surveillance. Much as they are not surprised by the near-constant presence of anthropologists who stalk the Territories' borders because of the long history of anthropological interest in Natives outlined in chapter 1, years of FBI and federal monitoring of indigenous communities have conditioned the novel's Native characters to expect state surveillance. FBI agents appear at several moments in *The Bird Is Gone*, conducting illicit drug trials on Natives, including Mary Boy, "Back when the FBI could still park on the side of the road and wave Indians over, on the pretense that some crime had allowed them jurisdiction," as well as in the archive of "Artefacts" that closes the novel, including a FBI memo from 1972 and a transcription of a confiscated tape recording (17, 176–79). Throughout, Native characters articulate their understanding of the FBI as antagonistic to Native individuals and communities (107).[30]

The Bird Is Gone also repeatedly references Pine Ridge, as the site of the FBI's illicit drug study and as a museum and reliquary for, among other artifacts, "the faded red truck in the display case, one stray bullet crossing the bed, leaving a federal hole in each side" (72). While Pine Ridge is an Ogala Lakota reservation in South Dakota with a long history independent from the FBI and federal force, the contexts of the narrative's references invoke the history of clashes between federal agents and Natives, especially American Indian Movement (AIM) activists in the 1960s and 1970s. Most famously, the 1973 Wounded Knee incident, in which AIM activists occupied the village of Wounded Knee, close to Pine Ridge, in response to the US's failure to respect treaty rights, lasted more than two months:

---

30. As Owen82 remarks on a tape once confiscated by authorities and stolen back by Back Iron that contains only intermittently intelligible language: ". . . thing about wanting to see if one was better than a half, if the FBI was going to win this time, or the Indians. Bullshit if you ask me" (107, ellipses in original).

> Two Indians were killed and several others wounded as the military fired more than half a million rounds of ammunition into the AIM compound. At one point, the government considered launching an open assault on the village, but after protracted negotiations between AIM and the FBI, the Indians finally agreed to end their occupation on condition that the government hold a full investigation into their grievances and demands. (Calloway 462)

As AIM activist Russell Means explains, however, the federal government never sufficiently fulfilled their promise (Calloway 462). Federal antagonism in Pine Ridge continued after the end of the siege, perhaps most famously in an event Jones recalls in his description of the faded red truck encased in the Pine Ridge museum, as a vehicle with a similar description factored prominently in the federal pursuit of Leonard Peltier, an AIM activist accused and ultimately convicted of murdering two FBI agents at Pine Ridge in 1975 (Calloway 462). The two "federal bullet hole[s]" on which Back Iron slices his finger when examining the truck, therefore, are imagined as historical evidence of federal violence and abuse of federal power. As Colin Calloway explains, Peltier "was arrested, tried, convicted, and sentenced to double life imprisonment on what many regarded as the shakiest of evidence. . . . Peltier remains in jail and his case remains a source of heated controversy and, for many, a symbol of America's continuing oppression of its Native peoples" (462). In Jones's novel, the faded red pickup truck in the Pine Ridge museum, scrubbed of explicit mention of Peltier, serves as a similar symbol of pervasive federal surveillance and policing of Native communities and individuals.

While Jones's specific references to Pine Ridge and Peltier's case suggest that the investigating agents in *The Bird Is Gone*, Chassis Jones and Blue Plume, are likely FBI agents, he notably declines to specify what agency they represent. "Federal agents" on Native land, historically speaking, could be representatives of the FBI, of the Bureau of Indian Affairs (BIA), the US Marshals Service, military personnel, or agents of multiple other federal organizations infringing on Native sovereignty over the years, a subject chapter 4 explores in more detail. While implicating the FBI, therefore, Jones also gestures toward more widespread state surveillance and policing, even in his speculative "Indian Territories." Relative to only brief references to 9/11—Denim Horse and Back Iron's high-school nickname of "the Twin Towers," for instance—Jones's engagement with histories of federal surveillance and use of force suggests that while the FBI may be a central target of the narrative, the federal government's sustained policing of Native individuals and communities spans more than one Bureau and a longer history than just the twenty-first century (37, 38). Perhaps because of this shared history, Jones's Native characters are not fooled by Chassis Jones's undercover disguise.

In her account of her ongoing investigation to fellow agent Blue Plume, Chassis Jones describes her undercover persona in the third person. She predicts that Blue Plume would "see her blonde hair and Indian eyes and she would nod a private nod to the locker where this folder is going to be, this report, and if she brushed up against you in the concession line it would be accidental, not a plea, but she won't show anything on her face, and you won't either" (123).[31] Chassis Jones remains fully convinced that she remains undetected as non-Native or as a federal agent, even after she mistakenly leaves her red contacts on a hotel sink while travelling with Back Iron. His acknowledgement of her white eyes the following day leave her nonplussed: "Miles later I caught Back Iron watching me in the vanity mirror. 'Your eyes,' he said. My contacts. He was the only person in the world who would have noticed" (71). Back Iron is not the only person who notices, however. Once Chassis Jones returns to Fool's Hip without her contacts or the sunglasses she takes from Back Iron, she attracts further attention:

"Your eyes," Nickel Eye said then, tapping his own.
I had my sunglasses off. My eyes. (146)

Neither Back Iron nor Nickel Eye appears surprised by Chassis Jones's white eyes, but rather seems to be reminding her that her disguise is compromised. The regulars at Fool's Hip appear to tolerate Chassis Jones and her investigation much as they tolerate LP Deal's eccentricities. At several points in the novel, women characters, including Chassis Jones, show each other LP Deal's stash of notebooks, hidden in the women's restroom wall, and the regulars are aware that LP Deal keeps a microphone up his sleeve. Courtney Peltdowne, in particular, keeps track of LP Deal, explaining that he "talks down his sleeve and then writes deep into the morning on notebooks he's obviously keeping in locker 32b. Everybody knows" (22). As she editorializes, however, "Sometimes she has to tell herself not to laugh. To take all this seriously. But sometimes it's better to just pretend, too" (23). While Chassis Jones recognizes the group's awareness of LP Deal's surveillance, her narration does not provide any indication that they see through her disguise—that sometimes it's better to pretend—as well.

Jones is not alone in implicating the FBI into his fiction or even incorporating humor in his writing at the expense of federal agents. Along with anthropologists, as evidenced in chapter 1, federal agents provide fodder for

---

31. Chassis Jones's entire account of her investigative work appears ripped from television: "I stayed up until dawn transcribing Cat Stand's sentence, then drawing lines from her to Denim Horse, to Back Iron, to LP Deal, and from LP Deal to Mary Boy, and then to Owen82 and Bacteen. And from Bacteen to Nickle Eye" (122).

a range of Native North American writers, including Gerald Vizenor, Louise Erdrich, and Toni Jensen, to name only a few. Jones's treatment of the FBI, like his characters' treatment of Chassis Jones, is at once good natured and decidedly political. In a wink to his readers, Jones narrates a poker game taking place at the end of the novel during Blue Plume's arrival and subsequent conclusion of the investigation. Chassis Jones, reflecting on the crowd watching the simultaneous poker game and federal intervention, observes: "It's not like we couldn't all see their cards. Like we didn't know it had been a misdeal, a cowboy hand: that there was one black hat among all these white. One bad guy" (154). Chassis Jones's description of the game not only maps onto the regulars of Fool's Hip—who knew all along there was an agent among them—but speaks to an awareness so common in Native and ethnic literatures as to almost be a trope. Like Doña Ramona in *Crossing Vines* anticipating her son's expectations, or Nam's father in "Love and Honor" and EMF in *The People of Paper*—and unlike characters in the post-9/11 fictions Banita describes—these characters are intimately familiar with the experience of being watched, tracked, and policed.

Acknowledging the multiple forms of surveillance to which Natives have been historically subject, *The Bird Is Gone* illuminates the tight historical—and literary—links between various forms of surveillance by having Chassis Jones collude with anthropologists, who run the Aborigine Hotline (69).[32] Chassis Jones suggests a larger economy of trade between federal agents and anthropologists as she examines the palimpsest of labels on a tape she finds in Back Iron's truck: "It was padded, though—the tape—insulated with names, four layers of adhesive labels stacked like stairsteps. The outermost was *The Bad River Band: Hoopin' it Up,* then right under that *Naming Ceremony: 38.R-934b,* then *Algonquin Phonics: Getting Primitive,* and then the original, a handwritten *Trading Buckets,* with the date" (104). Describing the labels to Blue Plume, Chassis Jones focuses on the one on which "*38.R-934b*" is written: "The files we used to trade the Hotline for had the same hierarchy of numbers and letters, right? Meaning the anthropologists had wanted this tape—how Owen82 got his name. And somebody had rubbed that *Phonics*-label on and carried it across to them. Some tomato.[33] And then Back Iron had dropped down into their data warehouse on the narrow beam of a penlight, done his thing" (104). Not only does Chassis Jones suggest that the anthropologists and federal agents actively trade information on Natives, but that the practice is central

---

32. According to LP Deal's "Terms": "**telepawn**—1. To call the Aborigine Hotline—*v.* 2. To sell your soul to the devil—*v., colloq.*" (172).

33. According to LP Deal's "Terms": "**tomato**—*n.* red on the outside *and* the in-, yet white just the same" (172).

to their information economy. By "doing his thing," however, Chassis Jones means that Back Iron slipped into the anthropologists' data warehouse to steal back the recording, much as he breaks into the Pine Ridge museum and steals the faded red truck. His theft is not unlike Federico de la Fe's instructions for members of EMF to "steal the plot lines and the hundred and five pages that have been written" should they come into contact with Saturn, or Nam's father's theft of the manuscript (Plascencia 105).

Chassis Jones not only delivers information to the anthropologists on the other end of the hotline, but it is clear that they—and their discipline more broadly—serve as her framework for understanding the people she investigates. At one point, after listening to the tape insulated under layers of labels, she describes the recording of Back Iron's and Denim Horse's high-school basketball game in distinctly anthropological terms: "It was like in one of those old black and white ethnology documentaries, where they're in some elder's house, and he's playing wise and savage all at once for them, but then, as he's walking out the door, he stops to straighten the rug with his cane. And the camera lingers, unsure" (106). Even as she maintains a dismissive attitude toward the anthropologists she includes in her narrative—she explains that the Councilmen "were so Indian the anthropologists launched themselves past with catapults, shutters clicking. It was like a plague of locusts" (145)[34]—her familiarity with their information economy reinforces the novel's close link between anthropological and state power. For Natives in the Territories, in fact, exile to the border, where they will be subject to anthropologists' interrogations, is a worse fate than capital punishment. As Item 2 in the "Artefacts" section of the novel explains, Native guards assigned the task of exiling a fellow Native to the border offer the exiled the possibility of suicide as an act of mercy (178).

In a scene resonant with the end of "Love and Honor," *The Bird Is Gone* concludes with a trashcan fire. LP Deal and Naitche, Cat Stand's son, destroy LP Deal's manifesto after Blue Plume's arrival at Fool's Hip. Chassis Jones describes the scene:

> In the toilets and smoking in the trashcan were all of LP Deal's notebooks. To keep them from the anthropologists. The only one I'd be able to salvage would be his unfinished manifesto, the terms he was dictating to America— transcriptions of clippings from newspapers and history books, done up in alphabetical order, like entries in a dictionary. It was written on the back of

---

34. Chassis Jones also describes the "flying anthropologists" as landing, then "breaking their chairs down into go-carts and driving fast for the border" (146).

an aborted series of profiles he'd written on Mary Boy and Back Iron and Denim Horse and Cat Stand and Nickel Eye and Owen82 and himself. Written back when they were all suspects. And he was first, had been the one standing over the body with the gun. (158)

The portions Chassis Jones manages to salvage—a series of profiles, the terms he was dictating in the form of dictionary entries—frame *The Bird Is Gone*, which opens with the profiles and concludes with the "Terms," a glossary of terms specific to post-Conservation Act Territories. LP Deal's suspicion that his writings would be disseminated through the linked state and anthropological information economies was not unfounded paranoia, therefore, but rather a valid fear. Like Nam's father in "Love and Honor" and de la Fe in *The People of Paper*, LP Deal would rather his intimate accounts be destroyed than be circulated beyond his control. Like Le, Jones affords his character narrative privacy by protecting those portions of his story he manages to destroy from curious readers. The novel's subtitle, "A ~~Monograph~~ Manifesto" indicates that *The Bird Is Gone* is LP Deal's manifesto, which is largely destroyed; as a result, the novel is one of absence, the missing portions of the manifesto filled in with Chassis Jones's incomplete surveillance of Fool's Hip regulars wise to her plan. Like Nam's account of My Lai, her story is only "close enough." In explicitly revising his subtitle, Jones draws attention to precisely what he isn't offering: a full account of what goes on in the Territories, or the information anthropologists and federal agents—and readers—desire.

While Jones shares only his last name with his narrator[35]—unlike a full name and biography like Plascencia or a first name and biography like Le—Jones still implicates himself in the novel's critique of how literature might function as a surveillance technology. Nestled in the author's website on a lengthy list of almost one hundred extradiegetic, or real-world, interviews with Jones conducted by news outlets, other authors, and websites is a document titled "LPTape 1," dated January 4, 2011—eight years after the publication of *The Bird Is Gone*. The editor's note indicates the interview's origin as Fool's Hip:

---

35. According to LP Deal's "Terms": "**chassis jones**—*n.*, *Psychol.* the distinct and undeniable need for a frame. [back-formation from 'basketball jones,' 'cigarette jones,' etc.]" (164, brackets in original). Even though Chassis Jones does not share the author's biography, full name, or gender, the name's definition suggests a metafictional nod toward Jones's need for a deliberate narrative frame in the form of his primary narrator. Alternatively, one might read the definition as an explanation for Chassis Jones's need for a frame—for LP Deal's manifesto—that bookends the novel and revises the novel's subtitle from "a monograph" to "a manifesto."

Editor's note: The following tape is one of many confiscated from the locker of LP Deal in the back of the Fool's Hip Bowling Alley in the Dakota Territories by Federal Agents during their investigation into the murder of tourists in the region. The publisher acquired the tapes through legal means and now has made transcripts of them available to the public so that more can be understood of the incident in question and the man who claims not to have been involved at all, Stephen Graham Jones. ("LPTape 1")

The note further indicates that the following transcript is "Taping session number four. Chassis Jones: female, "Indian," interrogator. Stephen Graham Jones: male, Blackfeet, author, interrogated. No relation" ("LPTape 1"). The interview, or interrogation, that follows barely acknowledges *The Bird Is Gone*, focusing instead on Jones's other fiction as well as his writing process. In one sense, the interview is Jones interviewing himself, perhaps a tongue-in-cheek way of circumventing frequent interview questions while reliving a former character for a moment. In another, however, the Editor's note subtly echoes the patient awareness—the pretending—modeled by the Native regulars at Fool's Hip: Chassis Jones is "Indian," a scare-quoted, general term in direct contrast to Jones's Blackfeet identification and the tribally specific identifications of the Native characters in *The Bird Is Gone*. The interview also raises questions about the novel's logic: why would an interview between Chassis Jones and anyone be part of LP Deal's collection of tapes? Even if understood as a playful move on Jones's part—because surely his claim "not to have been involved at all" is untrue—the interview's position on his author website elevates the novel's suggestion of pervasive surveillance to another level: even a Native author can't escape deposition by a federal agent. Jones's refusal of responsibility for his narrative also resonates with Plascencia's and Le's self-deprecating condemnations of their eponymous author–characters; like them, he acknowledges the complicity of authorship.

Like *The People of Paper* and "Love and Honor," *The Bird Is Gone* links state surveillance with the commodification of Otherness. The regulars of Fool's Hip are in fact guilty of the crime Chassis Jones and Blue Plume investigate; the final pages of the novel describe Chassis Jones's discovery of the missing tourists on the roof of the bowling alley, dead, "mounted to crossed poles, their eyes sewn open" (159). In a novel structured by multiple forms of surveillance, the image places additional critical pressure on what tourists visit the Territories to see. As LP Deal explains in the novel's opening profiles, "Denim Horse [was] the kind of Lakota that would have been kidnapped for the movies twenty years ago, just on principle, just because his black braids and chiseled face fit with the shirtless Indians of romance-book covers. . . .

The tourists can't get enough of him" (28). Cat Stand is similarly targeted for her familiar image, as she was famous in her youth as the "Lactose Tolerant Indian," whose face was printed on milk cartons across America (29). Both characters reject their commodified representations—Denim Horse refuses to pose for postcards, though his twin Back Iron takes his place, and Cat Stand ultimately leaves the commercial business and punishes herself for her participation by drinking a glass of bleach (30). Just as characters in *The People of Paper* and "Love and Honor" wrestle with the commercialization and dissemination of their representations, so too do Natives in Jones's Territories acknowledge and reject the commodification of their images for curious tourists. In sewing the dead tourists' eyes open—making them into "American scarecrows" (159)—regulars at Fool's Hip violently reject not only the observations of anthropologists and surveillance of federal agents, but also the persistent gazes of curious ("American") consumers.

Chapter 3 takes a closer look at Plascencia's and Le's responses to the commodification of the "ETHNIC STORY" to illuminate critiques of commodified otherness in fiction and film, focusing particularly on the way race and indigeneity serve as commercial spectacles in literary Hollywood. Reading Viet Thanh Ngyuen's account of a fictionalized *Apocalypse Now* in *The Sympathizer* (2015), chapter 3 explores how writers theorize narrative privacy when their representations circulate as material commodities and as entertainment in the context of a long history of cultural appropriation.

CHAPTER 3

Selling/Out and the Commodification of Difference

Contemporary authors in the US work within a long history of commodified ethnic and indigenous representations. Chapter 3 focuses squarely on a contradiction at the heart of the fiction in this project: although narratively and formally invested in privacy, every text circulates as commercial fiction. Authors, after all, must sell their stories to make a living, and commercial marketplaces make literature available to reading audiences. Truly private texts that remain uncirculated among literary audiences or free narratives that avoid marketplaces altogether certainly exist, but fall outside of principal articulations of narrative privacy. More interesting for the purposes of this chapter are the processes by which authors of commercial fiction literarily critique commodified visibility even as they materially support themselves in the literary marketplace. Whereas ethnographic exploitation and state surveillance, the organizing institutions of the first two chapters, are widely treated with opprobrium by fiction writers and literary critics alike, commercial representations complicate straightforward critique. Certainly, writers of color and indigenous writers still face barriers in the literary marketplace and are disproportionately undercompensated for their intellectual and creative production. The answer is not necessarily to stop selling fiction, even if the readerly curiosity on which the market relies does not escape critique.

This chapter approaches the contradiction between privacy and commercial entertainment from two perspectives. It opens by returning to fiction by two writers who style their metafictional texts as self-aware ethnic commodities: "Love and Honor and Pity and Pride and Compassion and Sacrifice," a short story from Nam Le's collection, *The Boat* (2008), and Salvador Plascencia's *The People of Paper* (2005), both considered at length in chapter 2 for their interrogation of literature as a surveillance technology. Both Le and Plascencia narratively linger on the discomfort of selling stories about one's own community, particularly when it involves commodifying and circulating familial or traumatic stories. Their desire to tell conflicts with their reluctance to reveal characters' intimate struggles. Both Le and Plascencia consider the relationship between *selling* stories and *selling out* their subjects. The chapter then pivots to Viet Thanh Nguyen, who considers questions of selling out and producing ethnic commodities from a different perspective: the racial optics of Hollywood that profit from, alternately, the erasure and spectacularization of people of color and indigenous people. In *The Sympathizer* (2015), a novel explicitly framed as a confession from one Vietnamese man to another to circumvent white US audiences, Nguyen centers the simultaneous erasure and explicitly violent depiction of Vietnamese characters in Francis Ford Coppola's *Apocalypse Now* (1979), as well in as other US-centric Hollywood films about the Vietnam War. Le, Plascencia, and Nguyen all diegetically consider what privacy entails when their characters—like their authors—are in the business of selling their stories.

Following the concerns about privacy and access articulated by writers in the first chapters of this book, Le and Plascencia each self-deprecatingly consider the ways in which they betray their families and communities by making a living as a writer. Le considers the risks of publishing about Vietnam and the Vietnamese diaspora in terms of familial and generational guilt; as chapter 1 argues, ethnographic imperatives in literature increase the risk that such stories will be read as personal testimony rather than fictional approaches to difficult subjects, an intimacy Le rejects in "Love and Honor" and "The Boat." For Plascencia, selling depictions of fieldworkers in Southern California—including undocumented workers—for readers' entertainment constitutes a form of colonial betrayal in the gendered tradition of la Malinche, Pocahontas, and Rita Hayworth, tropes he threads—and critiques—through the novel.

Le and Plascencia expose the politics of market expectations for depoliticized, palatable ethnicity and draw attention to the various limits of what representations they—or their author–characters—are willing to sell. In these acts of narrative privacy, the authors acknowledge readers, rupturing the objectifying process of commodification by asserting their characters' subjectivity, and refuse exoticism by having their characters look up at their audiences.[1] In his work on exoticism in postcolonial literature, Graham Huggan asks if it is possible "to construct an object of study that resists, and possibly forestalls, its own commodification" (32). This chapter argues that the formal technique of narrative privacy works to diminish the appropriative and political power of commodification. For example, Le narratively destroys a character's story, offering readers only an (diegetic) account of the story passing between two diasporic Vietnamese men, not the (metadiegetic) story itself. Plascencia writes characters who recognize that an omniscient narrator writes and manipulates them and who actively seek to escape his surveillance and readers' curious gazes, illuminating the power relations behind their visibility.[2] Le's and Plascencia's characters desire narrative privacy because they understand that if their stories are sold, they will circulate as entertainment in a process they feel compromises and trivializes their life experience. Facing charges from their characters of "selling out" by publishing their stories, Le and Plascencia balance desires for privacy with the necessarily commodified, public form of commercial fiction by highlighting the limits of readers' access to the worlds they create in order to underscore what audiences cannot purchase or know.

Nguyen, in his engagement with Hollywood's canonical war films, takes a different approach to the commodification of racial representations, focusing instead on the representations that audiences can purchase in the form of Hollywood spectacle. Adopting the language Min Hyoung Song, Plascencia, and Le use, Nguyen's narrator grapples with charges of "selling out" by working as a cultural consultant on the set of a film that depicts Vietnamese individuals as alternately silenced or subjected to spectacular violence. In directing his narration to another Vietnamese man—his interrogator—the narrator marks

---

1. Huggan explains, "Exoticism describes a political as much as an aesthetic practice. But this politics is often concealed, hidden beneath layers of mystification. As a technology of representation, exoticism is self-empowering; self-referential even, insofar as the objects of its gaze are not supposed to look back" (14). Treuer's Bimaadiz and Eta, as parodies of "Euroamerican fantasies" of Native people, fully inhabit their roles as exotic—albeit accessible—characters. Like Treuer's Apelles, however, characters in *The People of Paper* do reference their readers; they look back. Le also implicates readers in his fiction when Nam's father anticipates readers' reactions to his story.

2. Drawing on Fatimah Tobing Rony, A. Gabriel Meléndez describes the "experience of the third eye" as the experience of "becoming conscious, sometimes painfully so, that one hails from a cultural community that has been under some kind of quasi-anthropological surveillance and scrutiny for some time. Ancestors and forebears, one discovers, have been spied upon for purposes not solely filmic and not solely incidental. It is the sense of having been studied that is particularly disconcerting to members of historically excluded populations" (4). The characters in *The People of Paper* experience similarly painful realizations that they have been written into a narrative, spied upon by an omniscient author and reading audiences.

his story as private, a departure from the racist spectacle he helped produce. All three texts metafictionally navigate the implications of making a living as a writer while offering up their stories as entertainment to the marketplace, profiting from subjectivities that are, frequently, economically marginalized. Through narrative privacy, Le, Plascencia, and Nguyen suspend their fiction in the tension between commercial products and private stories to disrupt conventional processes of commodification.

SELLING AUTHENTICITY

Le and Plascencia focus their discomfort with the commodification of their fiction on the way ethnicity circulates in literary marketplaces as niche and—as chapter 1 argues is often the case—self-evident, authentic expressions of culture. Working within a US context in which publishers and authors have historically profited from representations of Otherness without regard for—and sometimes with antagonism toward—the peoples who produced or inspired such representations, Le and Plascencia suggest a colonial genealogy for contemporary literary markets that continue to monetize commercial ethnicity despite persistent social, political, and economic inequalities for people of color in the United States. These writers approach through a literary form difficult questions about how writers of color and indigenous writers might participate in contemporary literary economies that often value their work for their "cultural" and assumed ethnographic quality rather than their literary merit or political efficacy. Both texts imagine unsympathetic audiences who consume the fictions, including characters' hardships, as easily dismissed entertainment, part of what A. Gabriel Meléndez terms "the spectacle of cultural viewing" (16). Le and Plascencia contend with these issues, paying particular attention to their roles in producing commodities marked and marketed as ethnic in particular colonial histories, and also to contemporary racial and literary politics that perpetuate this literary market. Nguyen, on the other hand, considers the spectacle of cultural viewing by at once narratively reproducing the filmic gaze and ascribing a Vietnamese identity to the story's audience. In doing so, he extends Le's and Plascencia's self-deprecating critiques of production to examine consumption of commercial spectacles of difference.

Producing literary representations of peoples, locales, and encounters for profit was always part of European exploration and colonization of the Americas. Early forms of representation included the records of colonial exploits kept by explorers, missionaries, traders, and ethnographers that were later published and circulated. "By the end of the nineteenth century," Meléndez writes, ethnography and commercial entertainment were so interchangeable "it was impossible to sort out what part of early photography and cinema representing native others was entertainment and what part was science" (17). He explains that early cinema was "complicit in representing the Other as savage, exotic, hypersexual, or quaint, that is, anything but real," practices which "conditioned the American public to anticipate exotica, foreignness, and spectacle" in depictions of cultural others, expectations Hollywood continues to satisfy for profit (5, 16). When understood in terms of global markets, contemporary practices of representing colonial others for profit is part of what Linda Tuhiwai Smith terms "trading the Other," a "vast industry based on the positional superiority and advantages gained under imperialism" that circulates commodified artifacts, ideas, and representations of colonized or previously colonized peoples (93). "As a trade," she writes, "it has no concern for the peoples who originally produced the ideas or images, or with how and why they produced those ways of knowing" (93). Key to Smith's definition of trading the Other is the cultural and economic disconnect between commodified representations—including the content of the representations but also the profit they generate—and the people from whom the representations originated. Smith's theory of "trading the Other" shares the critical thrust of cultural appropriation, "a contradictory behavior with a colonial history," which Coco Fusco describes as "the simultaneous embrace of a culture and rejection of the people who originate it" (66). Smith's and Fusco's theorizations hinge on the contradiction between the two halves of the processes they identify: the welcome reception of commodified, palatable representations and the rejection of or disregard for originating peoples' lived experiences.[3] That is, one symptom of ongoing colonial processes is the profiteering from images of Otherness while those who originated that intellectual, cultural, or artistic capital remain excluded from economic and social equality.[4] For Nguyen, for example, this profiteering manifests itself in

    3. One historical example Fusco offers is of Native dances: "American history from the late nineteenth and early twentieth century is rife with examples of how black and Native American cultural expression was regulated by a white power structure and removed from its sources to serve as entertainment for whites. Many Native American dances, for example, were outlawed on reservations while they were regularly performed for whites at fairs and circuses" (68).
    4. Smith positions the practice of trading the Other in a global context of colonization and exploitation of indigenous peoples. Fusco focuses more closely on the US, particularly consumer habits of appropriating adequately depoliticized, decontextualized ethnic commodities and art. At their cores, however, both Smith's and Fusco's concepts point to the colonial process of disassociating the widely circulated forms of commodified visibility colonized peoples experience from the ongoing in/visibility of the political and economic realities of their lived experiences.

the spectacular suffering and complete silence of Vietnamese people in US films about colonial wars in Vietnam. The animating conflicts of both "Love and Honor" and *The People of Paper* center on author–characters Nam and Sal contending with their own relationship to the processes Smith and Fusco theorize. In a market whetted for ethnographic or exotic portraits of Otherness, Nam and Sal turn to narrative privacy as a means of theorizing how authors might represent Latinx and diasporic Asian communities with explicit attention to corresponding progress toward social justice for those communities by drawing deliberate attention to the politics of selling entertaining representations on the page and in the world.

US capitalism has a long and vexed history with racial inequality, not only in terms of labor exploitation but also in the marketing of and—increasingly—toward ethnic groups. Susan L. Mizruchi explains of US capitalism's rapid expansion between the Civil War and WWI, "On the one hand, an expanding capitalist industry, far from being inimical to cultural difference, welcomed it, taking advantage of the tremendous diversity of American society to identify and pitch products to consumer groups. On the other hand, American capitalism aggressively manipulated racial hostility, fanning the flames of nativism, devaluing and excluding through various means blacks and ethnic others and defending the social Darwinism that legitimated claims of Anglo-Saxon superiority" (3). The rest of the twentieth century followed a similar pattern of exploiting nonwhite labor and purchasing power while excluding racial Others from political and social equality. Even as corporations cater to the purchasing power of "special markets," as Arlene Dávila explains, they reinforce highly compromised forms of ethnic visibility—as marketable products, as consumers, and as exterior to the US mainstream market. She explains, for example, "Latinos are continually recast as authentic and marketable, but ultimately as a foreign rather than intrinsic components of US society, culture, and history, suggesting that the growing visibility of Latino populations parallels an expansion of the technologies that render them exotic and invisible" (4).[5] Speaking of the rise of multiculturalism in the 1980s and 1990s, Fusco clarifies that the US's "projection of racial diversity as desirable, and our sophisticated consumer's attraction to commodified otherness have done little to stop increasing the polarization of wealth along racial lines. In fact, they parallel the intensification of xenophobia and nativism in government policy throughout the nations of the First World" (70). The decades since Fusco's

---

5. In *Latinos, Inc.: The Marketing and Making of a People*, Dávila expands her study of the marketing of Latinx culture to various other racial and ethnic groups in the US. There, she explains more fully how targeted marketing strategies, in addition to affirming particular stereotypes, also reinforce the centrality of whiteness in US commercial imaginations (219).

writing have only confirmed her observations. Despite increasing globalization and interconnectivity and sustained "attraction to commodified otherness," wealth gaps persist in the US and xenophobia and nativism continue to intensify, particularly post-9/11.

US history offers enough diverse and sustained examples of selling race and difference as spectacle to support a tremendous amount of historically situated scholarly work on the subject.[6] Observing patterns across specific instances of these commodified and decontextualized spectacles, however, suggests two primary critical stakes: control over cultural representations and stories, and the implications of various forms of visibility for nonwhite people in the US, from political surveillance to the lived experience of "looked-at-ness."[7] Central to the commercial success of representations of nonwhite peoples in the United States is the palatability of their decontextualization. As Amy Tang explains, the "institutionalization of multiculturalism" rewards depoliticized and dehistoricized representations, made appealing and non-threatening to commercial audiences, who can then consume such narratives as entertainment (1). The texts throughout this volume disrupt expectations of entertainment by refusing to offer their stories or, similarly, by insisting on the performative, fictional nature of the stories they tell; in either case, they draw attention to the limits of readers' access. Recognizable, domesticated ethnicity represents what audiences have come to expect by fulfilling familiar stereotypes or tropes; they depict ethnic subjectivities that are contained and know-

---

6. In addition to Fusco and Smith, some of the most prominent scholarly work in literary and race studies in the past several decades has centered on historically specific issues of the commercialization of racialized spectacles. For instance, Saidiya V. Hartman's *Scenes of Subjection: Terror, Slavery, and Self-Making in Nineteenth-Century America* (1997) explores the spectacle of performance at US slave auctions, public violence against African Americans, and minstrel shows. Eric Lott also considers the appropriative nature of minstrelsy in *Love and Theft: Blackface Minstrelsy and the American Working Class* (1993). Toni Morrison's *Playing in the Dark: Whiteness and the Literary Imagination* (1992) considers the representation and exploitation of blackness in American literature, particularly its strategic in/visibilities that advance primarily white narratives. Eleanor Ty theorizes North American "scopophilia" toward Asians and Asian North Americans as a destructive form of cultural consumption in *The Politics of the Visible in Asian North American Narratives* (2004), and Colleen Lye historicizes "American Orientalism" as historical, social, and literary appropriation in *America's Asia: Racial Form and American Literature, 1893–1945* (2005). Philip J. Deloria tracks non-Native appropriations of Native images from the Boston Tea Party through the twentieth century in *Playing Indian* (1998). Charles Ramírez Berg's work with Latinx stereotypes in pop culture extends critical work on commodification to Hollywood, critical territory later shared by Mary Beltrán and Camilla Fojas's anthology on Hollywood's commercialization of mixed-race images, representations meant to herald an ostensibly postrace or multicultural era or, more cynically, to market to a consumer base interested in generic—thus likely depoliticized and palatable—ethnicity.

7. I consider Rey Chow's adaptation of Laura Mulvey's theories of visuality, including "looked-at-ness," in chapter 1 (Chow, *Primitive Passions* 180).

able, safely under surveillance. For instance, the romanticized story of Ojibwe youths David Treuer weaves through *The Translation of Dr. Apelles,* considered at length in chapter 1, parodies the sort of palatable ethnicity often rewarded by publishers and consumers. In his critique of problematic ways in which US audiences consume images of Native peoples, Treuer reworks the Greek pastoral *Daphnis and Chloe* into a commercially attractive story about Ojibwe youths Bimaadiz and Eta by explicitly drawing on canonical and historical US stereotypes about Natives, particularly narratives about Native nobility and innocence. Catering to "Euroamerican fantasies of Indians," Treuer's omniscient narrator delivers Bimaadiz and Eta for his readers' consumption with descriptions of their bodies and exploits that drip with romantic idealism (Yost 64). Unlike Apelles, Treuer's protagonist in the other narrative in *Translation,* and Plascencia's characters, Bimaadiz and Eta never look up to confront their author or audience; they contentedly live out a perfectly consumable and nonthreatening Native romance.[8]

Withholding private stories, rather than anti-representational, is a political act that acknowledges and deflects expectations of palatable intimacy. As chapter 1 contends, familiar markers of difference—often stereotyped and therefore recognizable—increase ethnic and indigenous US fiction's value to publishers and, often, readers. Writing in the heyday of the multiculturalism of the 1990s, bell hooks argues, "The commodification of Otherness has been so successful because it is offered as a new delight, more intense, more satisfying than normal ways of doing and feeling. Within commodity culture, ethnicity becomes spice, seasoning that can liven up the dull dish that is mainstream white culture" (181). Commodified otherness allows US consumers "imagined access to the cultural other through the process of consumption," what hooks terms "eating the other," a process that invites the embrace of particular cultural representations while allowing—perhaps even requiring—consumers to reject or ignore the subjectivities, politics, and histories behind the representation (Huggan 19, hooks 21).[9] Domesticated, palatable representations of ethnicity are nonthreatening in part because they focus on issues of dehistoricized, depoliticized authenticity rather than authors' political goals or aesthetic achievements, but also because they allow readers uninhibited, unchallenged access to the lives of Others.

---

8. When Bimaadiz and Eta meet their omniscient narrator, in fact, they treat him deferentially, not as a "sell out" as do Plascencia's characters, and the narrative awards the narrator deity status.

9. Mize and Swords, among others, articulate this relationship: "consumption in the era of global capital accumulation is heavily rooted in the marginalization and exploitation of immigrant labor" (xxv).

"SELLING IT": MEMORY IN "LOVE AND HONOR"

To make a living by writing, however, authors must sell their stories. Le and Plascencia each contend with their own implication as writers in environments in which selling fiction can be understood as at once the measure of their success as writers and as a form of betrayal as they contribute ethnic commodities for circulation, observation, and consumption in a history of cultural appropriation and pervasive surveillance of nonwhite peoples. Their situations are more complicated than that of a native informant delivering insider information to a white audience in exchange for money, however, as audiences of commercial fiction are by no means monolithic and, as the authors in chapter 1 illustrate, literature accomplishes far more than transparent cultural translations for curious audiences. Further, many factors other than a story's potential commercial success influence what writers include in their fiction, even as editors and publishers wield influence over those writers hoping to publish their work.[10] However, both Le and Plascencia focus the stories under consideration in this chapter on the complications and contradictions of producing fiction for a commercial market. In his work on contemporary Asian American writers, Song considers authors' struggles with the constellation of critical questions raised by publishing fiction in the current literary industry as "the dilemma facing contemporary Asian American writers as ethnic writers at the dawn of the twenty-first century" (90). I extend the dilemma Song identifies not only to include indigenous and Latinx authors, but also to specific concerns about writing intimacy and trauma in responsible and nuanced ways in an industry that commodifies these features as intrinsic to ethnic and indigenous literature.

In his recent multidisciplinary study, Song supplements literary analysis with interviews and statistical information on the publishing industry and literary award processes. He raises several questions central to this chapter, asking for instance how writers contend with producing texts that will be—for the talented and fortunate individuals who reach commercial success as writers—turned into objects and received as ethnic commodities. He explains the dilemma the writers he interviews face:

---

10. In exploring the pattern of contemporary writers refusing the label of "Asian American," Song theorizes: "perhaps resistance to being labeled comes from working in a field dominated by assemblages of creative-writing programs, talent agents, editors, and marketing departments that relentlessly seek to commodify all that is different about a writer and that is thus also compromised in a way a writer might want to work against. Or perhaps such resistance emerges because writers, precisely in being writers, are intimately aware of the ways in which representation seems always to be invading personhood" (14).

They can embrace a position prepared for them by a literary marketplace with a whetted appetite for stories that can operate as a form of ethnography, but in doing so they can feel as if they are selling out to the marketplace and not engaging in anything more meaningful than an economic transaction. . . . Likewise, in refusing to embrace such a position, writers might find themselves narrating this refusal to be identified with their ethnic background, as if there is something shameful in it. Such a refusal may also feel like a turning of their backs on communities whose experiences continue to be squeezed through the distortion of powerful extant narrative frames about Asian Americans, and about Asian diasporics more generally. (90–91)[11]

Song argues that ethnic writers are forced to contend with expectations placed on their ethnicity in an industry in which "their ethnicity is converted into a kind of commodity that helps attract attention to the stories they have to tell" (75). Often, these expectations are in the form of ethnographic imperatives, depoliticized and packaged as entertainment.

While I depart from Song's interdisciplinary methodology to focus more narrowly on how several contemporary writers use literary form to contend with the commodification of their work by the publishing industry, I share his interest in how writers negotiate market expectations in nuanced ways—that is, without catering to publishers' interest in familiar, palatable representations or resorting to equally confining reactionary roles against ethnic or racial representation. I draw on Song's use of the phrase "selling out" as a loaded but critically useful term that resonates with the central anxieties in "Love and Honor" and especially in *The People of Paper*, in which a character charges the author-character with betraying his family, friends, and hometown "for fourteen dollars and the vanity of [his] name on the book cover," and *The Sympathizer*, in which the narrator is labeled a "sellout" (Plascencia 138). I appreciate the discomfort associated with the term "selling out," as it illuminates

---

11. Ty makes a similar point about Asian North American fiction writers: "In my study of works by Asian North Americans, I argue that the ambivalent claims and powers of visibility create tensions and disturbing positions for authors who attempt to represent difference without falling prey to Western scopophilic fantasies. To resist the visible and the pleasures of scopophilia, to resist performing typically Oriental or ethnic roles without rejecting the everyday little acts that constitute one's self, become some of the biggest challenges of self-representation" (10). In his work on exoticism and postcolonial literature, Graham Huggan voices a similar conclusion: "Exoticist spectacle, commodity fetishism and the aesthetics of decontextualization are all at work, in different combinations and to varying degrees, in the production, transmission and consumption of postcolonial literary/cultural texts" (20).

the uncomfortable tension between betrayal and economic exchange that Le, Plascencia, and Nguyen explore in their metafictions.

Le's and Plascencia's use of self-referential metafiction to explore the relationships between literature, commodification, and surveillance historically situates their critical projects. In his work on contemporary ethnic literary form, Ramón Saldívar critically engages with Plascencia's *The People of Paper* and Junot Díaz's *The Brief Wondrous Life of Oscar Wao* (2007) to theorize "a radical turn" in American literature in the twenty-first century. He writes, "in the twenty-first century, the relationship between race and social justice, race and identity, and indeed, race and history requires these writers to invent a new 'imaginary' for thinking about the nature of a just society and the role of race in its construction. It also requires the invention of new forms to represent it" ("Historical Fantasy" 574). While I depart from Saldívar's theorization of a historical fantasy genre emerging in a "postrace" era,[12] I pay similar attention to the way literary form can reckon with historically specific concerns, such as the places in the twenty-first century marketplace for literature by writers of color and indigenous writers. Saldívar characterizes this "postrace aesthetic" as both urgent and necessary: "*The People of Paper* forcefully insists upon us a different question—of the *possibility* and the *necessity* of an aesthetic idiom sincerely (not ironically) committed to social justice, an aesthetic idiom not fixed, debased, counterfeited, fetishized, or commodified precisely because not yet pinned to particular formal or historical referents which might *never* come to be" ("Historical Fantasy" 584). The aesthetic Saldívar describes manifests in Plascencia's self-deprecation, his emphasis on his own culpability, and his indictment of his power. Jennifer Harford Vargas terms this formal aesthetic "*author*itarian," in which Plascencia "dramatizes the power dynamics of authorial creation and narration by riffing on the author-as-god analogy with an author-as-dictator analogy" (64).[13] Arguing that "Saturn functions as a general symbol of power, whether that power is wielded by an individual,

---

12. The language central to Saldívar's argument is a bit misleading. He clarifies: "the term 'postrace' does not mean that we are *beyond* race; the prefix 'post' here does not mean a chronological 'superseding,' a triumphant posteriority. Rather, the term entails a conceptual shift to the question of what meaning the *idea* of 'race' carries in our own times. The *post* of postrace is not like the *post* of post-structuralism; it is more like the *post* of postcolonial, that is, a term designating not a chronological but a conceptual frame, one that refers to the logic of something having been 'shaped as a consequence of' imperialism and racism" ("Historical Fantasy" 575).

13. "In doing so," Vargas continues, "Plascencia's representation of the borderlands of dictatorship usefully illuminates the relations of domination that exist in the production of fictional worlds, in the surveillance of undocumented subjects, in the exploitation of migrant laborers, and in the capitalist circulation of the novel as a commodity in global literary markets" (63).

group, or nation," Anne Mai Yee Jansen reaches a similar critique by reading power relations between diegetic author and metadiegetic characters in terms of labor histories, particularly the farmworker strikes of the 1930s (109, 106). Metafictionally highlighting issues of commodification and surveillance in literary form, the fictions in this chapter answer Saldívar's call for aesthetic innovation by deploying the formal technique of narrative privacy as a way of negotiating processes of appropriation in the twenty-first century.

The moral center of "Love and Honor and Pity and Pride and Compassion and Sacrifice," as explored in chapter 2 in terms of state surveillance, is whether Nam (as opposed to the author, Le) should share—through commercial fiction—his father's story of surviving the My Lai massacre. Nam's initial resistance to writing about Vietnam is a resistance to the expectations placed on "ethnic authors" to sell the traumas and stories of their own background and life experience as intimate testimonies marketed as ethnic commodities rather than political representation. Nam understands that publishers expect him to write stories about Vietnam or Vietnamese people, but he worries that writing such stories will prevent him from gaining the respect of his peers, who will not take his story seriously as anything other than a self-evident ethnographic account. He is unmotivated to write deeply personal stories that will be read as entertainment, rather than as sophisticated literary engagements with histories and ideas, yet, as Le emphasizes, he still faces the very practical concerns of deadlines and making a living.

Nam's community at the Iowa Writers' Workshop serves as a microcosm of competing advice about how Nam should negotiate his position as an "ethnic" author. Instructors and visiting publishers warn that to sell books he must set himself apart from other writers, suggesting he write about Vietnam because "Ethnic literature's hot. And important too," an assessment more concerned with salability than the aesthetic or political importance of his work (9). Song describes the advice Nam receives as "explicit exhortations to turn native informant, to sell one's life's story as a commodity for literary enjoyment and, decidedly as an afterthought, for serious contemplation" (88). Nam's colleagues evidently share the sentiment that much of ethnic writing's value stems from its place as a cultural commodity rather than serious literature, as they list—perhaps out of jealousy or anxiety about their own commercial futures—what they see as the limitations of ethnic writing: "it's full of descriptions of exotic food"; "the characters are always flat, generic"; "You can't tell if the language is spare because the author intended it that way, or because he didn't have the vocab" (9). A recent graduate, "The workshop's most recent success," however, offers evidence for the publishers' and instructors' claims about the desirability of ethnic literature without substantiating Nam's colleagues' concerns about quality. She is "a Chinese woman trying to immigrate to America who had written a book of short stories about Chinese characters in stages of immigration to America. The stories were subtle and good" (8). As a result, rumor has it, "she'd been offered a substantial six-figure contract for a two-book deal" (8–9). Amongst Nam's community, however, the question remains as to whether it was the "subtle and good" writing or the Chinese content that earned the author recognition and financial success.

Several of Nam's colleagues interpret the Workshop's recent success story as a direct result of her selling her culture and taking what they perceive as the easy route. One of these colleagues ignores the "subtle and good" quality of the Chinese graduate's writing to illustrate a knee-jerk reaction to the way "ethnicity is converted into a kind of commodity that helps attract attention to the stories they [ethnic authors] have to tell," as he dismisses ethnic literature as "a license to bore" (Song 75, Le 9). He praises Nam for not relying on his "*background* and *life experience*" for material: "You could *totally* exploit the Vietnamese thing" (9, 10). Of course, "the Vietnamese thing" to which the colleague refers is Nam's experience as a refugee and as the son of a massacre survivor and former political prisoner. Operating from an unacknowledged position of privilege, he looks past Nam's actual experiences to consider market expediency, much as in the same way he discounts the Chinese author's success as taking the easy route, a conclusion that omits practical consideration of her "*background* and *experiences*" struggling to immigrate to the United States. Another colleague trivializes Nam's difficulty writing a story by assuming Nam's niche knowledge of Vietnam diminishes the challenges of crafting fiction: "'Writer's block?' Under the streetlights, vapors of bourbon puffed out of his mouth. 'How can you have writer's block? Just write a story about Vietnam'" (8). Nam's anxiety over writing about Vietnam or Vietnamese characters illustrates that for him—as for the recent Chinese graduate of the Workshop—writing about his background and life experience is perhaps the most difficult option, especially when writing in a medium understood, at least in part, as entertainment. As Nguyen explains, "the Vietnamese American author who writes about Vietnamese Americans is seen as only writing about who he or she knows, which is not as impressive. It's definitely true that Vietnamese American authors have a hard time escaping the racial binds of authenticity in literature, which exist because of racial contradictions in American society overall" (Hong). Rather than a lens through which to consider William Faulkner's universal verities listed in the story's title, Nam's family's traumatic past will serve as "authentic" entertainment for audiences who have come to expect trauma and hardship—along with "descriptions of exotic food"—from ethnic literature. The easier route for Nam would be to protect his and his family's background and life experience from being commodified and circulated as entertainment.

In the midst of the ideological debate raging in the Workshop, Nam faces a very practical problem: an end-of-term deadline for a short story. Pressed for time because of his father's visit, Nam decides to write a story he remembers from his childhood, one he overheard his father telling to a group of friends. He recreates his father's account of surviving the My Lai massacre as a youth as best he can from memory, acknowledging that, as a story about Vietnam, the narrative appears to capitulate to one of the Workshop's ideological camps. Nam's father, however, reads a draft of the story and dismisses it as inaccurate. In response, Nam asks his father to tell him the true account:

> He [Nam's father] was silent for a long time. Then he said, "Only you'll remember. I'll remember. They will read and clap their hands and forget." For once, he was not smiling.
>
> "Sometimes it's better to forget, no?" "I'll write it anyway," I said. It came back to me—how I'd felt at the typewriter the previous night. A thought leapt into my mind: "If I write a true story," I told my father, "I'll have a better chance of selling it."
>
> He looked at me a while, searchingly, seeing something in my face as though for the first time. (24)

The language, as critics have noted, is specifically capitalist. No longer is Nam interested in finishing an assignment for a course; rather, he seeks commercial success as a writer through his father's past. Donald Goellnicht explains, "In this uncanny perception that plays upon the double meaning of 'selling it,' truth becomes translated into saleability, authenticity in Asian diasporic fiction a commodity in a late-capitalist market of cultural products. Nam operates on the assumption that, in this marketplace, memories have become commodities that must compete for customers" (199).[14] Nam's father expresses concern over the commodification of his story, imagining an audience that, instead of remembering and thoughtfully considering the narrative, will treat the story as disposable entertainment. Nam's father's warning echoes hooks's declaration that the "overriding fear is that cultural, ethnic, and racial differences will be continually commodified and offered up as new

---

14. Goellnicht observes the tangled decisions writers such as Nam must navigate: "On the one hand, Nam has decided to sell his father out, to turn a profit from this story; on the other, he decides to inject a decidedly un-American narrative—My Lai from a Vietnamese civilian's perspective—into American cultural memory in the belief that Americans will 'buy' (believe as well as purchase) a true story" (199).

dishes to enhance the white palate—that the Other will be eaten, consumed, and forgotten" (200).[15] Like hooks, and not unlike Plascencia's characters in El Monte, Nam's father resists the commodification of his specifically Vietnamese trauma as entertainment for a Western audience.

Whereas Nam believes the act of writing gives his father's story meaning beyond its commodity value, Nam's father understands the written story as reducing his memories to a marketable—and ultimately forgettable, disposable—commodity. Nam's father does have words for his trauma—as evidenced in his telling of the story to Nam—but deliberately refuses to share those words as entertainment. In the conclusion of the story, explored at length in chapter 2, Nam's father tells him the story, only to burn the sole copy the following day to protect his memories from circulating as entertainment for curious readers. Le leaves unresolved, however, the central anxieties of the story: should Nam write stories from his "*background* and *life experience*"? How does commercial fiction shape storytelling economies? How might Nam make a living as a writer? That such questions about the basic economies of authorship permeate the story illuminates the uneven ways in which the specter of selling (out) haunts writers of color.

"SELLING OUT": BETRAYAL IN *THE PEOPLE OF PAPER*

Plascencia takes a similarly metafictional approach to anxieties over commodification of his stories and the possibility of "selling out." In *The People of Paper*, Plascencia's characters decide that their author–narrator, Saturn, has too much control over their lives. Sensing Saturn as an oppressive force looking down from the sky, the characters wage a "war on omniscient narration (a.k.a. the war against the commodification of sadness)," elsewhere in the novel named a "war for volition" (218, 53). The characters' grievances against Saturn, who reveals himself to be a writer named Sal Plascencia, link issues of omniscient surveillance, commodification, and volition in the post-9/11 context of Mexican immigration to the US. Plascencia implicates in this context his readers and his role as author to consider how his narrative mimics US processes of commodifying Otherness while surveilling and restricting nonwhite bodies. By crafting a metafiction that explicitly lays open several diegetic worlds, Plas-

---

15. Nam worries about commodifying his father's trauma himself when he considers how his stories might be marketed if he writes about Vietnam and Vietnamese people. He imagines the image publishers will use on his book's dust jacket: "I pictured myself standing in a rice paddy, wearing a straw conical hat. Then I pictured my father in the same field, wearing his threadbare fatigues, young and hard-eyed" (9).

cencia explores the traitorous implications of selling his hometown through literature; he considers how offering paying audiences a view into the lives of the Mexicans and Mexican Americans whom he controls constitutes profiting from the ongoing political and economic struggles people experience on the US–Mexico border.[16] In doing so, Plascencia extends the same anxieties undergirding Le's story throughout his novel.

In turning a critical—metafictional—lens on the relationship between characters and their author, Plascencia positions his author–character, Sal, as a traitor for selling his omniscient perspective to paying audiences. Sal intends to sell his diegetic novel about EMF "as entertainment," profiting off particular forms of commodified Mexicanness even as he continues to invade the privacy of the subjectivities that animate his novel. Plascencia invites comparison between Sal's plans for publication and the pervasive cultural appropriation in the US that consumes palatable images of Latinidad on television and in film while building a fence along the US–Mexico border and supporting unfair labor practices in Mexico and throughout Latin America. The US government imposes inconsistent and unjust legal and economic obstacles on the lives of Mexican Americans and Mexican migrants to the US, such as racial profiling, limited work opportunities, and few legal avenues for relief—almost all of which work in the US's favor economically. Sal's characters understand the narrative obstacles he drops in their stories in a similar light; their strife creates a more compelling story, and Sal profits by commodifying their sadness. As is too often the case, the undocumented Latinxs and immigrants who populate the novel's pages have no means of speaking back to the oppressive forces that structure their lives.

On a separate diegetic level, however, characters are not only able to speak back to Sal—and Plascencia—but they explicitly engage in discourses of betrayal. In fact, betrayal—selling out—not only consumes the relationships in Sal's world but becomes the lens through which Sal understands everything from colonialism to his novel-in-progress about de la Fe and EMF. In Sal's logic, betrayal on the part of Liz, his former partner, created the heart-

---

16. In *The Book of Want* (2011), Daniel Olivas similarly contends with anxiety about commodifying stories of Mexican Americans by breaking narrative distance and having characters interview each other about their respective decisions to participate in the novel. One character, La Queenie, feels disrespected in the interview, so removes herself from the novel, asserting the same agency exhibited by characters in Plascencia's El Monte. As she leaves the interview and the novel, La Queenie denigrates *The Book of Want* by distinguishing it from "a great novel like *The Hummingbird's Daughter* or *The People of Paper*" (99). Rather than acquiescing to the literary space Olivas authorizes for her, La Queenie pulls herself from the novel in a distinctly political act that confronts the economic and social inequalities faced by the subjectivities that populate Plascencia's and Olivas's novels.

break that caused him to go to war with his characters. Existing not only on the first of the novel's dedication pages but also in the world in which Sal is a struggling writer rather than an omniscient force in the sky, Liz bears the brunt of Sal's anger. Sal charges Liz with betraying him and their race by leaving him for a white man, whom he aligns with North American colonialism. He similarly couches his other grievances against Liz in an explicitly colonial context, accusing her of being a "sell-out," "Worse than Rita Hayworth . . . You are worse than the Malinche, worse than Pocahontas" (118). By invoking Malinche, Rita Hayworth, and Pocahontas—all women who partnered with white men under various conditions—Sal taps into a long tradition of masculinist discourse in which women of color are to be either conquered and enjoyed as spoils of conquest, or protected as symbols of their race. In this formulation, women are either passive objects, or, as in Sal's examples, traitors.

As a historical figure, Malinche was a Nahuatl woman twice exchanged as property, the second time to Hernán Cortés (Rebolledo 62). Because she was able to speak Maya and Nahuatl, she became an important translator for Cortés. As Tey Diana Rebolledo explains, "She later became Cortés's mistress. Her name became so closely identified with that of the conqueror (and his with hers) that in Mexico, by the twentieth century, the word 'Malinche' or 'Malinchista' became synonymous with a person who betrays her or his country" (62). Feminist Chicana scholars reclaimed the historical figure, however: "Chicana writers do not view La Malinche as the passive victim of rape and conquest but instead believe her to be a woman who had and made choices. Because she possessed the power of language and political knowledge, for them La Malinche is a woman who deliberately chose to be a survivor" (Rebolledo 64). While Chicana scholars have contextualized Malinche's decision to have a child with Cortés as an act of survival by an intellectual woman who had been exchanged as a commodity, Sal clearly intends his comparison of Liz to Malinche as an epithet. As with Pocahontas, another indigenous woman who later paired with a European invader, Malinche stands in for gendered, cultural betrayal. Writing in the mid-1990s, Rebolledo explains that calling someone a Malinche can have even broader connotations, riffing on the multiple meanings of "selling-out," as it "specifically refers to those Mexicans who relate excessively to American-produced commercial goods" (62). In charging Liz with being "worse than the Malinche," Sal calls on a long history of linking commodification with betrayal or "selling out" to project his own anxiety about selling out his characters to readers who will consume their sadness as entertainment.

As another character Sal writes as a manifestation of betrayal, Rita Hayworth shares with Malinche the specific connotation of gendered cultural betrayal, also with the implication of "selling out," but this time in the context of Hollywood representation. Rita Hayworth, born Margarita Carmen Cansino, starred in Hollywood films in the early twentieth century (Ovalle 70). Born in New York to a Spanish father and white American mother, Rita entered the entertainment industry as a Latina, only to undergo a "process of publicized commodification and transformation (from Margarita Carmen Cansino to Rita Cansino, ethnic starlet, to the all-American Rita Hayworth)" (McLean 3).[17] While Sal's biography of Hayworth is inaccurate—she was not a plum farmer from "a coastal town in Jalisco"—his account of her transformation succinctly mirrors the biography Hayworth scholar Adrienne L. McLean offers (Plascencia 41–42). Sal explains:

> Rita Hayworth bleached her jet-black hair into a light shade of auburn. To emphasize her widow's peak, she used needle-shaped electrodes to push back her hairline. She pinched her cartilage until her mestizo nose was pointy. The in-house linguist at Fox Pictures touched Rita's tongue, teaching her to unroll her *r*'s and pronounce words like *salamander* and *salad* without sounding like a wetback. (47)

Contextualizing Hayworth's career in patriarchal Hollywood and theorizing Hayworth's image as spectacular commodity, McLean understands Hayworth as a complex figure, "both agent and object" (28). To Sal, however, Hayworth is another "Rita Vendida," in the same vein as Malinche (Plascencia 78). "Too good to fuck us lettuce pickers," Sal's Hayworth chooses white men over Mexican men, and literally sells herself to Hollywood by transforming into an American celebrity (45). Sal interprets Liz's betrayal—leaving him for a white man who lives in Hollywood—as a similar form of whitening and selling out. Like de la Fe, who was resigned to a town of farmworkers fifteen miles east of Hayworth's mansion, Sal sees himself as left behind with the lettuce pickers as Liz whitens herself for her new lover.

Using the figures of Malinche, Pocahontas, and Rita Hayworth as shorthand for racialized, feminine betrayal reinforces negative stereotypes of women as objects or as deceptive and traitorous. It also ignores the substantial bodies of Chicana, Native, and feminist (especially woman of color feminist) scholarship that contest historical use of these figures through more nuanced, less reductive, and more politically useful readings.[18] Sal—and by implication,

---

17. Hayworth's all-Americanness is acknowledged in the novel by her image's implication in colonial processes, as Sal points out, "her pinup shot was airbrushed to the first test bomb dropped on the island of Bikini Atoll" (42).

18. Rebolledo's *Women Singing in the Snow: A Cultural Analysis of Chicana Literature* (1995) offers an important overview of some of this scholarship. Rayna Green's classic essay,

Plascencia—pushes his use of masculinist depictions of colonialism to the point of parody, however, such as when he equates Liz's boyfriend's semen with imperialism: "He would not think of her [Liz] or of the white boy who colonized his memories. He who had spread his imperialism everywhere. All over her, spilling it on her chest and stomach, coating her lips, and throat, lining the esophagus and intestines" (124). Even in the emotional hyperbole accompanying heartbreak, Sal's masculinist depiction of imperialism is extreme enough to suggest at least self-awareness, if not irony, in his reliance on gendered, colonial tropes.

In several instances, Sal allows the women characters he accuses of betrayal to speak back to their creator—and audience—to contest Sal's problematic depiction of women as "sell-outs." Rita Hayworth sporadically enjoys the novel's narrative focus and eventually adopts the occasional role of first-person narrator. Through the narrative in her dedicated columns, Rita's characterization as a traitor to her race becomes complicated by discourses of racism and capitalism on the US–Mexico border in entertainment spaces that "help US tourist-consumers assume and sustain a sense of cultural superiority through the exhibition of exoticized non-white bodies" (Ovalle 73). Sal narrates Rita's/Margarita's entrance into the entertainment industry: "In Tijuana, as she danced in anchored gambling ships and casinos,"[19] where Hollywood executives evading Prohibition "asked Margarita to dance in front of their celluloid motion machine" (44).[20] Ovalle argues that these nightclubs on the Mexican side of the border, usually co-owned by wealthy Americans, positioned "Latina bodies as readily available objects and commodities of first world tastes," as they "indulg[e] the pleasures of an Anglo-American male clientele operating from a wholly US perspective" (73). While Sal gets little of Hayworth's biography correct, his attention to her entrance into Hollywood's entertainment industry through border nightclubs is historically accurate and contextualizes her choices as a Latina performer historically and politically; her decision to "sell out" might be better understood as a negotiation of an industry that had already positioned her as a racialized commodity. Speaking in the first person, Rita responds to her popular characterization as a trai-

---

"The Pocahontas Perplex" reconsiders Native women archetypes. More recently, Alicia Gaspar de Alba considers Malinche in *[Un]framing the 'Bad Woman': Sor Juana, Malinche, Coyolxauhqui and Other Rebels with a Cause* (2014).

19. While Plascencia fictionalizes much of Hayworth's biography in Rita's character, Hayworth did perform "at venues such as the Foreign Club in Tijuana, and on the *Rex*, a notorious gambling boat off the coast of Santa Monica, California" (Ovalle 72). She was "discovered by a Hollywood producer named Winfield Sheehan in a Tijuana club co-owned by Twentieth Century Films' cofounder and amusement park pioneer Joe Schenck" (73).

20. Plascencia narrates the colonial processes of erasure and renaming: "'Rita, you're fabulous,' they said, and from that point onward her first name was condensed" (44).

tor, a trope Sal exploits: "it is not elephants that never forget, but those we betray, those we hurt. . . . Unable to excuse a change of address or wardrobe. Telling their children and grandchildren that I am their sellout whore" (214). Rita directly engages with the way an individual woman's historically specific decisions—glossed as "a change of address or wardrobe"—become overwritten by familiar narratives of cultural betrayal. While Sal problematically relies on Rita as a trope of feminine treachery, her sympathetic character has space to refute her flat characterization and to contextualize her decisions in the political and social histories of Hollywood and continuing US racism.

Cameroon, Sal's new girlfriend, also offers the novel's audience an alternative to Sal's narrative. For instance, she points out to readers as number sixty-three on her sixty-four-page list of lies Sal tells in the novel, "Rita Hayworth was never Mexican" (136). She contends that Sal abuses his power as narrator to manipulate the lives of the women he crafts as characters, punishing them for hurting his pride. In addition to Rita's revised biography, Sal depicts his relationship with Cameroon unfairly by depicting her as "A clingy and desperate girl sitting on a bidet" (226). Cameroon outlines her grievances about the unfairness of his fiction in a letter "written in a cursive so angry that it broke through the paper," which Sal includes in the novel (226–27). One of Cameroon's narrative columns depicts her in the future, finding an out-of-print *The People of Paper* on sale for two dollars in which she learns Sal has killed her off by narrating her dying in Africa, where locals feed her to sharks (227–28). She reflects on Sal's narrative misogyny and the death of her character as she wonders why "her fate was such an unimaginative one. But she knew why. This was the fate of women who know too much, women who can upset the pride of Saturn. Because ultimately Saturn is a tyrant, commanding the story where he wants it to go. That is why they fight against him, why they hide under lead and try to push him to the margins" (228). Cameroon's assessment of Sal—Saturn—as a tyrant illuminates the audacity of Sal's pretensions to omniscience and his abuse of the omniscient perspective. Echoing Sal's assertion that "I too am a colonizer . . . I can wipe out whole cultures, whole towns of imaginary flower people," Cameroon understands Sal's narration as manipulative and aligns the women in Sal's life whom he turns into characters with EMF's struggle against omniscient narration (238). Cameroon's challenge to her depiction as a character—and the ease with which a privileged author can write her fate—focuses critical attention on Sal's role as a writer and his decisions to diminish particular groups. In challenging how Sal characterizes her and the other women in the novel, Cameroon reminds audiences of his—and by extension, Saturn's, Plascencia's, and all authors'—biases and authorial privilege.

Liz takes up a similar critique of Sal's narrative decisions particularly as they relate to women by reversing his accusations of "selling out." Taking up Sal's insistence on framing their breakup in the language of colonialism and representation, Liz points to *The People of Paper* as a more serious form of selling out:

> So I have moved house and replaced you with a white boy, but that is nothing compared to what you have done, to what you have sold. In a neat pile of paper you have offered up not only your hometown, EMF, and Federico de la Fe, but also me, your grandparents and generations beyond them, your patria, your friends, even Cami. You have sold everything, save yourself. So you remain but you have sold everything else. You have delivered all this into their hands, and for what? For fourteen dollars and the vanity of your name on the book cover. (138)

Despite Sal's understanding of his omniscience as colonizing in nature, Liz's accusation rearranges Sal's relationship to colonization by naming him not as a colonizer, but as a sell-out to colonizers (his publisher and readers); she reverses the charges Sal once leveled against her. Central to Liz's complaint is that Sal is willing to exchange access to those closest to him for money and individual recognition. While she never names Sal's interlocutors—"their" might refer to the white colonizers Sal evokes with his pronouns, or publishers and readers—Liz literalizes Sal's frequent epithet, "sellout," in her accusation.

Plascencia's reliance on tropes of betrayal directs readers to a central anxiety of the metafictional novel: writing for commercial audiences as a traitorous act. By using *The People of Paper*'s form as a stage on which to play out the conflict between Sal and the women characters he betrays, Plascencia concedes his own implication as a Mexican American writer selling access to his hometown, family, friends, and characters. He also includes himself in Cameroon's indictment of omniscience as an arrogant and easily abused narrative privilege that, like the colonialisms undergirding the discussion, often obscures its own power dynamics. Saldívar explains that Liz, in confronting Sal diegetically, "foregrounds the fact that we are dealing with not so much an unreliable *narrator* as a totally discreditable *author*, 'Salvador Plascencia,' whose own sins, of selling out friends, family, community, and ideals for the sake of mere authorial vanity—the commodification of sadness—are wrapped in a veil of disingenuousness, at best, or deceitful bad faith, at worst" ("Historical Fantasy" 580). In allowing his characters to speak out against their representation and commodification—and the consequences of their compromised privacy—in terms of "selling out," Plascencia invites critical comparisons between writing commercial fiction and the acts of cultural betrayal of one's self and people that Sal vehemently opposes.

In fact, Plascencia styles *The People of Paper* as self-aware in its commodification of sadness, a commodification the characters recognize, detest, and in which they implicate both author and audience. From the start, de la Fe condemns Saturn's willingness to sell his heartbreak of abandonment—a despair so deep he burns himself daily for years—and his vulnerability as a legally and economically marginalized laborer relegated to working in flower fields because he does not have the necessary documentation for other opportunities. Similarly, his daughter, Little Merced, admits "her own resentment, not only toward Saturn, but also those who stared down at the page" (186). Little Merced's indictment of readers extends de la Fe's critiques of their author to the novel's paying audience who, against the explicit wishes of the characters, continue to read *The People of Paper* and peer into the private moments Saturn cultivates only to violate for profit. In wanting to protect her father by shielding him "from mockery, from the pity of strangers," Little Merced desires the protection of narrative privacy and indicts the practice of narrating sadness for commercial audiences (186). In this, she shares the sentiments of Nam's father in "Love and Honor," who would rather burn his story than have it sold as entertainment so that readers—or literary critics—can feel as though they can witness his trauma and extend him pity.

Tired of perpetuating legacies of betrayal by selling the lives of those he loves and creates, Sal destroys the novel he has written. Imagining himself in the role of Samson—yet another narrative of a man betrayed by a woman—Sal sacrifices himself and his work to demolish the system. Instead of the columns of a temple filled with Philistines, Sal pushes against the columnar structure of *The People of Paper*:

> At times debilitated by the thought of her, but still able to summon enough strength to press against the columns. Saturn's weight leaned against the structure. At first there was only a single crack at the base of the column. He thought of her, of her perfidy, and then of the others throughout the story: Delilah, Merced, Ida. The lone crack splintered into a web of fractures, buckling the structure and crumbling it to rubble. Once the first support was down the others were easily tipped, all the columns falling. (242)

Rita contextualizes Sal's evocation of Delilah as he tears down the story by pointing out the irony in the masculinist traditions that devalue women as weak, yet reveal them to be more powerful than God: "[Delilah] chose her people and a bag of silver over her love of Samson, cutting his locks of hair with a borrowed razor and delivering him to his enemies. Samson was consecrated by God Almighty and defeated by the weakest of the sexes" (232). Rita continues, "It is Delilah who is the hero, the one who brings the brute down. Avenging the deaths of the thousands he killed" (235). As Rita points out, Delilah's betrayal of her lover for her people, while grouped together by Sal with other anecdotes of feminine "perfidy," is actually the reverse of Rita's and Malinche's ostensible betrayal; Rita performs the sort of feminist reading of Delilah Sal explicitly denies Rita, Malinche, and Pocahontas. In identifying Samson's own brutish betrayal that preceded Delilah's, Rita focuses for Sal his own complicity in selling out by profiting from social and economic systems that continue to commodify and consume images of women like Liz and workers like de la Fe. Sal responds by destroying his novel to prevent it from circulating as a commodity or as merely entertainment. *The People of Paper* ends with Little Merced and her father walking "south and off the page," concluding simply: "There would be no sequel to the sadness" (245). Like Nam's father, Sal appears to find narrative privacy incompatible with published narratives, as writing is implicated in processes of commodification, and selling a story is akin to facilitating these processes.

Unlike Sal, who destroys his diegetic novel to protect his characters from further omniscient meddling and commodification, Plascencia chooses to publish the novel readers hold in their hands. In doing so, he appears to fulfill Liz's prediction that Sal would sell out El Monte for fourteen dollars and the vanity of his name on the cover. Whereas Sal concedes complete narrative privacy to his characters by allowing them to walk off the page and destroying the narrative he has crafted, Plascencia, despite self-reflexively implicating himself in his own critique of omniscience and commodification, exposes his characters—including Sal—to the curious gazes of paying audiences. He makes explicit, in other words, his characters' desire for privacy only to publish their story anyway. Through the novel's formal self-referentiality, however, Plascencia at least allows his characters a stage to speak back to his privilege and to destabilize readers' positions as literary consumers.

SELLING AND NOT SELLING: REPRESENTATION IN THE MARKETPLACE

In reflecting on the politics of Plascencia's formal innovation in *The People of Paper*, Saldívar turns to the last line of the novel to illuminate the stakes of writing fiction sincerely committed to the cause of social justice ("Historical Fantasy" 584). He asks, "How could there be a sequel to sadness? To its commodification? To the colonization of the racialized mind?" ("Historical Fantasy" 584). Saldívar reinforces Sal's understanding of literature as a colonizing tool. Saldívar and Plascencia each consider the act of accessing and influencing characters' intimate thoughts or secrets as colonizing acts, implying writers' and reading audiences' complicity in ongoing, if vaguely defined, colonial projects. In explicitly divulging his characters' intimacies, Plascencia self-deprecatingly positions himself as a literary colonizer, a role Le avoids by destroying Nam's father's story. Saldívar argues that, as Plascencia narratively illustrates, selling a story about the sadness of marginalized people risks "reducing sadness and the people who experience it, into objects, or worse, of participating in the naturalizing of social inequalities in relation to the ways that commodities are produced and consumed" ("Historical Fantasy" 583). Consequently, he contends, nonwhite writers' only chance at political progress toward social justice is to adapt new literary forms. Plascencia and Le, along with the other writers throughout these chapters, use narrative privacy to mitigate the invasiveness of their narratives, as well as the politically regressive effects of commodification.[21]

Both *The People of Paper* and "Love and Honor" use narrative privacy as a tool for approaching narratives of sadness responsibly and negotiating readers' access and subjects' exposure. While Plascencia illustrates de la Fe's and Little Merced's motivations for desiring a narrative privacy he does not grant, Le honors his character's insistence on privacy by describing but declining to tell a narrative of trauma; he deploys narrative privacy to illustrate for readers what he was not willing to narrate for a commercial marketplace. As Goellnicht points out, "There is something obscene in trying to make art out of such experiences, especially when that art is directed to a Western audience who . . . will co-opt, appropriate, and transform the memory into entertainment" (202–3). "Love and Honor" makes clear that Nam's father's reticence is not a refusal or inability to testify, as he shares his story completely with his son; it is a refusal to offer his story as entertainment for readers (26). By withholding Nam's father's full account from readers, Le prevents the story's knowability and readers' opportunity to "clap their hands and forget" (24). Plascencia's evocation of "the commodification of sadness," while treated playfully in *The People of Paper,* similarly expresses concern about the at-times devastating conditions facing undocumented Mexicans on the US–Mexico border and in California and the US Southwest. His explicit refusal to allow

---

21. As bell hooks succinctly argues, "When commodified it is easy for consumers to ignore political messages" (194).

his characters a sense of privacy and control draws into focus the historically situated political realities of the subjectivities that populate his novel.

Saturn's decision to destroy his story and Plascencia's decision to publish *The People of Paper* model two divergent approaches to a central anxiety of the novel, that authors directly benefit from representing ongoing struggles still being fought by real people. Plascencia's title and his dedication to Liz, "who taught me that we are all of paper," point to this anxiety over the distance between lived experiences of people and writers' literary—paper—representations. As Vargas observes, "The novel interrogates capitalist literary markets, racialized transnational labor exploitation, and nationalist politics of exclusion through a fictional allegory about people made of paper, people trapped in paper, and people without papers" (83). Specifically, Plascencia draws attention to the privileged position of writers who, often having escaped or survived experiences similar to those they depict, now consider them from the safety and comfort of literary distance while the conflicts and struggles they narrate continue to permeate others' lives. Put differently, the novel's tension between characters and author illustrates the fraught relationship between commodified otherness "sold as entertainment" (to the benefit of publishers and authors and for the entertainment of readers) and the possibility of mobilizing literary representations for political and social equality for living people at the margins of US society. Whereas Saturn reacts to this tension by destroying his story, Plascencia publishes *The People of Paper*, purposefully inviting critique of the access he offers readers.

The People of Paper's reception balances Plascencia's critique of authorial privilege and selling out, however, by illuminating what representations literary industries—and Hollywood—reward. Plascencia's difficulty getting his novel published and the subsequent appropriation of his fiction clarifies Song's claims that the commercial fiction market has a "whetted appetite for stories that can operate as a form of ethnography" (90). The market may desire apolitical depictions of ethnicity, perhaps, but Plascencia's experience suggests that it does not yet reward discussions of race, and certainly not racial politics. While Liz and several other characters assume Saturn's or Sal's novels will reach reading audiences, Plascencia found it difficult to get *The People of Paper* published. He eventually placed the manuscript with McSweeney's, a press willing to reproduce his unusual typography and visuals, including holes in the page and large blocks of ink. Four years after the novel's publication, Shane Jones, a confessed fan of Plascencia's, published *Light Boxes* (2009) to much critical acclaim; the novel was optioned for film almost immediately by Spike Jonze. *Light Boxes* explicitly mimics *The People of Paper*, though Jones never acknowledges Plascencia's influence in a text that does acknowledge the influence of several other sources, including other contemporary authors.[22] *Light Boxes* earned Jones a deal with Penguin Publishing group and was popular enough to raise the profile of Jones's subsequent novels.

The two books share a stunning degree of overlap, both in form and narrative details. Like *The People of Paper*, *Light Boxes* makes use of innovative typography, columnar text organization, and extensive white space. Both novels also rely on shifting perspectives, with different columns representing the perspective of characters listed at each column head. More significantly, *Light Boxes* also contains two diegetic levels: a brokenhearted author and, metadiegetically, the story he tells about characters whom he submits to constant surveillance and the sadness of an unending February. As in *The People of Paper*, the characters declare war on their narrator in hopes of escaping sadness and regaining control over their lives. Jones borrows narrative details from Plascencia, as well: a character climbs through a hole in the sky to confront the author–character, characters hide under tortoise shells, the author-character's lover smells of smoke and honey (much as Cami smells of honey in *The People of Paper*, and is at one point singed, so also smells of smoke), kites are extracted from workshops where they were hidden so investigating priests could not find them, mattresses are stuffed with mint, and the adult protagonist loses his wife because of the author's heartbreak at losing his romantic partner. However, Jones's novel is based in a racially unmarked New England, where the characters are made to suffer an endless February by their heartbroken author rather than the systematic economic and political inequality Mexican and Mexican American characters suffer in Plascencia's El Monte, California.[23]

---

22. Jones devotes an entire page to a "List of Artists Who Created Fantasy Worlds to Try and Cure Bouts of Sadness," naming "1. Italo Calvino / 2. Gabriel García Márquez / 3. Jim Henson and Jorge Luis Borges—Labyrinths / 4. The creator of MySpace / 5. Richard Brautigan / 6. J. K. Rowling / 7. The inventor of the children's toy Lite-Brite / 8. Ann Sexton / 9. David Foster Wallace / 10. Gauguin and the Caribbean / 11. Charles Schulz / 12. Liam Rector" (83).

23. As Plascencia writes in the comment thread of a glowing review of *Light Boxes*, written by Jones's personal friend and in which Jones, his fiancée, and their friends participate in the comments, "'Light Boxes' reads like _The People of Paper_ disemboweled of its Mexicans and hung out to drip dry in a Sanrio Store. Sure, there's some distortions: Your February is taller than Saturn. Your farmers win the war, my farmers lose. The bee addict's hair in *PoP* is singed by the heat of her halo, while in 'LB' there's no justification why the girl smells like honey and smoke. Some things stay the same: you also put dead bees in mason jars, seek comfort in turtle shells, contemplate the same exact act of violence (knife to the throat, which then drips into the air) against the powerful entity that lives disheveled and heart-broken up in the sky. You declare war on sadness. Your sky shreds pieces of papers. On page 14, a rectangle of black even thought blocks much like Little Merced and Baby Nostradamus do. And this is just the shit off the top of my head" (Young).

Jones's novel affords a unique comparison opportunity to consider the implications of race in contemporary literary marketplaces outside of metafictional, diegetic discussions. *Light Boxes* and *The People of Paper* are similar in form and in narrative, yet it was Jones's novel—a story scrubbed of racial politics, ongoing social inequality, and immigration policy—that was immediately optioned by Hollywood and earned its author a Penguin deal. Despite *Light Boxes*'s explicit borrowing from *The People of Paper*, Jones's appropriation of Plascencia's work was widely defended as artistic license or coincidence and reviewers and online forums condemned Plascencia's defense of his intellectual property as impolite and immature.[24] Facing accusations of plagiarism, Jones explains he was "cleared of the accusations by my agency William Morris Endeavor, my publishers Penguin, here in the US, and Hamish Hamilton in the UK, and a slew of independent lawyers brought in by Penguin" (Jones "Now That" 2). Recounted in a *VICE* article condemning frivolous plagiarism charges, Jones clearly intends the list of legal counsel to reinforce his claims of innocence. The list also illuminates, however, the tremendous resources available to Jones in a system he admits favors his position.[25] Legally, he says, "Plagiarism in literature is difficult to prove. Unless passages are lifted word for word, no judge will side with the plaintiff," and that legal precedent says "ideas, images, tone, style, characters, and structure are all fair game" (2). Jones insinuates that as a result of the minor controversy, Spike Jonze dropped the option, a decision officially blamed on the script, "which wasn't developing on time" (4). Jones wrote his editorial on plagiarism on the occasion of Dave Eggers's *The Circle* facing similar charges of borrowing from an earlier, less-known fiction. Aligning himself with Eggers, whom he interprets as telling the accusing author "Go fuck yourself," Jones suggests that as in his own case, the matter can be reduced to jealousy, when a "bigger author with a bigger publisher . . . gets all the praise—or that the other guy's book is better and yours is just forgotten" (4). The arrogance of Jones's dismissal is matched only by the indignation of his online supporters,[26] many of whom accuse Plascencia

---

24. Some examples of the heated debate can be found in Blackburn, Young, and Vorgefuehl.

25. Jones continues his complaint, however: "That wasn't the end. There were more lawyers for the American edition (by my count, five different lawyers looked at the two books and it cost more than $10,000, which indirectly affected my advance for my next book—my agent expressed their disappointment to me over the phone, not only about the sales but the legal troubles). I wasn't allowed to correspond with my editor and work on edits for more than a month" (3).

26. The feud is heated: as one Jones supporter writes (and then reiterates later in the post), "I'm not saying I will beat Salvador Plascencia's ass if anything bad comes out of his assholery here, but I'm going to beat Salvador Plascencia's ass if anything bad comes out of his assholery here" (Young).

of indicting Jones in an attempt to ride his coattails into the mainstream, or of fabricating plagiarism charges for cheap attention.

Conspicuously absent from most responses to Plascencia's comparisons of the text is attention to the racial politics of Jones's revision of *The People of Paper*. Even as Jones protests, "The books are really different," neither he nor his supporters cite as evidence the most striking difference between the books: the ethnic differences between their characters and geographies (Vorgefuehl). The choice to ignore racial and colonial power structures at play, however, is a privilege contemporary Mexican American authors like Plascencia do not enjoy. Jones's novel, which Plascencia describes as *The People of Paper* "disemboweled of its Mexicans and hung out to drip dry in a Sanrio Store," offers its characters a happy ending unavailable in a historically and politically contextualized El Monte (Young). In *The People of Paper*, de la Fe and Little Merced walk off the page and surviving members of EMF grow old, nursing their losses and dreaming of someday conquering Saturn. *Light Boxes*, in contrast, resolves happily when the protagonist, Thaddeus, defeats the author-character, February, freeing the other characters from February's surveillance and manipulation (140). In addition to regaining volition and freedom from fickle surveillance, the characters in *Light Boxes* enjoy a fresh start in New Town, an ending February's partner, the Girl Who Smells of Honey and Smoke, surreptitiously writes into their story (129). The ending the Girl Who Smells of Honey and Smoke writes also allows the dead to return to life and the missing to reappear and reunite with their families (134). "Everyone smiled in New Town," characters report, because February is no more and "the sun came out big and glorious and the leaves on trees looked like they were on fire. Crop fields and flower beds bloomed" (134, 133). The last pages of the novel are adorned in flowers; flowering vines drape from the sky with blossoms "the size of [characters'] heads," and flower-covered babies cry "huge white flowers [that] unfold from their little mouths and float like balloons up into the sky" (145). Ending with a scene of rebirth in which flowers appear from nowhere and characters are granted privacy and volition, *Light Boxes* safely confines the surveillance, manipulation, and lack of freedom characters experienced in the narrative to a singular aberration caused by an individual author's heartbreak.

De la Fe, Little Merced, and EMF already live in a town of flowers, but the flowers in El Monte do not magically appear, though they may seem to for the annual tourists from Pasadena and Arcadia. Instead, they grow from EMF's labor in harsh working conditions in which "Crop dusters mist the petals with insecticide and plant food is tossed at the foot of the stalks, spread by the hands of flower pickers" (91). Even if Cami or Liz intervened in the story's ending to allow de la Fe to kill Saturn and free El Monte from omniscient surveillance and commodification, and even if she wrote a conclusion in which Merced returns to de la Fe and other deceased or missing characters returned home, El Monte would still not approximate Jones's New Town. In a historically and politically situated El Monte, Cami or Liz would also have to distribute "laminated cards with the stamp of a bald eagle" to many of the characters so they could work legally without fear of deportation, end the widespread practice of racially profiling Mexicans and Mexican Americans that became law in parts of the country soon after *The People of Paper*'s publication, and curtail government surveillance on the border and in agricultural centers throughout the West coast conducted in the name of national security (33). She would also have to address centuries of pervasive racism targeting people of color and recently heightened US nativism. As at-best-marginally legal, laboring Mexicans or Mexican Americans living in California and frequenting the US–Mexico border, de la Fe, Little Merced, and EMF have larger problems of surveillance, volition, and commodification than Saturn and their inclusion in a novel. Whitewashing *The People of Paper*—a move the novel anticipates with its depiction of Hollywood's historical and fictional whitening of Rita Hayworth—does more than change the location and the names; it shapes the characters' possibilities. To not see the racial politics at play in Jones's rewriting of Plascencia's story—this time stripped of race, racialized geography, and surveillance politics—is not to read vulnerably, but from a place of privileged epistemic blindness.

The irony that Plascencia's characters accuse him of selling out even as he struggled to publish *The People of Paper* and was unable to option it as a film like Jones's extraordinarily similar novel—selling out, that is, before ever selling anything—raises questions about what representations Hollywood audiences want to see, questions taken seriously by a range of writers, critics, and filmmakers. In crafting literary Hollywoods, or engaging nonfictional elements of the film industry in their fictional worlds, writers of color and indigenous writers craft critical, pedagogical stages on which they metafictionally examine the politics of visibility, especially in the highly mediated, highly lucrative form of Hollywood film. These literary Hollywoods are certainly not a new phenomenon—as scholars and activists have astutely documented[27]— but recent fictions help illuminate ways of thinking about filmic visibility and

---

27. For instance, see *Reel Asian: Asian Canada on Screen*, ed. Elaine Chang; *Latina/o Stars in US Eyes: The Making and Meanings of Film and TV Stardom*, Mary Beltran; *Hidden Chicano Cinema: Film Dramas in the Borderlands*, Gabriel Meléndez; *Latino Images in Film: Stereotypes, Subversion, and Resistance*, Charles Ramírez Berg; *Chicanos and Film: Representation and Resistance*, Chon Noriega; *Celluloid Indians: Native Americans and Film*, Neva Jacquelyn Kilpatrick; and *Reservation Reelism: Redfacing, Visual Sovereignty, and Representations of Native Americans in Film*, Michelle Raheja, among others.

representation in terms of narrative privacy. Among them, Nguyen's *The Sympathizer* theorizes the importance of audience and the conditions under which readers and viewers consume characters' stories.

SELLING TICKETS: LITERARY HOLLYWOODS IN *THE SYMPATHIZER*

Nestled in the middle of Nguyen's Pulitzer-Prize winning novel about a Vietnamese double agent who negotiates the appearance of loyalty to the South Vietnamese police forces, the Communist revolutionaries, and a cast of friends and associates is a scathing critique of Hollywood's depiction of Vietnamese people. In a relatively isolated episode, the story's unnamed narrator agrees to work as an on-set cultural expert for *The Hamlet*, an *Apocalypse Now*-esque war film about Vietnam. Through his interactions with the Auteur, a thinly veiled Frances Ford Coppola, the narrator reflects on the almost totalizing power of Hollywood in terms of popular and political representation. The Auteur, much like the author–figure in Plascencia's and Le's fiction, retains control over how characters appear to audiences and what shape their narratives take; so too does he profit from providing appetizing depictions of the individuals, communities, and nations in his film. In the case of the Vietnamese characters on set, the narrator learns, that means Vietnamese who are either wholly good or wholly evil and are, in either case, silenced and often subjected to spectacular violence.

The narrator first contributes to the Auteur's film project by critiquing the way the script spectacularizes Vietnamese individuals at the cost of their humanity. He reflects, "I was flummoxed by having read a screenplay whose greatest special effect was neither the blowing up of various things nor the evisceration of various bodies, but the achievement of narrating a movie about our country where not a single one of our countrymen had an intelligible word to say" (123–24). After learning that spectacle was precisely the Auteur's aim with the film, the narrator confesses, "Ever the industrious student, I had read the screenplay in a few hours and then reread and written notes for several more hours, all under the misguided idea my work mattered. I naively believed that I could divert the Hollywood organism from its goal, the simultaneous lobotomization and pickpocketing of the world's audiences" (129). The way the narrator describes the systemic silencing and objectification of Vietnamese individuals, their transformation from subjects to spectacle, also reminds readers that Nguyen frames the novel not just as a first-person narration, but as a confession by a Vietnamese man to his Vietnamese confessor.

The narrator does not just claim Vietnam and Vietnamese people for himself, but also on the part of his interlocutor, describing "our country," and "our countrymen." That is, while the Auteur's audience may be non-Vietnamese Americans—as his assistant producer remarks, "[what] it boils down to is who pays for the tickets and goes to the movies. Frankly, Vietnamese audiences aren't going to watch this movie, are they?"—Nguyen's is *specifically* Vietnamese (127–28).[28] The Hollywood spectacle of violence against racialized bodies, in other words, is for non-Vietnamese eyes; the book, however, formally assigns its audience as Vietnamese.

In an act of narrative privacy, Nguyen mitigates the actual diversity of his global audience by framing his narrator's story as a private—albeit compulsory—address to another Vietnamese individual. As in Nam's father's account of surviving My Lai, delivered to his son in "Love and Honor and Pity and Pride and Compassion and Sacrifice," or the other private texts throughout the fictions in these pages, the narrator directs audiences' attention to the limits of our inclusion. Nguyen explains the novel's framing as a response to the racial climate of the publishing industry:

> And the other reason why the confession became really important to the novel is that it's a confession written from one Vietnamese person to another Vietnamese person who was the interrogator. And what that meant was that what I could do in the novel was to construct an implied audience of Vietnamese people. So it was Vietnamese people talking to Vietnamese people, which is not how minority literature typically works in this country. Typically if you're a minority writer in this country you're expected to write towards the white audience. I mean, the literary industry is 89 percent white. They're the first line of defense in terms of getting published in this country and minority writers understand that. And I really did not want to write this novel with a first audience of white Americans. I wanted to write it with a first audience of other Vietnamese people. And I knew that this would fundamentally change the way that the novel was written and how it would situate the American readership. (Gross)

Nguyen's understanding of his place in the US literary marketplace literalizes the advice Nam receives from instructors and publishers in "Love and Honor." It also draws Song's conclusion that Asian American writers are writing in "a literary marketplace with a whetted appetite for stories that can operate

---

28. Notably, when the narrator does watch the film, he does so with his friend and compatriot, Bon, in Bangkok, "in a movie theater full of locals" (274).

as a form of ethnography" into context: whose appetite, exactly, desires such representations (90)? In writing his audience into his novel, Nguyen creates for himself a pedagogical stage for more precisely interrogating questions of audience and access.

A material effect of privileging a Vietnamese audience is that the novel, like many of the texts in chapter 1, critiques the industry's policing of cultural authenticity. Displacing the question from the literary onto the filmic, Nguyen interrogates not only the emphasis on "authenticity," but the hollow means by which those in power determine who and what merit authority on a given subject. To the Auteur—and by extension Hollywood—white people, as consumers and producers of the representation, get to decide who and what constitutes authority on Vietnamese history and representation. For the Auteur, the answer is, in part, material found in published books. In response to the narrator's critique of his depiction of Vietnam, the Auteur retorts, "I researched your country, my friend. I read Joseph Buttinger and Frances FitzGerald. Have you read Joseph Buttinger and Frances FitzGerald. He's the foremost historian on your little part of the world. And she won the Pulitzer Prize. She dissected your psychology. I think I know something about you people" (125–26). Disregarding his earlier confession that "You're the first Vietnamese I've ever met. Not too many of you in Hollywood. Hell, none of you in Hollywood," the Auteur privileges published source material over the narrator's lived experiences in a move consistent with the multiculturalist conflation of text and human Amy Tang critiques (125). That is not to say he disregards lived experiences altogether, however; he boasts, "I had a Green Beret who actually fought with the Montagnards vet the script. He found me. He had a screenplay. Everyone has a screenplay. Can't write but he's a real American hero. Two tours of duty, killed VC with his bare hands. A Silver Star and a Purple Heart with oak leaf clusters. You should have seen the Polaroids he showed me. Made my stomach turn" (125). A decorated US veteran's experiences, likely based on violence spectacular enough to make the Auteur's "stomach turn" and probably not unlike the massacre Nam's father declines to describe for audiences in "Love and Honor," confirms Hollywood's expectations of Vietnam and so are accepted as accurate. As the narrator learns on set, however, the Auteur's skepticism of Vietnamese cultural knowledge runs deep enough that he and his assistant, Violet, dismiss as unqualified Vietnamese actors for all roles except for extras. As the narrator laments, "What Violet was telling me was that we could not represent ourselves; we must be represented, in this case by other Asians" (152). Unqualified to speak about Vietnam, Vietnamese individuals are also apparently unqualified to represent themselves in *The Hamlet*.

In a narrative that takes the form of a double agent's confession, explorations of loyalty and betrayal are to be expected. One of the most memorable discussions of betrayal, however, occurs in the register of representation. After disagreeing with the narrator about his directorial decision to include a spectacular, violent rape of a Vietnamese woman in the film, the Auteur labels him a "sellout."

> This is war, and rape happens. I have an obligation to show that, although a sellout like you obviously would disagree.
> The unprovoked attack stunned me, "sellout" vibrating in my mind with the electrical colors of a Warhol painting. I am not a sellout, I finally managed to say. He snorted. Isn't a sellout what your people would call someone who helps a white man like me? Or is "loser" a better term? (157)

Perhaps in part because the preceding conversation—much like the narrator's understanding of his role as a consultant—centered on critically considering the real-world effects of representations, the narrator reacts viscerally to the Auteur's charge of selling out. Later, when giving instructions to four extras playing the part of interrogators, the Auteur tries to get them into character by reminding them that in his perception of Vietnam, at least, "There's nothing worse in your eyes than someone who sells out his country for some rice and a couple dollars" (159). The stage directions only reinforce for the narrator the Auteur's perception that he is disloyal, selling out his country and countrymen not for "fourteen dollars and the vanity of [his] name on the book cover," as does Sal, but for "some rice and a couple dollars." The narrator's stated intent in becoming involved with the film's production—besides leaving town for a time after carrying out an assassination—is to develop numerous and nuanced representations of Vietnamese and Vietnam within Hollywood's powerful economy of representation. To be charged with selling out, therefore, undermines his purpose much as Liz's charge leads Sal to abandon his literary project.

The narrator finally sees the finished film more than a year later when travelling with his friend and compatriot, Bon, in Bangkok. Watching the film with locals, the narrator observes the actors he helped manage, especially "the Viet Cong who looked, if not exactly like me, fairly close to me. They certainly looked exactly like my fellow spectators, who whooped and laughed as a variety of American-made weaponry vaporized, pulverized, lacerated, and splattered their not-so-distant neighbors" (275). Afterward, he pressures Bon for a response: "He finally looked at me, his gaze a mix of pity and disappointment. You were going to make sure we came off well, he said. But we weren't even human" (277). He continues, "All you did was give them an excuse, he said. Now white people can say, Look, we got yellow people in here. We don't hate them. We love them. He spat out the window. You tried to play their game, okay. But they run the game. You don't run anything. That means you can't change anything. Not from the inside. When you got nothing, you got to change things from the outside" (278). Bon echoes the narrator's initial reaction to having his screenplay revisions largely rejected by the Auteur, when he lamented, "I had failed and the Auteur would make *The Hamlet* as he intended, with my countrymen serving merely as raw material for an epic about white men saving good yellow people from bad yellow people. I pitied the French for their naiveté in believing they had to visit a country in order to exploit it. Hollywood was much more efficient, imagining the countries it wanted to exploit" (129). Bon's conclusions, like his own, reinforce the narrator's anxiety over his complicity in Hollywood's profitable, exploitative representation industry.

The narrator is not alone in his worry about selling out by participating in Hollywood's representation of Vietnam. The extras he is tasked to enlist are wary of the roles they will play, despite knowing their background roles will remain uncredited. Filming in the Philippines, the narrator finds refugees willing to play civilians, "(i.e. Possibly Innocent but Also Possibly Viet Cong and Therefore Possibly Going to Be Killed for Either Being Innocent or Being Viet Cong)," and soldiers in the Army of the Republic of Vietnam, i.e. "Possibly Friend but Also Possibly Enemy and Therefore Possibly Going to Be Killed for Being Either a Friend or an Enemy," but he finds populating roles for the National Liberation Front fighters "most troublesome": "Nobody wanted to be the Viet Cong (i.e. the freedom fighters), even though it meant only playing one. The freedom fighters among the refugees despised these other freedom fighters with an unsettling, if not unsurprising, vehemence" (156–57). The desperation of life in refugee camps, however, means that money solves the problem: those extras playing National Liberation Front guerillas earn twice the rate of other characters. The actors' reticence toward accepting undesirable roles even as they need to earn money to survive, however, reinforces the narrator's own anxieties about his role in the film's production and, extratextually, implicates Nguyen's role as an author.

In framing the narrator's role on set in terms of selling out, especially in a novel that is, among many other things, a palimpsest of betrayal, Nguyen invites critical introspection into the stakes of popular, commercial narratives that treat race as spectacle. That is, of all of the narrator's confessions, why does he linger on the accusation of selling out while working on *The Hamlet* in the same way he reflects on moments of violence, in which he killed or tortured individuals? That is, why equate betrayal and violence, especially as a spy? In interviews, Nguyen explains that his narrator understands that representations have real effects in the world:

> And he understands it very intellectually and viscerally that what is happening here is that Hollywood is the unofficial ministry of propaganda for the Pentagon, that its role is to basically prepare Americans to go fight wars by making them focus only on the American understanding of things and to understand others as alien and different and marginal, even to their own histories, right? And so his belief is that he can somehow try to subvert this ministry of propaganda, this vast war epic that is going to continue to kill Vietnamese people in a cinematic fashion, which is simply the prelude to actually killing Vietnamese people in real life. (Gross)

In other words, representations often become the groundwork for reality. As the narrator reflects, "Movies were America's way of softening up the rest of the world, Hollywood relentlessly assaulting the mental defenses of audiences . . . It mattered not what story these audiences watched. The point was that it was the American story they watched and loved, up until the day that they themselves might be bombed by the planes they had seen in American movies" (166). His fear is that in helping produce *The Hamlet,* he became part of the US imperial project. Indeed, as the Auteur addresses the film crew before the culminating explosion scene, he argues not only that representations precede reality, but that the two ultimately conflate. "When your grandchildren ask you what you did during the war, you can say, I made this movie," he explains, "Long after this war is forgotten, when its existence is a paragraph in a schoolbook students won't even bother to read, and everyone who survived it is dead . . . the work of art will still shine so brightly it will not just be about the war but it will be the war" (172). By the Auteur's logic, not only is Hollywood part of the US military-industrial complex, but the narrator is complicit, if not an active participant, in colonial warfare against Vietnam. The stakes of the Auteur's charge that he is a "sellout," therefore, increase dramatically.

The narrator's anxieties about being a "sellout" echo Liz's charge against Sal in *The People of Paper,* as well as Nam's understanding of the importance of "a true story" in "Love and Honor." Liz's complaint to Sal, "You have delivered all this into their hands, and for what?" explicitly frames Sal's betrayal as sharing in-group ("your hometown, EMF, and Federico de la Fe, but also me, your grandparents and generations beyond them, your patria, your friends, even Cami") knowledge and experiences with "them," publishers and audiences (Plascencia 138). Whereas Plascencia never metafictionally speculates on his audience's identity other than Liz's in-group/out-group binary, Nguyen explicitly identifies his narrator's interlocutor as Vietnamese. The story reading audiences consume, therefore, is a private confession between Vietnamese individuals, not—as with *The People of Paper* and the story Nam writes in "Love and Honor"—fiction written with the intention of selling it, nor is it a commercial spectacle like the Hollywood film in the novel. In framing *The Sympathizer* as a confession between two Vietnamese individuals ultimately on the same side of the novel's political and ideological divides, Nguyen not only cuts out, as he notes, the expected "white audience" and predominantly white publishing industry, but also characterizes the story as private (Gross). In doing so, he moves toward circumventing the commercial processes his narrative critiques in Hollywood representations. Even so, the narrator's suspicion of representation extends even to the economics of his confession,[29] as he admits, "I cannot help but wonder, writing this confession, whether I own my own representation or whether you, my confessor, do" (187). Both possibilities, at least, result in Vietnamese control over his story. As Saldívar asks of *The People of Paper*, "what is it that novels may do to alter the conditions of commodification and reification, especially within the historical conditions of postmodern late capitalism in a supposedly postrace era?" ("Historical Fantasy" 583). For Nguyen, at least, narratively framing his story as a private accounting between Vietnamese individuals and under Vietnamese ownership and control disrupts the normal processes of commodified representations of Vietnamese individuals and communities.

Ultimately, however, *The Sympathizer* circulates as commercial fiction and, despite its international popularity, the majority of readers are not Vietnamese or part of the Vietnamese diaspora. The narrator's concerns about ownership and representation, therefore, remain unresolved. He reflects, "Not to own the means of production can lead to premature death, but not to own the means of representation is also a kind of death. For if we are represented by others, might they not, one day, hose our deaths off memory's laminated floor?" (187). The narrator experiences this discursive death when he realizes that the Auteur had excluded him from *The Hamlet*'s credits. "Failing to do away with me in real life," the (notably, unnamed) narrator confesses, "he had succeeded in murdering me in fiction, obliterating me utterly in a way that I was becoming more and more acquainted with" (277). The tension between the novel's form as an expression of narrative privacy and its realization in the world as a successful commercial product recalls the same bind Plascencia, Le, and other writers throughout these pages experience. In an interview reflecting on *The Sympathizer*, Nguyen remarks, "There are no conventional happy endings here

---

29. The framing of *The Sympathizer* as a confession brings to mind Mohamedou Ould Slahi's *Guantanamo Diary* (2015). Though not a confession, *Guantanamo Diary* accounts for Slahi's time in US custody at Guantanamo Bay.

". . . Conventional happy endings are the property of Hollywood. And that's propaganda—propaganda for the American dream. I don't believe in that" (Streitfeld). Instead, readers are left to negotiate the politics of purchasing and reading a story not meant for audiences to read.

Like Nam, Nguyen's narrator finds extra-monetary meaning in his work. In addition to trying to subvert the Auteur's dismissive, reductive depiction of Vietnam, he uses the graveyard in the set's "Vietnamese hamlet" as a means of finally paying tribute to his mother, who died while he was away at college. Selecting the largest gravestone as hers, he attaches her image and birth and death dates to the memorial. Before the set's destruction in the culminating explosion scene, he returns to the graveyard for a final goodbye—cut short, as it turns out, by the Auteur's intentionally premature explosion that sends the narrator to the hospital and ultimately back to the US. Before he is blown up, however, the narrator reflected on the insufficiency of his memorial to his mother as he walked through the artificial graveyard: "Melancholy slipped her dry, papery hand into mine as she always did when I thought about my mother, whose life was so short, whose opportunities were so few, whose sacrifices were so great, and who was due to suffer one last indignity for the sake of entertainment" (174). Like de la Fe in *The People of Paper*, who especially disliked the thought of being "sold as entertainment," and Nam's father in "Love and Honor and Pity and Pride and Compassion and Sacrifice," who warned his son that "they will clap their hands and forget," Nguyen's narrator is specifically troubled by the thought of his mother's image becoming entertainment (Plascencia 53, Le 24). Written into these fictions—a medium understood, at least in part, as entertainment—questions of the relationship between memory, representation, and entertainment further contextualize authors' formal impulses toward privacy.

Chapter 4 takes up similar issues of literary representation and historical witness in Monique Truong's *The Book of Salt* (2003). Drawing on de la Fe's belief that "some things are better kept hidden," and Nam's father's question to his son, "Sometimes it's better to forget, no?," I read Truong's evasive protagonist as embodying anti-documentary desire as he negotiates the confining quality of narrative. *The Book of Salt* asks how readers and writers might respect gaps in literary and historical records—gaps such as Nam's father's burnt story or the lives de la Fe, Little Merced, and EMF shield from Saturn. Truong's protagonist shares Nguyen's narrator's suspicion of any representation outside of his control, so avoids becoming a character in anyone else's story—including Truong's.

CHAPTER 4

Textual Archives and Anti-Documentary Desire

Narratives in which characters and narrators actively pursue illegibility as a form of privacy provoke the animating question of this chapter: how can literature—itself a form of historiography, archive, and institutional verification—approach gaps in literary and historical records without reinscribing the centrality of literature and archival documentation as validating authorities? Conventional academic practices try to recover or imagine ways into such gaps in the record—or, following critics such as David Eng, to name such gaps as melancholic—but the fiction throughout *The Politics of Privacy* suggest literary and political value in leaving some gaps unfilled (Eng 59).[1] Salvador Plascencia and Nam Le, for example, each acknowledge the limits of their craft by having their respective characters explicitly reject inclusion in textual records. In *The People of Paper*, Federico de la Fe explains that "some things are better kept hidden" from writers and readers, a sentiment shared by Nam's father in "Love and Honor and Pity and Pride and Compassion and Sacrifice" before he burns the sole manuscript of his story about surviving the massacre at My Lai: "Sometimes it is better to forget, no?" (Plascencia 186; Le 24). In both texts, Plascencia and Le employ narrative privacy to negotiate

---

1. Eng offers insight into how he understands melancholia in *The Feeling of Kinship*: "Racial melancholia thus describes a psychic condition by which vexed identification and affiliations with lost objects, places, and ideals of Asianness, as well as whiteness, remain estranged and unresolved" (116).

the limits of representation for their characters and, by extension, for various modes and sources of knowledge strategically left out of written records. This chapter draws on these and other instances of narrative privacy from earlier chapters to contextualize Monique Truong's *The Book of Salt* (2003), which anchors the chapter, to provoke questions about the limits of literature.

Literary attention to the limits of literature and to the potential undesirability of textual inclusion seems self-defeating, a theoretical concession not unlike de la Fe and Little Merced's self-erasure from *The People of Paper*, from which they walk "south and off the page" (245). Narrative privacy in the face of ethnographic imperatives, state surveillance, and exploitative markets of exchange make much more sense than privacy from reading audiences of literature. Reading, after all, connects audiences with ideas, and literary and historical archives recover and preserve those ideas over time and across space. If the previous chapters illustrated the historical and ongoing problems of ethnographic, state, and market visibilities for people of color and indigenous people, chapter 4 contends with literature itself. Rather than a form of self-erasure, however, narrative privacy pushes readers to look critically at the politics of access in literary studies.

Truong uses the form of *The Book of Salt* to shield characters from readers. She crafts Bình, the protagonist and narrator of the novel, from a marginal account in modernist archives—the brief mention of Gertrude Stein and Alice Toklas's "Indochinese cooks" in *The Alice B. Toklas Cook Book* (1984)—then tells the story of Bình's almost complete absence from historical and literary records as a deliberate act of agency, rather than the inevitable outcome for a queer Vietnamese man laboring in Parisian kitchens in the early twentieth century. From the first page of the novel, when he describes his aversion to photographers, Bình privileges ephemerality; he understands food as both a nutritive and sensuous experience and considers his work as a cook to be a series of artistic acts that can only be appreciated for a short time, in direct contrast to Stein's art (tangentially including Toklas's *Cook Book*), which contributes to and helps establish the American modernist canon. Within the novel's logic, forgetting is as powerful a tool as remembering for surviving and thriving, and Bình is suspicious of all forms of permanence—photographs, ink, fame. Sharing the concerns of Plascencia's, Le's, and Stephen Graham Jones's characters, he considers at length the way the French Empire and the Catholic Church serve as surveillance technologies that enforce particular stories over others. Within this context, Bình's near-absence from historical and literary records—his illegibility—can be understood as an exercise of his agency and an expression of his anti-documentary desire, not just as an inevitable fate for multiply marginalized colonial subjects.

Truong, like the other authors in this book, insists on narrative privacy and declines to order the events and repercussions of imperialism into a knowable, containable, static narrative—if such an account was even possible—that would allow readers to come to terms with the consequences of historical and ongoing imperial projects and, therefore, begin to justify them or relegate them to the past. While conventional recovery scholarship identifies and fills gaps in historical and literary records—itself vital work—Truong raises the possibility of reading such gaps as spaces of privacy. She exposes the limits of literature, itself a form of institutionally authorized narrative, to tell particular stories without reinforcing the historical authority of literature and archival documentation, an authority that often enables imperialism and oppressive political practices. In doing so, she challenges assumptions that historical and literary inclusion—no matter how well-meaning—is desirable for marginalized and historically excluded subjectivities.

Characters' resistance to the textual visibility that animates the fiction under consideration in this chapter emerges in a fraught history of state-instituted documentation and highly compromised, canonical literary representations of people of color. Textual documentation of people of color and indigenous people in the US, in its many forms, has always been implicated in dramatically unequal power relations.[2] For instance, textual documentation has formed the basis of legal identity for people of color and indigenous people, a prerequisite for the recognition of individuals as human or as citizens in the US. It also has been and continues to be a method for valuing different classes of people. Individuals marginalized by legal systems because of their ethnicity, class, race, gender, ability, nationality, citizenship, or sexuality have historically developed tools for negotiating those systems either from compromised positions of inclusion or, at times, strategic exclusion. Government officials can manipulate, invalidate, or revoke official documentation; when documentation stands in for the individual, these manipulations impose external conditions—such as shifting political climates, geographical location, or the whim of a law enforcement officer—on individuals' humanity.

Early examples of the ways in which documentation has historically stood in for individuals in the US are Africans' and African Americans' "free papers" during slavery. These documents, which protected free black people from pervasive assumptions that they were slaves, were the difference between individuals being considered chattel or human. Recent films, including *Django Unchained* (2012) and especially *12 Years a Slave* (2013), which is based on an

---

2. Minh-ha explains the processes by which classification is death for people of color, especially women, in the US (48).

1853 memoir by Solomon Northrup, as well as canonical accounts by writers such as Frederick Douglass and Harriet Jacobs, underscore the tangible importance of free papers to individuals and the devastating effects of losing or not obtaining such documentation. As historically important and liberating as free papers were to individuals, their necessity remains insulting and dehumanizing, as they reduce peoples' recognized humanity to paper documents. Not recognizing paper's authority to name one a human would be both righteous activism and entirely untenable for individuals in deeply compromised deficits of power.

While US political and social systems have transformed dramatically since the era in which African Americans required paperwork to establish they were fully human, the systemic legal marginalization of groups of people persists even in a twenty-first-century context. For people of color—including citizens—along the US–Mexico border, particularly in Arizona, which in 2010 passed SB1070 or the "Support Our Law Enforcement and Safe Neighborhoods Act," paperwork remains a prerequisite for human rights. Ronald L. Mize and Alicia C. S. Swords explain that SB1070 requires law enforcement to check the papers of any person suspected of being in the state illegally if they "lawfully stop any person who is operating a motor vehicle if the officer has reasonable suspicion to believe the person is in violation of any civil traffic law" (183). They continue, "Some critics fear the act will lead to racial profiling; on closer read it is clear the act does mandate racial profiling and provides a how-to manual for police on how to profile those who look like immigrants" (183). Proponents of racial profiling defend the practice by appealing to what Leo Chavez calls the "Latino Threat Narrative" perpetuated through media spectacles that represent Mexicans and Central Americans in the US as "illegal immigrants" or "aliens" threatening American jobs and draining US social programs, "an invading force from south of the border that is bent on reconquering land that was formerly theirs (the US Southwest) and destroying the American way of life" (2). Humanity, citizenship, or residency is not enough; a class of people defined by phenotype, language, and economic class also requires paperwork for freedom and human rights. Furthermore, the requirement to carry papers compromises any sense of inclusion that possessing the proper documentation purports to afford. Especially in the last two decades, "documented" and "undocumented" have become a new vocabulary for classing groups of people; to not have documents is to be less than human in US public discourse.

Documented identity takes on a different—but no less vital and complicated—meaning for American Indians in the US. As Brian Klopotek explains, "American Indian identity is formed, expressed, and policed in many subtle ways in a variety of contexts, but the federal government's tribal recognition decisions provide a uniquely explicit, public, and potent arena for the dramas of identity to be enacted" (1). Klopotek describes the tribal recognition process that requires Native communities to submit documents attesting to their "history, race, culture, and genealogy" to the Office of Federal Acknowledgement (OFA) of the US Bureau of Indian Affairs (BIA) (1). This process, Klopotek explains, "mak[es] this tiny federal office the unelected arbiter of Indian identity in many ways" (1). The OFA, in other words, assesses whether the tribe's documentation—evidence which must accord with dominant US systems of knowledge and which must account for ruptures in Native history, language, residency, and knowledge created by the US government—justifies their existence as a recognized people.[3] "To lack status [recognition] as a tribe within the meaning of federal law," Klopotek explains, "means to live without the limited protections and benefits available for tribes under that law—tribes must be federally recognized to exercise legal jurisdiction over their own land, be exempt from state taxes, or operate high-stakes gaming facilities, for example" (3).[4] More than asking Native peoples to accomplish the impossible, the recognition process uses documentation as a tool of erasure. Joanne Barker explains:

> The United States escapes the consequences of its own historical sins by having real Indians situated in a far distant past before colonialism and imperialism mattered and embodying those cultures and identities today as though colonialism and imperialism have had no substantive or significant long-term consequences. Native peoples are confronted with the impossible task of representing *that* authenticity to secure their recognition and rights as sovereigns. (35)

---

3. Klopotek explains in more detail: "At its most basic level, federal recognition (also called, more formally, acknowledgement) establishes a political and legal relationship between a tribe and the United States that carries particular rights and responsibilities for both parties under federal law: it affirms the status of a tribe as an indigenous nation with inherent rights to self-government in its homeland, but it simultaneously validates the colonial authority of the United States over the nation. While the federal-tribal relationship has routinely been a means through which the United States has exerted control over tribes, the government-to-government relationship also affords tribes unique standing to protect their political, legal, and cultural rights" (2–3).

4. He continues, "But because federal recognition has been as much a means of domination and subjugation as a means of protection for tribal sovereignty, its appeal to tribes has ebbed and flowed with shifts in federal Indian policy and race relations in the United States more generally" (3).

To be federally recognized, in other words, Native communities have to conform to ideas of Nativeness that are inherently racist, that relegate Natives to the past, and that obscure the traumas of imperialism. Requiring documentation that contemporary Native communities closely resemble their pre-contact ancestors—documentation of which often comes from missionary and other imperial sources—the US government assigns value to Natives based, in part, on their production of documents complicit with the erasure of the nation's violent imperial history.

Not all Native tribes undergo the federal recognition process, however, because the General Allotment Act of 1887 recognized many Native nations in the process of divesting Natives of their land. In doing so, the Act generated census rolls of officially registered Natives, which "recorded their blood quantum paternally and maternally, marriage and dependency status, and age. This information was used by the BIA to evaluate the 'competency' of the individual to manage the demands of private property ownership and so earn the rights and privileges of citizenship that came with being issued full land title" (Barker 88).[5] The government also used the information to develop and issue Certificate of Degree of Indian Blood, or CDIB cards, still in use today (92). Barker explains, "Quickly, being enrolled and being able to document descent to someone on the rolls became the only mechanism within federal and tribal law by which individuals qualified for tribal membership status and rights (and were so counted by tribes when applying for federal funds that were dependent on population totals)" (91). The census rolls were fraught with errors, however, as a result, in part, of the bad faith and deep ignorance of the US government. "Many [Natives] refused to be registered (enrolled), give up their names or the names of their families, provide personal information, or accept the patent certificates they received in the mail following the closure of the rolls," Barker explains (91). She continues, "Further, federal officials were often grossly ignorant of tribal languages and social politics and so accepted information about individuals on the word of others, some of whom spoke from the context of intense family and interpersonal conflicts, providing false or incomplete information" (91).[6] As a result, the official documentation that

---

5. "'Competency' was determined by theories of social evolution and human genetics that fused race, biology, and culture. The theories went that the *less* Native blood/biology a person possessed, the more socially assimilated into U.S. society she or he was; the *more* Native blood/biology a person possessed, the less she or he was socially assimilated" (89).

6. Barker explains that many individuals "defied the political contexts informing the production of the rolls, the use of the rolls in tribal dispossession, and the fact that tribes did not have an administrative history of keeping and preserving written documents like certificates of birth, marriage, and death that were required after the rolls closed. This forced Native people born after the rolls were closed—for instance in Indian Territory in 1906—to go to federal, state,

continues to define legally many Natives' political identities, which in turn affords individuals specific legal rights and communities specific resources guaranteed by treaty, is deeply flawed. In part, this inaccuracy stems from historical actors'—Native and non-Native—understanding of and in some cases resistance to the power of state documentation. Some refused to participate in a system bound to marginalize and suppress their rights (or to attach their indigeneity to paperwork), while others entered into the system and manipulated the rolls to their advantage.

A particularly compelling example of historical agents manipulating the US government's oppressive practice of conflating people with their documents comes in the aftermath of the 1906 earthquake and fires in San Francisco, which destroyed the local public records. At the time, Asian immigration to the US was tightly restricted, and Asian women were almost entirely excluded from entering the country as a result of the Page Law of 1875.[7] As part of a history in which the US initially recruited Asian men as laborers, particularly along the West Coast and on the railroad lines, only then to exclude further immigration, bar Asian men from owning land, and relegate Asian laborers to specific, conventionally feminized professions, the disaster created a space for Asians and Asian Americans to challenge their state-imposed isolation.[8] Lisa Lowe explains, "According to U.S. law, the children of Americans were automatically citizens, even if they were born in a foreign country. After the 1906 San Francisco earthquake and fires destroyed municipal records, many young men purchased the birth certificates of American citizens of Chinese ancestry born in China and then claimed they were citizens so as to enter the United States" (125). Fae Myenne Ng narrates the social implications of the resulting surge in immigration, including relationships between "paper sons" and "paper fathers," or people who were related on paper despite often being otherwise linked only through an economic transaction, in her novels *Bone* (1993) and *Steer Toward Rock* (2008).[9] In the novels, she illustrates the

---

and local government offices and churches to secure documentation of their lineality. For those who could not do so—for whatever reason—they and their descendants were granted neither legal status nor rights in their tribes" (92).

7. "The Page Law of 1875 and a later ban on Chinese laborers' spouses had effectively halted the immigration of Chinese women, preventing the formation of families and generations among Chinese immigrants; in addition, female U.S. citizens who married an 'alien ineligible to citizenship' lost their own citizenship" (Lowe 11).

8. Lisa Lowe offers a more expansive historical context in *Immigrant Acts*.

9. Ng's project in *Bone*, in particular, resonates with my articulation of narrative privacy. The narrative progresses backward through time as characters try to solve the mystery of their sister's or daughter's suicide. Documents fail to provide any answer or comfort. Also, Ng details and explores the historical practice of many Chinese who saw the US not as home but as an economic opportunity, who wished for their children to "dig up" their bones after they'd died,

ways in which Asian American communities transformed documentation—so frequently a source of oppression and alienation—into a means of empowerment. For Ng's characters, paper relationships and paper identities came to have meanings of their own, but did not supplant other forms of self- and community-identification. Narrative privacy, then, has a long history in North America in its deliberate manipulation of textual identification.

Truong engages with issues of historical and contemporary privacy in texts through metafiction, specifically her strategic deployment of narrative privacy. Self-reflexively conceiving of the novel as a textual record, Truong withholds and obscures particular elements of her story, rupturing the historical unity of her narrative and prohibiting audiences from consuming her characters as spectacle. Truong self-consciously centers her narrative on a historical figure preserved in an archive that has marginalized and trivialized his life experiences by characterizing him through tropes and inserting him into a predetermined narrative. Truong engages with the archival figure by imagining Bình as a more human, more sophisticated historical subject. She carefully avoids overwriting the historical structure with her own narrative, however; *The Book of Salt* is Truong's formal experiment in writing an account that does not allow narrative or documents to stand in for or erase the individual. Rather, the novel represents a way of imagining and conceiving of the past without relying on or wishing for a complete historical—or literary—record. *The Book of Salt* does not offer readers the opportunity to feel reassured or self-congratulatory because Truong imaginatively resuscitates Stein and Toklas's Vietnamese cook from the confinement of archival records, nor does it offer, as critics suggest, a means of mourning historical subjects lost to incomplete and politically compromised historical records. Instead, Truong invites readers to question the validity and desirability of—and our own reliance on—textual and narrative records altogether, given their complicity with historical structures of power.

In the service of his larger project on queer liberalism, Eng develops the concept of "historical catachresis" to explain *The Book of Salt*'s relationships with history and archives. Unlike many reviewers and critics who understand Truong's novel as a historical revision or recovery, Eng reads *The Book of Salt* as disclaiming the possibility of a singular history altogether. For Eng, historical catachresis describes the ruptured relationship between reified versions of history and the "unknowable and unthinkable" possibilities of "what-could-have-been," and asks "who must be forgotten and what must be passed over,

---

then "send them—no, accompany them—back to the home village for a proper burial" (79). They wished, in other words, not to leave a trace of their physical presence in the US.

homogenized, and discarded, in order for history to appear in the present as a stable object of contemplation" (63). Historical catachresis, he explains, "works to dislodge a particular version of history as 'the way it really was' by denying the possibility of a singular historical context in which the past has transpired and reemerges in the present as a reified object of investigation" (63). He argues that by highlighting the impossibility of the story she tells, Truong "shifts our attention from the problem of the real to the politics of our lack of knowledge"; rather than filling or suturing gaps in the historical record, Truong denies the possibility that the record can ever be complete (65). Eng concludes that the novel "saturate[s] the what-can-be-known with the persistent, melancholic trace of the what-might-have-been, the what-could-have-been," and that the melancholic traces evoke "the possible, albeit unverifiable ... the forgotten, albeit persistent" (59, 65). In highlighting Truong's critical project of questioning the possibility of comprehensive historical recovery projects and the persistent scholarly blindness toward historically invisible actors, Eng productively shifts critical conversations around *The Book of Salt* away from evaluations of Truong's historical acumen.

Truong's critical project exceeds the scope of Eng's argument, however. I understand Truong's privileging of persistent, unverifiable possibilities not as melancholic but as undermining the processes of authorization that determine what and who is verified. *The Book of Salt* does not generate an alternative, subaltern archive, but questions the desirability of archival presence altogether. In other words, Truong suggests being unverifiable or illegible in literary and historical records is not a "melancholic loss" for subjects who may not have recognized literature or documentation as having the authority to verify their existence. Rather, she deploys narrative privacy as an expression of anti-documentary desire.

Anne Anlin Cheng articulates the critical concept of "anti-documentary desire" in her work on Theresa Hak Kyung Cha's experimental novel, *Dictee* (1982). *Dictee* outlines the stakes of historical and literary inclusion and offers one model for rethinking colonial archives by refusing a clear narrative that would render the events it covers—multiple imperialisms, an invasion of Korea, diaspora—legible.[10] Cheng, who reads *Dictee* as "a critique of the desire for documentation," explains, readers "are allowed neither the complacency of spectatorship nor the consolation that bearing witness effects change" (142, 150). Cheng argues that *Dictee* "indicts our very desire to know

---

10. Lowe also looks to *Dictee*, as well as Jessica Hagedorn's *Dogeaters* (1990) and Ng's *Bone* (1993) to theorize "antirepresentational" and "antinarrative" form in Asian American women's literature as "an alternative aesthetic to the realist mode, and in that alternative, the text opens space for a different historical subject engaged with that aesthetic" (119, 120).

and see the 'other' through reading—implicates, in fact, our positions as private, historical, or literary witnesses of submerged histories" (150). Illustrating anti-documentary desire, Cha declines to offer audiences a coherent narrative of violence, fragmentation, and cultural rupture that would allow readers to comprehend the effects of European and US imperialism in Asia. Ordering the events and repercussions of imperialism into a singular narrative would represent them as contained and knowable artifacts to be consumed as entertainment, or as (contained and knowable) penance. Worse, such ordering may allow for the possibility of imperialist nostalgia or politically conservative justifications of imperial projects (Rosaldo 69).[11]

Cheng defines and contextualizes anti-documentary desire within scholarly desires for representations and complete histories. She cautions her academic colleagues:

> We need to step back and look at the desire for history, especially in minority literature. The desire to know and to bear witness as some kind of "redemptive" act has fueled many of the recent academic moves to recognize and understand the various histories and forms of colonization—a desire, in other words, for the documentary. . . . This documentary impulse as a mode of knowledge also carries certain pedagogical assumptions that reinforce the academic tendency to conduct "corrective re-readings." (143)

The same processes of narration that may allow victims of uncontainable, unintelligible events to heal can also be a means for readers to satiate guilt, "bear witness," and feel as though they have comprehended the consequences of imperialism and racism on people of color. Furthermore, the desire for documentation is a product of the modern state and institutions implicated in the modern state; in other words, when scholars long to recover documentation, they do so for historical and political reasons intimately tied to the very institutions responsible for historical and literary erasure, including universities. Like Eng's historical catachresis, Cheng's theorization of anti-documentary desire critically undermines universal views of history and implicates academ-

---

11. For example, the Law of 23 February 2005, passed by a conservative majority in the French Parliament, required high school teachers to "recognise in particular the positive role of the French presence overseas, notably in North Africa" (Henley). Conceiving of imperial narratives and history as linear, lawmakers articulated technological and educational advancement in territories previously occupied by France as the result of French occupation. Refuting narratives—such as the one French conservatives constructed in 2005—helps prevent historiographical justifications of empire.

ics' desires for recovery.[12] Intentional illegibility—as opposed to the inarticulable as experienced in trauma or other challenges to the limit of language—is an act of defiance, and in the case of *The Book of Salt*, an act of narrative privacy.

Saidya Hartman and Y-Dang Troeung point to the political and psychic risks of critical approaches to literature that insist on textual representations when writers, characters, or contexts require otherwise. In her study on the spectacular nature of violence and power in representations of US slavery, Hartman opens *Scenes of Subjection* (1997) by metacritically describing her decision to omit Frederick Douglass's description of his aunt's beating. She does so "to call attention to the ease with which such scenes are usually reiterated. . . . Rather than inciting indignation, too often they immure us to pain by virtue of their familiarity . . . and especially because they reinforce the spectacular character of black suffering" (3). Naming repetition as potentially politically and emotionally destructive,[13] Hartman joins Cheng in asking scholars, writers, and audiences to reflect on the desire to witness:

> Are we witnesses who confirm the truth of what happened in the face of world-destroying capacities of pain . . . ? Or are we voyeurs fascinated with and repelled by exhibitions of terror and sufferance? What does the exposure of the violated body yield? . . . Or does the pain of the other merely provide us with the opportunity for self-reflection? At issue here is the precariousness of empathy and the uncertain line between witness and spectator. (3–4)

Evoking similar issues of visibility and looking Nam Le raises in "The Boat" and echoing Mary Louise Pratt's challenge to curiosity, Hartman cautions readers not to put uncritical pressure for visibility on communities already under other forms of surveillance. Similarly, Troeung argues "that the impetus to keep certain wounds open and alive in the public sphere—to keep our gazes focused on a difficult past in order to combat historical erasure—must be tempered by a consideration of the psychic and material costs of such acts" (91). Persistent efforts in investigating ways to fill historical and textual gaps, despite politically sympathetic intentions, may be forms of academic narcis-

---

12. Cheng is not refuting the importance of recovery work or new approaches to history but—like this project—asking for a fuller consideration of what visibility entails. These discussions are made possible by the tremendous work accomplished by scholars and authors who have insisted on visibility and voice for previously marginalized or erased histories.

13. Plascencia similarly critiques the destructive potential of repetition in Cameroon's complaint against Sal in *The People of Paper*. While treated more playfully, Cameroon's indictment of Sal's narrative of their sexual relationship focuses on the undesirability of documentation also at stake in *The Book of Salt* (226).

sism that blind critics, writers, and readers to other possibilities, such as what Trinh T. Minh-ha terms "opaqueness" (48). She writes, in the context of critiquing masculine, invasive anthropological study, "I may stubbornly turn around a foreign thing or turn it around to play with it, but I respect its realms of opaqueness. Seeking to perforate meaning by forcing my entry or breaking it open to dissipate what is thought to be its secrets seems to me as crippled an act as verifying the sex of an unborn child by ripping open the mother's womb" (48–49).[14] Truong's protagonist, Bình, for example, insists on his right to remain opaque, even to himself. He sums up his philosophy of self-aware forgetting by explaining to readers, "I choose to remember these things only. The rest I will discard" (36). For Bình, as for Le's protagonist in "The Boat," looking away and forgetting are important survival strategies often overwritten by zealous writers, scholars, and readers seeking understanding, equality, and—in the worst cases—spectacle, justification, or absolution. In directing attention to spaces of privacy and diegetic struggles with representation, *The Politics of Privacy* risks the invasive critical attention against which Hartman and Minh-ha warn. The private spaces in the texts throughout this volume, however, are pedagogical theorizations; as published fictions made available to readers, they are performative assertions of privacy modeled diegetically on fictional characters. Narrative privacy focuses critical attention on the ways in which writers imagine visibility and looking strategies in their fictional worlds to help readers understand the political stakes of visibility and privacy in the world outside of literary texts to better respect the lived experiences of human beings. Offering their narratives as practice arenas, these writers help audiences exercise deliberation and responsibility in our extradiegetic, or real-life, worlds.

Narrative privacy allows Truong to approach the critical commitments of her project and to address the central question of this chapter: how can literature approach gaps in textual records without reinscribing the privileged position of literary and archival documentation? That is, how can fiction account for the historical exclusion and marginalization of groups of people without retroactively inscribing a belief system that values inclusion in permanent records despite the potential political costs of that inclusion? Further, Truong's project provokes critical attention to who gets to decide what stories are recovered or imagined and highlights the potential costs of mediating narratives, even by well-meaning scholars. Through narrative privacy, Truong

---

14. Driftpile Cree author Billy Ray Belcourt similarly describes a "trauma of description": "Everywhere in the colonial archive there are a plethora of descriptions that sought and seek still to hold the position of the Indigenous in a state I can only describe now as against opacity, as against the right to be unseen and unseeable" (Belcourt).

models a formal approach to creating space for extratextual, private sources of knowledge, even as she confronts the exposure inherent in commercial narrative. *The Book of Salt* also engages questions of who owns and controls stories. Bình frequently uses language of ownership when talking about stories or life events and shares with Treuer's narrator in *The Translation of Dr. Apelles* a pervasive concern about how his audience will receive his story. As with Apelles, Bình's desire to retain control over his story is greater than his desire to share in a complex negotiation Truong explores through narrative privacy.

TO TELL, TO EMBELLISH, TO WITHHOLD

The Book of Salt opens with Bình's reflection on the departure of GertrudeStein and Miss Toklas—Truong's fictionalized Gertrude Stein and Alice B. Toklas[15]—from Paris in February 1934 for an extended speaking tour in the US, but most of the story takes place through Bình's recollection of his time in Paris and, before that, his youth in Vietnam and subsequent sea voyages. Born in Saigon as the fourth and last son in his family, Bình endures the abuse of his alcoholic father and enjoys the affections of his long-suffering mother, with whom he labors in the family kitchen. Bình secures a position as a *garde-manger* in the Governor-General's kitchen, where his oldest brother, Anh Minh, is the *sous-chef*. There, Bình learns to speak French and to cook French dishes before being fired from the staff once a jealous secretary discovers and reports Bình's affair with the new *chef de cuisine*, Jean Blériot. Disowned by his homophobic father, Bình takes to the sea as a galley cook aboard the *Niobe*,[16] where he meets Bão, a fellow Vietnamese man with whom he becomes close. Several years and many sea voyages later, Bình trades sea travel for Paris, where he works as a live-in cook for a series of employers and otherwise survives through barroom bets and casual prostitution. In the fall of 1929, Bình responds to an ad in the paper, posted by GertrudeStein and Miss Toklas for a live-in cook at 27 rue de Fleurus and subsequently takes the position, his memories of which provide the bulk of *The Book of Salt*'s narrative.

---

15. Truong's characters are named GertrudeStein and Miss Toklas, whom I distinguish from the historical figures Gertrude Stein and Alice B. Toklas.

16. Niobe, a figure in Greek mythology, is widely associated with mourning and the tears she wept after her fourteen children were executed as punishment for their mother's boastfulness (Plato 163). Bình's self-exile begins on a ship associated with sadness, a characterization Truong contrasts with GertrudeStein's and Alice Toklas's triumphant return journey to America.

Bình inhabits a fairly comfortable position in the Stein-Toklas household, where he cooks for GertrudeStein and Miss Toklas six days a week, observes their large following of artists and devotees, and lives an otherwise solitary life. He is a curiosity to GertrudeStein, who frequently engages him in conversation and, Truong playfully suggests, adopts her famed reticent literary voice from Bình's poor use of French and frequent failed attempts at communication.[17] Bình accompanies his employers on their annual summer escape to Bilignin, France, and is privy to the intimacies of their daily lives, including their slowly building fame and their growing desire for public recognition. Bình's access to his employers' secrets and his occasional disclosures of their private moments to readers underscores his power as narrator; he has his Mesdames under narrative surveillance even as he protects his own narrative privacy. GertrudeStein and Miss Toklas desire fame, however, and negotiate issues of privacy—like issues of queerness—from positions of privilege not available to Bình.

After several years in the Stein-Toklas household, Bình attracts the attention of Marcus Lattimore, a black man passing as white in Paris. Lattimore hires Bình to cook on Sundays, and initiates a weekly tryst through which they develop a relationship of dubious intimacy and because of which Bình dubs Lattimore "Sweet Sunday Man." Bình is fascinated by Lattimore, with whom he can only communicate through food, sex, and their mutually insufficient French, and realizes that Lattimore's interest in him stems primarily from his position of intimacy in the Stein-Toklas household. "The honey that he craves is the story that he knows only I can tell," Bình acknowledges (149). His suspicions are confirmed when Lattimore asks him to "borrow" a manuscript from GertrudeStein's collection so that he can study the work of a genius. Bình reflects, "You want to see GertrudeStein's handwriting, her crossed-over words, the discarded ones. She *is* the twentieth century, you tell me. What she keeps and what she does not will tell you about the future, you insist. My Madame is not a soothsayer, I think" (209). Nevertheless, Bình steals "a thin notebook that says to [him] it is small, insignificant, forgettable even," and opens the manuscript, which he later learns is titled *The Book of Salt,* to discover that GertrudeStein has written a story about him (214).[18]

---

17. Speaking about GertrudeStein's rough French, Bình observes: "I think it a companion to my own. I think we will exchange one-word condolences and communicate the rest with our eyes. I think *this* we have in common" (34). She is fascinated with his ability to use the language in minimal ways to express his point.

18. See, for example, Min Song's chapter, "The Trope of the Lost Manuscript," in *The Children of 1965: On Writing, and Not Writing, as an Asian American* (2013).

Bình understands his inclusion in GertrudeStein's literary repertoire not as honorific, as Lattimore might, but as alternately terrifying, restrictive, and invasive. He describes the discovery of his Anglicized name, "Bin," among other English words as a form of drowning:

> I find my American name written again and again on the following pages as well. With each sighting, I am overwhelmed by the feeling that I am witnessing myself drowning. There . . . I am, I think. Here . . . I am again. I am surrounded on all sides by strangers, strung along a continuously unraveling line that keeps them above the water's surface. It is a line that I cannot possibly hold onto. GertrudeStein knows it, and she has cast me in there anyway, I think. (214–15, ellipses in original)

In contrast to the string of aspiring youths who frequent GertrudeStein's salon in hopes of gaining her favor and for whom such literary inclusion would entail a form of desirable immortality, Bình moves quickly to anger. Imaginatively evoking GertrudeStein, he rebukes her narrative as theft: "I did not give you my permission, Madame, to treat me in this way. I am here to feed you, not to serve as your fodder. I demand more money for such services, Madame. You pay me only for my time. My story, Madame, is mine. I alone am qualified to tell it, to embellish, or to withhold" (215). Bình reiterates language of ownership when he imaginatively delivers the manuscript to Lattimore: "Here, Sweet Sunday Man, here. This notebook may belong to my Madame, but the story, it belongs to me. Look, it has my name all over it" (215). He uses the sensation of drowning to articulate his anti-documentary desire and is later appalled when he learns from Lattimore, who left town after Bình delivers the manuscript to him, that "Stein captured you, perfectly" in *The Book of Salt* (238). Textual inclusion, for Bình, is tantamount to drowning and captivity, both sensations that entail a loss of control and a loss of freedom.

Bình's reaction to the discovery of his story in GertrudeStein's canon illustrates two components of Truong's articulation of narrative privacy in *The Book of Salt*. Bình considers his inclusion in literature as undesirable in part because he understands GertrudeStein's textual narrative as inescapable and a form of destructive permanence, akin to drowning or captivity; throughout the novel he reiterates his preference for the freedoms of ephemerality, fleeting moments in the present unconcerned with archival or textual preservation. Second, Bình desires ownership and control over his story, including those versions constructed on stereotypes, literary conventions, and dominant historical practices. Facing the impossibility of controlling or owning a story once it circulates in the world, Bình opts instead to dissimulate, like Treuer's Apelles; he alternately tells, embellishes, or withholds the story he narrates.

Truong foils Bình's anti-documentary desire with GertrudeStein's and Miss Toklas's explicit pursuit of fame. Throughout the narrative, Bình reflects skeptically on his employers' delight in being photographed and interviewed for publication: "Every visit by a photographer would be inevitably followed by a letter enclosing a newspaper or magazine clipping with my Mesdames' names circled in a halo of red ink. The clippings, each carefully pressed with a heated iron, especially if a crease had thoughtlessly fallen on my Mesdames' faces, went immediately into an album with a green leather cover" (2). GertrudeStein and Miss Toklas fill the album with "family photographs of the most public kind," gleefully accumulating material evidence of their growing fame (2). For GertrudeStein, the attentions of journalists and photographers confirm and complement her role in curating American modernist art, the evidence of which Bình observes filling the bookshelves in 27 rue de Fleurus, her cabinets of personal writing, and the chairs in her weekly salons. He understands her documentary desire as intimately connected to her sense of professional, artistic, and historical becoming: "My Madame is staring into the camera so intently that I imagine it was she who willed the shutter to close and open back up again, fixing her in that moment when she declared, '*I am the one*'" (213). Through Bình's skepticism, Truong critiques the overwhelmingly dominant position documentation has in creating and reinforcing historical importance.

For Bình, in contrast, photographs have the capacity to violate subjects' privacy. Truong bookends the novel with Bình's ruminations on the two photographs he possesses of the day GertrudeStein and Miss Toklas left the Gare du Nord in France for the US on the SS *Champlain*. The first line of the book reads, "Of that day I have two photographs and, of course, my memories," and the final page of the novel describes the images in Bình's two photographs (1, 261). Bình observes at several points in the novel the degree to which photographers invade GertrudeStein's and Miss Toklas's privacy. "Photographers," he explains while acknowledging his own privileged access to his employers' lives, "are even more curious than servants. The only difference is that photographers practice their invasive art while my Madame and Madame are still in the room" (233). GertrudeStein and Miss Toklas are unconcerned with potential invasions of privacy, as they crave the recognition they associate with photographs: "Photographers, my Mesdames believed, transformed an occasion into an event. Their presence signaled that importance and fame had arrived, holding each other's hands" (1). Bình, however, is far more suspicious. "At the Gare du Nord that day," he recalls, "all I could think about were the flashes of the cameras, how they had never stopped frightening me. They were lights that feigned to illuminate but really intended to blind" (2–3). Bình points to his Mesdames' naïve fascination with photographers and the fame photographs offer as a model of the blindness cameras' flashes produce. In analyzing the two photographs of the Gare du Nord in the final pages of the novel, Bình illuminates the degree to which the images inadequately represent an experience by fixing in a specific moment something dynamic and complex. In doing so, they blind viewers—like readers and critics—to other possible narratives.

Truong's critique of photography resonates with Susan Sontag's thesis that despite their constructedness and ability to objectify or dehumanize their subject, and despite years of theorization to the contrary, photography has eclipsed other ways of remembering or knowing (89). She writes, "Photographs objectify: they turn an event or a person into something that can be possessed. And photographs are a species of alchemy, for all that they are prized as a transparent account of reality" (81). They are also a form of surveillance. John Tagg writes, "Like the state, the camera is never neutral. The representations it produces are highly coded, and the power it wields is never its own" (63–64). Specifically, photography has historically objectified and surveilled people like Bình who are marginalized and considered by photographers, viewers, and/or the state "only as someone to be seen, not someone (like us) who also sees" (Sontag 72).[19] Truong critiques GertrudeStein's and Miss Toklas's insistence on self-preservation through photography in part by contrasting their philosophy with Bình's privileging of embodied experiences and sensations over confining, highly selective historical accounts. In doing so, she illuminates the vastly different stakes of visibility for someone like Bình and someone in a more protected position, such as Stein and Toklas.

Only once does Bình reveal a desire to be photographed; in exchange for obtaining one of GertrudeStein's notebooks, he asks Lattimore for a photograph together. When Lattimore leaves town with the notebook—and after paying only the deposit for their photograph together—Bình is at first crushed. Noticing an image of the Man on the Bridge hanging in the photography shop, however, Bình instead prefers to forego the picture of Lattimore and himself and obtain one of his elusive scholar-prince. An aberration in an

---

19. Sontag makes this point with more specificity: "Generally, the grievously injured bodies shown in published photographs are from Asia or Africa. This journalistic custom inherits the centuries-old practice of exhibiting exotic—that is, colonized—human beings: . . . the exhibition in photographs of cruelties inflicted on those with darker complexions in exotic countries continues this offering, oblivious to the considerations that deter such displays of our own victims of violence; for the other, even when not an enemy, is regarded only as someone to be seen, not someone (like us) who also sees" (72).

otherwise ephemeral existence, Bình's desire for a photograph with Lattimore, while powerful, quickly fades.

Bình's desire for invisibility and privacy stems in part from his understanding that the French Empire and the Catholic Church constantly monitor him as a poor, queer Vietnamese man. He resents the moment in every job interview when prospective employers require him to account for his whereabouts over the course of his lifetime as a precondition of assessing his value as a cook and his reliability and safety as a presence in the household. Bình withholds from his accounting three years in which he was not in Vietnam, Paris, or on ships moving between imperial ports. He recalls interviewers' almost universal reaction:

> Three years unaccounted for! you could almost hear them thinking. Most Parisians can ignore and even forgive me for not having the refinement to be born amidst the ringing bells of their cathedrals, especially since I was born instead amidst the ringing bells of the replicas of their cathedrals, erected in a far-off colony to remind them of the majesty, the piety, of home. As long as Monsieur and Madame can account for my whereabouts in their city or in one of their colonies, then they can trust that the République and the Catholic Church have had their watchful eyes on me. But when I expose myself as a subject who may have strayed, who may have lived a life unchecked, ungoverned, undocumented, and unrepentant, I become, for them, suspect. (17)

Like Federico de la Fe in *The People of Paper*, Bình understands constant surveillance as limiting his opportunities; like Plascencia, Truong underscores the importance of imperial and state surveillance—and, importantly, documentation—in historically contextualizing contemporary discussions of visibility for people of color. For the Parisians who pay Bình's wages, the *République* and the Catholic Church constitute legitimizing institutions with the capacity to validate Bình's subjectivity.

Bình shares his preference for the ephemerality of lived, shared experiences not only with de la Fe, but also Nam's father in Le's short story "Love and Honor" and Doña Ramona in Rigoberto González's *Crossing Vines*. Nam's father, for instance, tells stories of his youth to his son in what is for him a traumatic, embodied, intimate experience. Le describes Nam's father contorting himself into shapes to illustrate torture methods for Nam, and as the pair drink scotch, they bond over a growing sense of intimacy fostered by sharing. Nam's father burns in a homeless man's fire the narrative Nam records in typewritten form, however, to keep the story from circulating among audiences who will read the story divorced from the context of the night of sharing and storytelling. For Nam's father, "Sometimes it's better to forget" than to record stories for unchecked, decontextualized consumption (Le 24). Doña Ramona, in *Crossing Vines,* similarly prefers her son to listen to her stories and engage with her embodied storytelling than to record and transcribe her words for inclusion in the academic record. The preservation of her stories holds no interest for Doña Ramona; she would much rather Leonardo have paid attention over the years for the sake of listening to her stories, rather than demanding she tape her musings so that they can outlive her and move beyond the contexts she provides. Like Nam's father and Doña Ramona, Bình privileges ephemeral, embodied knowledge and experiences over the permanence—and captivity—of the story he discovers GertrudeStein has written about him.

Lived experiences and ephemeral pleasures, long subordinated by European and American reliance on empirical evidence and documentation and Catholic doctrine focused on eternal salvation over earthly pleasures, are important sources of meaning for Bình. Lattimore considers Bình's relationship to GertrudeStein and Miss Toklas to be an economic relationship like any other unless Bình takes advantage of his proximity to a literary genius—by, for instance, procuring manuscripts. Bình rebukes Lattimore's assumptions by asserting the value he places on daily physical exchanges with his Mesdames:

> Sweet Sunday Man, please understand. My Madame and Madame sustain me. They pay my wage, house my body, and I feed them. That is the nature of our relationship. Simple, you may think. Replaceable, even. The morning meals, the afternoon repasts, the evening suppers, the day-to-day is what I share with them. You may think that that is just an unbroken string of meals, continuous but otherwise insignificant, but you would be wrong. Every day, my Mesdames and I dine, if not together, then back-to-back. (209)

In Bình's value system, sharing with his employers the food he labors to prepare offers intimacy and communion far more valuable than literary or critical inclusion. Unlike his discovery of his name in one of GertrudeStein's manuscripts, Bình's description of his place in the rhythms of daily life in the Stein-Toklas household is one of relative belonging forged through acts of communal meals and shared appreciation of Bình's labors. Bình actively resists inclusion in the modernist canon GertrudeStein curates and Lattimore reveres, and is uninterested in curating an alternative archive of his own; he finds value and satisfaction in the parts of life experienced very much in the present.

In direct contrast to GertrudeStein's and Miss Toklas's infatuation with fame, literary canonicity, and the permanence of their stature in the historical record, Bình seeks privacy and agency in remaining undocumented. The actions and materials he understands as giving meaning to his life are all ephemeral in nature. His labor in various kitchens, for instance, produces sensual meals that are consumed shortly thereafter; even if they were not, the dishes he prepares are perishable and hardly suitable as artifacts. His menus, moreover, shift with the changing Vietnamese and then Parisian seasons, as he cooks with fresh and available ingredients dependent on dynamic factors of weather, harvest, and seasonality. Unlike Miss Toklas, who dutifully records her recipes and insists on exact replication of her tastes, Bình cooks from memory and adapts menus according to his perceptions of his audience's tastes and moods. Rather than claiming a dish or method of preparation as his own by writing recipes as Miss Toklas does, Bình asserts his power in the kitchen and his participation in the human processes of creation and consumption by cutting his hands and lacing the meals he prepares with his own blood. "Blood," he declares, "makes me a man" (142). Blood, labor, and the resulting meals are all the ephemeral components of daily life that constitute Bình's sense of self, along with equally intangible, fleeting desires, fears, and tastes.

Bình cultivates ephemerality as a method of survival as well as a source of meaning. Each season, he trades his clothing at *le mont-de-piété*, or pawnshops, choosing utility over attachment to particular articles of clothing. He explains, "I have always thought it best to pawn my light-weight suits when the weather changed. It provided protection from hungry moths and a saving on mothballs. My own hunger also played a somewhat deciding role" (6). When he struggles with traumas of his past, he self-consciously jettisons portions of destructive memories and creates new memories for his psychic health. Shifting his attention to the beauty of narcissus bulbs blooming in the window, he notes to his readers, "I choose to remember these things only. The rest I will discard" (36). Even his memories are impermanent, not a personal archive but a strategy for survival, happiness, and health. Further, when his sense of alienation as a Vietnamese man in Paris becomes overwhelming, he finds solace in confirming his continuing presence by examining himself in "a small speckled mirror that shows me my face, my hands, and assures me that I am still here" (19). Bình relies on a fleeting, ephemeral record of himself—his image in a mirror—rather than official documentation or a lasting image such as a photograph for confirmation of his identity, a confirmation he treats as deeply private.

In his pursuit of privacy, Bình embraces various forms of invisibility. He learned the value of invisibility from his mother and older brothers, who escaped the worst of his father's wrath by staying out of his line of sight. From the beginning, invisibility serves Bình as a survival strategy. As a domestic, he can "move unnoticed" through the homes in which he works; unlike GertrudeStein's and Miss Toklas's adoring visitors who are denied access to the private rooms of 27 rue de Fleurus, Bình reminds readers "I can walk through them without being seen" (155, 26). While scholars generally identify Bình's invisibility as a racial and class injustice,[20] Bình also finds joy in being invisible in plain sight. He explains to readers, "Always discreet, almost invisible, I imagine that when the guests look my way they see, well, they see a floor lamp or a footstool. I have become just that" (149). From his place of invisibility within the Stein-Toklas household, he is free to move around, observe visitors, and avoid the prying inquiries GertrudeStein and Miss Toklas joyfully endure. Bình similarly enjoys the invisibility of anonymity in Parisian markets, where his Vietnamese phenotype shields him from individuation, marking him as an "Indochinese laborer, generalized and indiscriminate, easily spotted and readily identifiable all the same" (152). While not preferable to the way he could "take [his] body into a busy Saigon marketplace and lose it in the crush," where he "was just a man, anonymous, and at a passing glance, a student, a gardener, a poet, a chef, a prince, a porter, a doctor, a scholar . . . above all just a man," Bình takes comfort in the invisibility afforded him by Parisians' dismissive assumptions about Vietnamese (152).[21] Bình's race, class, and occupation—the very elements that preclude meaningful inclusion in the literary and historical archives GertrudeStein curates—offer him a measure of privacy in his daily life.

Even as his racialized body affords him the ability to remain invisible as an individual in Paris, Bình's body ultimately betrays him when Lattimore sees him in passing one day at the market. Bình imaginatively and ironically confronts his lover: "I believe that my relationship to this city has now changed. I have been witnessed. You have testified to my appearance and demeanor. I have been sighted. You possess a memory of my body in this city, ink on a piece of paper, and you, a magician and a seer, could do it again. How can I carry my body through the streets of this city in the same way again?" (110). Up until this point in the novel, Bình has imagined himself invisible in Paris, even if that invisibility is by virtue of Parisians' presuppositions about Vietnamese men in the city. Rather than incurring loneliness or despair, as might be expected, this invisibility is comforting to Bình, who believes it makes him

---

20. For example, see Coffman (153).

21. Bình's desire for the anonymity he enjoyed in his home country resonates powerfully with Franz Fanon's claim, in his essay on the white gaze, that "I wanted to be a man, and nothing but a man" (92).

freer to embody places and senses; his experiences are not corrupted by matters of record. He equates Lattimore's sighting of him, however, to "ink on a piece of paper," a descriptive recording—albeit in memory form—of his "appearance and demeanor" in the city. Bình enjoys and even desires Lattimore's attentions in the privacy of Lattimore's apartment and the relative intimacy of the Stein-Toklas salon; it is specifically a public sighting that upsets Bình, in part because he was unaware Lattimore saw him.[22]

Bình weighs Lattimore's sighting so heavily in part because he understands bodies, experiences, and physical senses as highly important forms of embodied knowledge. Although literate in Vietnamese and able to communicate with his limited knowledge of French, Bình frequently relies on a range of physical senses to accumulate information and discern meaning.[23] When his brother Anh Minh writes to him at 27 rue de Fleurus, for instance, he engages with the letter first as he would a culinary dish:[24]

> I sniffed the envelope before opening it. It smelled of a faraway city, pungent with anticipation for rain. If my Mesdames had not been in the room, I would have tasted it with my tongue. I was certain to find the familiar sting of salt, but what I needed to know was what kind: kitchen, sweat, tears, or the sea. I wanted this paper-shrouded thing to divulge itself to me, to tell me even before the words emerged why it had taken my brother almost five years to respond to my first and only letter home. (5)[25]

Bình understands that his brother's letter might divulge itself through taste or smell as well as narrative, a distrust in written language his brother shares, writing "it would have been better for [Bình] to hear it all in person" (8). Bình explains, "What he meant was that paper was not strong enough to bear the weight of what he had to say but that he would have to test its strength any-

---

22. Bình's first meeting with Lattimore, in fact, is marked by his sense of being seen: "After years of the imposed invisibility of servitude, I am acutely aware when I am being watched, a sensitivity born from absence, a grain of salt on the tongue of a man who has tasted only bitter" (37). Bình craves intimate visibility with his lover.

23. Truong pushes this emphasis on embodied knowledge further in her next novel, *Bitter in the Mouth* (2010), in which the protagonist, Linda Hammerick, experiences synesthesia; she can physically taste words.

24. Importantly, Bình rarely receives written correspondence: "They said that they had been startled to realize that they had never seen my full name in writing before. What probably startled them more was the realization that during my years in their employment I had never received a piece of correspondence until this one. I did not have to look at the envelope to know. It was from my oldest brother" (5).

25. Yet, they might have understood. Bình later explains of his Mesdames: "They never assume that words can tell them the whole story" (186).

way" (9). Anh Minh only writes to Bình as a last resort, understanding face-to-face communication as superior, if impossible given their distance.

Anh Minh's letter becomes one of Bình's few possessions, and its value exceeds its capacity as a written narrative. Unlike GertrudeStein's manuscripts, which remain neatly preserved among other texts in her cupboard, Anh Minh's letter physically changes because of its extended, intimate contact with Bình's body. Bình keeps the letter in his jacket pocket and reveals that "The oils on my fingertips, the heat of my body, had altered its physical composition. The pages had grown translucent from the repeated handling, repetitive rereading. The ink had faded to purple. It was becoming difficult to read. Though in truth, my memory had already made that act obsolete" (9). Bình's lived experiences erase the narrative fixed on the page, a narrative Bình would have rather discerned through taste and smell than reading in the first place. The permanence of the text, in other words, is inconsequential for the letter's meaning to Bình.

Bình's suspicion of documentation and recorded narrative does not diminish his reliance on stories as dynamic tools for survival and emotional health, however. Growing up by his mother's side in the kitchen in a city saturated with Catholicism, Bình experiences competing models of storytelling. From his mother, Bình learns to create or embellish the stories he needs to survive and to narrate paths of hope and survival into the story of his own life. For instance, she tells him stories about her former lover—and implicitly, Bình's biological father—a scholar-prince who treated her kindly and gently, unlike her abusive husband (174). Bình adopts the story as his own, using the promise of one day finding his scholar-prince as a source of hope despite, as critics suggest, the implausibility of his mother's story (Jones 121). From his father, "the Old Man" known around Saigon as a "holy man," a "proselytizer of the city's poor," and an ostensibly devout Catholic who converts locals by driving them to desperation through the gambling den he runs on the side, Bình learns storytelling can be absolute and confining, qualities he loosely associates with the Catholicism his father exploits.[26]

Truong draws into relief the novel's competing articulations of storytelling through the story of Father Augustine that Bình and his mother self-reflexively modify. Father Augustine was an emissary tasked with visiting Rome and escorting "a small fortune in gold chalices, a papal gift for the Bishop of Saigon" back to Vietnam (165). Bình and his mother dislike the official story, which ends with Father Augustine's death on a ship far from home—"a trag-

---

26. Norman W. Jones considers Truong's treatment of Catholicism in productive ways that complicate the straightforward assessment I offer here.

edy" to their minds—and his unwitting exchange with his ship's captain of the papal gold for a proper burial in France (165). Rather than preserving the story, meant to offer local Catholics a model of "fidelity and devotion to the Catholic Church," Bình and his mother "felt free to improvise" and to imagine other possibilities for the story's ending, including speculation about how the captain dealt with his newfound fortune (165). "My mother and I enjoyed this version because the last words did not belong to Father Augustine but to the man who took the gold chalices home with him," Bình explains (172). He adds, "We wondered how they must have looked displayed on the windowsill of the captain's house. We imagined that they must have caught the glint of the sun and poured its light all over the room. Beautiful, we thought" (172). Bình and his mother transform a tragic ending of Catholic piety into one of beauty as a means of negotiating their place in a deeply misogynist, homophobic household and city. In self-consciously relating her narrator's practice of embellishing stories, Truong metafictionally encourages readers to question her narrator's reliability.

As an adult, Bình briefly meets the scholar-prince he once dreamed of with his mother, who tells him yet another ending to Father Augustine's story. Bình meets the man, a fellow Vietnamese in Paris, on a bridge and throughout the novel refers to him as "the man on the bridge," though readers later learn his name is Nguyên Ái Quốc, a pseudonym used by Ho Chi Minh, the Vietnamese revolutionary, during his time in Paris in the 1930s (246).[27] The man on the bridge holds the same promise of hope, escape, and love for Bình as his mother's scholar-prince once held for her. Readers are no more assured of the veracity of Bình's encounter with the man on the bridge than we are of his mother's love affair with her own scholar-prince, but the account of Father Augustine he offers displaces questions of veracity with an illustration of the unreliability of even ostensibly static, permanent stories.[28] The man on the bridge describes to Bình what happened when Father Augustine's journal reached the Bishop of Saigon with news of the lost gold. The bishop, like earlier missionaries, "Understood the power of literacy. The written word never stops proselytizing, never dies of malaria, and has an uncanny tendency to reproduce" (173). Especially coming from a religious tradition reliant on textual history, the bishop understood that written accounts are upheld as authoritative and, as in the Old Man's worldview, absolute. "Enraged to learn that a simple

---

27. For examples of scholars who address the man on the bridge's pseudonym, see Norman Jones (118) and Eng (61–64).

28. "Here, the query, 'Did Ho Chi Minh *really* sleep with men?' is lost; the impossibility of the question and a response opens up a tear in historical time, a space of disappearance and forgetting in which time never quite coincides with itself" (Eng 64).

country priest had traded away his gold chalices for a burial in Avignon," the story goes, "The Bishop ripped out all traces of Father Augustine and kept the journal, with its remaining blank pages, for his own" (173). Even an ostensibly permanent form that continues to proselytize after the author and subject are long gone can be violently revised to reflect the needs of an individual. Father Augustine, a poor Vietnamese man, is forcibly removed from the official record by the blue-eyed bishop (173). Bình's and his mother's embellishments of stories for purposes of hope and survival, therefore, are no less valid than official records, kept by the same authorities tasked with surveilling and validating the existence of people like Bình for Parisian employers.

Despite the powerful ways in which Bình and his mother understand and embellish stories as a survival strategy, Truong makes clear that storytelling is not always a positive force for the less-privileged, as evidenced by Father Augustine's effacement. Bình is acutely aware of the "inevitable" stories that would be told or assumed about him as a poor, gay, Vietnamese man in Paris. Acknowledging the Orientalist tropes that confine Parisians' understandings of Asia and Asians, Bình tells the novel's audience of his encounters with the French, who unfailingly ask him to account for his past and his travels, implicitly calling for an account of his foreignness. In the aforementioned interviews with prospective employers, for instance, Bình explains, "To them, my body offers an exacting, predetermined life story. It cripples their imagination as it does mine. It tells them, they believe, all that they need to know about my past and, of lesser import, about the life that I now live within their present" (152).[29] As Isabelle Thuy Pelaud explains, "When he is seen, the color of his skin triggers exotic fantasies of Asia in the minds of the people he serves" (39). Despite believing they already know the story of Bình's life, written as it is in his Vietnamese features, employers demand his history. "I find myself again and again shamefully submitting," Bình admits:

> And so I stay on, eventually serving myself forth like a scrawny roast pig, only to be told, "Thank you, but no thank you." Thank you? Thank you? Madame, you should applaud! A standing ovation would not be inappropriate, I think each time. I have just given you a story filled with exotic locales, travel on the open seas, family secrets, un-Christian vices. *Thank you* will not suffice. My self-righteous rage burns until I am forced to concede that I, in fact, have told them nothing. This language that I dip into like a dry ink-

---

29. Bình understands that people read his body as a text; in other words, he is not the only character who recognizes embodied knowledge as a tool for negotiating and understanding the world. His employers, however, read his body in problematic ways by reading his Asian features as predetermining his life story.

well has failed me. It has made me take flight with weak wings and watched me plummet into silence. (17)"[30]

Armed with imperialist, Orientalist expectations, these employers interview and occasionally hire Bình because "They yearn for a taste of the pure, sea-salt sadness of the outcast whom they have brought into their homes" (19). The invisibility Bình's phenotype affords him in Paris comes at the cost of Parisian expectations and demands for his exotic stories of travel and trauma.

Truong empowers Bình narratively, as he avoids marginalization in histories such as Stein's and Toklas's by performing as a self-consciously unreliable narrator.[31] Truong's novel, told from Bình's perspective, threatens to itself capture Bình in literature in the same manner as Stein's diegetic *The Book of Salt*, albeit by his own volition. Truong metafictionally highlights ruptures in Bình's narration—examples of historical catachresis—by exposing him as telling a story, not an actual account of his life, as demanded of him by prospective employers. Truong makes clear that Bình freely embellishes his narration, revealing late in the novel that his father is still alive, despite his stories otherwise, and describing in detail scenes no one other than an omniscient narrator could have witnessed (229, 125). "I lie to myself like no one else can," Bình admits, "I always know what I need to hear. What else am I to do, revert to the truth and admit that I am a twenty-six-year-old man who still clings to the hope that someday his scholar-prince will come?" (80). Perhaps more pointedly, Bình declines to offer readers his given name, breaking the fourth wall to explain, "I never meant to deceive, but real names are never exchanged. Or did my story about the man on the bridge not make that code of conduct already clear?" (243). While he hints at several points that he changed his name from Bão ("storm") to Bình ("peace") for luck in his first water crossing, Bình makes clear that he playfully betrays his readers, the same way he does other characters in the novel (247, 242, 243).[32] Like Treuer's Apelles, Bình demonstrates that he is not aligned with his readers, but is rather alternately performing the story he knows readers expect and withholding his own story through narrative privacy.

---

30. "And so, like a courtesan, forced to perform the dance of the seven veils, I grudgingly reveal the names, one by one, of the cities that have carved their names into me, leaving behind the scar tissue that forms the bulk of who I am," Bình reflects, drawing on language of Orientalism (16).

31. Truong provokes the question: to whom and for what purpose do narrators owe reliability? What are the politics of these expectations, debts?

32. For example, see Jones (105), Eng (64), and Coffman (151).

In a move much like the ones Plascencia and Treuer make, Truong positions readers as akin to the prospective employers who demanded an account of Bình's life. He offers us the same "story filled with exotic locales, travel on open seas, family secrets, un-Christian vices"—the plot of *The Book of Salt*—while at the same time he has "told [us] nothing" (17). Bình highlights his interviewers' demands to know what happened in the three years unaccounted for in the life story he offers them, a secret he keeps for himself. Bình preserves what happens during his private time not only from his interlocutor but from readers as well; piecing together even his fabricated timelines still leaves three years missing. The novel's condemnations of the privileged and Orientalist desires Bình's Parisian audiences place on his stories, therefore, are transferable to the novel's readers.[33]

THE LIMITS OF LITERATURE IN CONTEMPORARY FICTION

Truong articulates narrative privacy through Bình's excessive concern for ownership and control over his own story and by explicating the consequences of his inclusion in histories like GertrudeStein's or Toklas's. Truong extends her critique of historical records by directly engaging Toklas's written archive. In the eponymous *The Alice B. Toklas Cook Book,* Toklas describes in passing several "Indo-Chinese" cooks who lived and worked in the Paris home she shared with Stein at 27 rue de Fleurus. As the bulk of scholarship on *The Book of Salt* centers on Truong's treatment of history, scholars have collectively traced the various moments in the novel inspired or explicitly lifted from *Cook Book,* including most famously Stein and Toklas's advertisement for a cook ("Two American ladies wish—").[34] Truong adapts Toklas's description of Trac—with Nguyen, one of their two primary "Indo-Chinese" cooks—in which "He would say, not a cherry, when he spoke of a strawberry. A lobster was a small crawfish, and a pineapple was a pear not a pear" into a scene in *The Book of Salt* that treats Bình's use of language with more nuance (Toklas 186). Truong writes:

---

33. Norman Jones makes a similar observation that he interprets more generously, noting "the narrative uncomfortably aligns the reader with Bình's employers by suggesting that the reader similarly misperceives him through a distorted colonizing lens, although Bình-as-narrator implicitly hopes for more from the reader in this regard by making the reader more aware of such distortions" (116).

34. For example, see Eng, Troeung, Jones, Coffman, and Truong, "Interview."

I wanted that afternoon to ask Miss Toklas whether the household budget would allow for the purchase of two pineapples for a dinner to which my Mesdames had invited two guests. I wanted to tell her that I would cut the first pineapple into paper-thin rounds and sauté them with shallots and slices of beef; that the sugar in the pineapple would caramelize during cooking, imparting a faint smokiness that is addictive; that the dish is a refined variation on my mother's favorite. I wanted to tell her that I would cut the second pineapple into bite-sized pieces, soak them in kirsch, make them into a drunken bed for spoonfuls of tangerine sorbet; that I would pipe unsweetened cream around the edges, a ring of ivory-colored rosettes. And because I am vain and want nothing more than the eruption of praises that I can provoke, I wanted to tell her that I would scatter on top the petals of candied violets, their sugar crystals sparkling.

"Madame, I want to buy a pear . . . not a pear."

Miss Toklas looked at me, recognition absent from her eyes.

I, yes, lost the French word for "pineapple" the moment I opened my mouth. (34–35)

Truong's deeply evocative (fictional) contextualization of Toklas's characterization of her cook as foreign and child-like, betrayed by language, powerfully questions the capacity of archives such as the ones Stein and Toklas curated to offer nuanced, textured insight into anything other than the subjectivities it privileges. Truong's project might be read as fictionally supplementing history or, as Eng argues, illuminating through historical catachresis "who and what must be forgotten" for history to take the form of a coherent narrative (63). The novel contextualizes and justifies Bình's preference for privacy—a vanity that resists reinforcement by dominant documentary methods—by demonstrating the other possible option for a queer Vietnamese man in Paris in the 1930s: a trace of Orientalist caricature in the historical records of the more privileged, like Toklas or Stein.

In part because of the stature of Eng's work on *The Book of Salt*, most scholars understand Truong's engagement with Toklas's archive in relation to history. They understand Truong's novel as expressing "a desire to create presence where absence has existed";[35] as "haunting" dominant historical

---

35. "Truong's account of the inspiration for her novel is informed by a desire to create presence where absence has existed; she sees the untold story of these Vietnamese servants as a gap in the 'official history' of the Lost Generation and creates a narrative to 'fill' it. In this sense, she demonstrates what Michel de Certeau, in *The Writing of History,* claims motivates historiographers: the need to fill or obliterate 'the lacunae' of history as well as the need for texts to have a 'structure of finality' that is 'organized by the need to finish'" (Fung 96).

narratives;[36] or a "postcolonial re-appropriation and subversion in the critical tradition of Ashcroft, Griffiths, and Tiffen's *The Empire Writes Back*." Fung raises the possibility that Truong challenges "the privileging of presence as the measure of historical notability," but concludes that "Even as the novel places this Vietnamese cook within the 'official history' of the Lost Generation, it constantly defines him by means of his absence and erasure" (96). Truong "embrac[es]" "absences in historical narratives," Fung argues, as she comes to terms with "the fact that no testimony, data, or any other sort of 'evidence' can be recovered to trace her protagonist's existence" (96). In other words, Fung argues Truong accepts the impossibility of accounting for historically marginalized subjectivities through conventional evidence, so, by default, questions positivist approaches to historical narratives that rely on textual records. More than accepting the impossibility of a complete, documented history—an argument Eng disclaims in his theorization of historical catachresis—I argue Truong *privileges* the intangible, unrecorded ephemera of Bình's life and narratively protects him from the exposure of historical inquiry. She does so by undermining the authority of conventional records and illuminating the stakes of representation—the limits of literature—not just for Bình, but for all socially marginalized individuals whose narratives are mediated by historically privileged authorities.

For example, Truong offers two accounts of Paul Robeson's visit to the salon at 27 rue de Fleurus in *The Book of Salt*, one from GertrudeStein and the other from Lattimore. After his visit, GertrudeStein recounts to Miss Toklas, in front of Bình, "I asked him why he insisted on singing Negro spirituals when he could be performing requiems and oratorios. Do you know what that curiosity in a suit said? In that basso profundo voice of his, he replied, 'The spirituals, theys a belong to me, Missa Stein'" (188). The couple shares a laugh over GertrudeStein's imitation, which Bình finds sobering, given GertrudeStein's position as a writer and likely an influential historical authority. Lattimore offers a different account, in which Robeson responded to the query by saying "'Miss Stein, with spirituals I can sing. The others I have to perform'" (189). In the difference between the two versions, Truong illustrates a version of the Bishop of Saigon ripping out Father Augustine's story; GertrudeStein records a depiction of Robeson which confirms existing, familiar, racist narratives, but which will likely be received with authority. In doing so, Truong confirms the basis of Bình's anxiety about entering GertrudeStein's record.

---

36. "Furthermore, just as the novel is haunted by the untold stories of Trac and Nguyen, the text is also haunted by its own future. Set in the 1930s but published in 2003, Truong's tale is inevitably inflected with our knowledge of what is yet to come in Vietnam" (Edwards 169).

GertrudeStein's oppressive power to mediate Robeson's story—much like the Bishop of Saigon's revision of the priest's journal—appears historically in Toklas's *Cook Book,* as well. Truong's engagement with Toklas's *Cook Book* as source material for the novel opens up another case study in the revisionary power of privileged narrative by attending to how Trac and Nguyen appear in Toklas's historical record. In a chapter titled "Servants in France," Toklas reports on the departure of one cook and the arrival of Trac: "It was then that we commenced our insecure, unstable, unreliable but thoroughly enjoyable experiences with the Indo-Chinese" (Toklas 186). She characterizes Trac as "childish," possessing "the gayest, most innocent and infectious laughter," but also deceitful with "amiable weaknesses" and an infantilizing accent, all stereotypes commonly associated with Asians, particularly in Orientalist constructions (187).[37] The few stories she tells reinforce her authority and knowledge in the kitchen, despite Trac's evident talent, further reinforcing the perception common to colonial ideologies that Europeans are intellectual while the indigenous or colonized are instinctual. When Trac leaves, Toklas reports that he warns her against hiring another Vietnamese cook: "In his pretty childish way he said we wouldn't like any other Indo-Chinese, none of them were nice like he was" (187). Toklas tried anyway, and found that "Each one in turn was either a gambler, which made him morose when he lost (and he always lost, for he did not work when he won), or he drank, which was unthinkable in our little home, or he loved women and would become dishonest, or he was a drug addict and he would not be able to work" (187). They eventually hired Nguyen, who they found to be "delightfully Chinese," before Trac rejoined them for another year (188). Throughout Toklas's account of her experiences with "Indo-Chinese" cooks, she consistently characterizes the men as childish and deceitful, given to vices, and desirably exotic. None of the rich characterization Truong offers in *The Book of Salt* appears in Toklas's record, which generalizes and dehumanizes the men who shared her home.

---

37. For examples of how these Orientalist constructions manifest themselves, see Colleen Lye, *America's Asia*. Toklas's story reads in full: "He made very few desserts and those were of the simplest. To his childish joy, I taught him several. But before this he served one evening a very dubious elaborately frosted and decorated cake. There was something familiar about the cake. Did you make the cake, Trac, I asked him. As he answered that he had, I remembered that I had seen it for years, or one like it, in the window of a very second-rate confectioner's. Are you sure, I ruthlessly continued. Trac nodded his head and broke out into the gayest, most innocent and infectious laughter. At once the three of us were laughing together. Nothing more was said that evening, but the next morning I said quite seriously, You must never make that cake again, we didn't care for it. All Trac said, but with a wide smile, was, Me know, me know" (Toklas 187).

Despite Miss Toklas's attempts to extract recipes from Bình—and, in *Cook Book*, from Trac—Bình's talents in the kitchen remain unreplicated in textual form. Recalling a pattern among past employers, many of whom insisted on learning his secret to making a delicious omelet, Bình relates an interior dialogue with his mistresses: "Do I look like a fool? I ask myself each time. Please, Madame, do not equate my lack of speech with a lack of thought. If there is a secret, Madame, I would take it with me to my unmarked grave" (153–54). Instead of telling them the real key to his success—"Repetition and routine. Servitude and subservience. Beck and call"—Bình explains to his employers that he adds nutmeg, an ingredient he confides to readers would destroy the flavor of eggs (154). If years of practice, as Bình tells readers, is the truth behind his omelet-making skills, no secret ingredient or technique can be captured in a cookbook like Toklas's. In *Cook Book*, Toklas admits, "Of course, there was no way of knowing how Trac prepared any of his delicious food. He was not secretive, but he was master in his kitchen. Much later, when he had left us and returned to us twice and then married, his wife told me the ingredients he used in some of the dishes he had cooked for us, but even she never knew the measurements. Trac said he didn't measure" (187). Trac's wife may or may not have known the secret to her husband's success in the kitchen, much as Bình's disclosure that years of practice may or may not be the key to his perfect omelets, a specific skill he uses to procure employment over other job candidates and a secret he is entitled to keep. Bình's evocation of an unmarked grave points to the two-fold nature of secrecy and ephemerality for a multiply marginalized subject. An unmarked grave is, Truong acknowledges, a likely resting place for an impoverished Vietnamese exile. She also suggests, however, that an unmarked grave is not a tragedy for Bình, but a hiding place where his secrets are safe from the curious covetousness of those, like his employers—and perhaps readers—who seek to extract those parts of him they consider valuable while discarding the rest.

Bình's archival origins inform his aversion to becoming a character in GertrudeStein's story. Since inclusion involves the interpretation to which Robeson, Trac, and Nguyen are subject, Bình insists on control over his story in order to maintain his privacy. Ironically, Truong's treatment of Bình's defiance in the face of reductive representation resonates in the novel's reception amongst publishers. Pelaud writes:

> Publishers at times make decisions based on their perceptions about the racist assumptions of the public. Although *The Book of Salt* garnered wide success, it initially encountered resistance from publishers. The first publisher that acquired the manuscript asked Truong to simplify the language because

they said a Vietnamese cook could not possibly have such sophisticated thoughts and the language was too poetic for an uneducated Asian character. "I cannot imagine a white writer being told that," laments Monique Truong. (125–26)

While publishers may have misjudged the novel's appeal, their perceptions of readers' racist assumptions were spot on, according to contemporary reviews of the novel that praised Truong's exoticism, instability, and unreliability. "Once published, this novel was loved for reasons the text itself seems to counter," Pelaud observes (126). Analyzing Christopher Benfey's review of the novel in the *New York Times,* Pelaud argues "Like reviews of Maxine Hong Kingston's *The Woman Warrior* thirty years before, Benfey measures the book to a certain degree against the stereotype of the exotic, and by extension inscrutable, and mysterious Oriental. His use of the adjectives 'insecure,' 'unstable,' and 'unreliable' is reminiscent of Orientalist attitudes aimed at defining Europeans as 'rational, peaceful, liberal, logical, and capable of holding real values without natural suspicion'" (Pelaud 126, quoting Said, *Orientalism,* 49).[38] As Pelaud notes, Benfey's review is not alone in its implicit reduction of Truong's novel, further substantiating Bình's anxieties—and those of the characters' in each of the texts in this study—over what happens to stories once they circulate in the world.

Bình, like Apelles, Nam's father in "Love and Honor," and de la Fe in *The People of Paper,* desires complete privacy from audiences who, like his various Parisian employers, will consume him as entertainment. He understands complete absence from literary circulation as preferable to how readers will treat his decontextualized story. For example, as he reels from GertrudeStein's theft of his story, Bình reflects, "A gift or a theft depends on who is holding the pen" (215). As if to confirm Bình's anxieties, scholars and reviewers have almost uniformly read the line as Bình giving his stories to readers, as a narrator. To do so, they must not only ignore the context of the comment—Bình's outrage and sadness over exposure and captivity by GertrudeStein and the canonicity she represents—but also, in the ethnographic tradition outlined in chapter 1, assume access to his story. Bình does tell readers a story, but he embellishes and withholds his story, as well. Truong critically highlights Bình's acts of

---

38. Ironically, Truong meant to distance readers from her characters through her poetic prose. Pelaud reports, drawing on a lecture Truong delivered to Karen Yamashita's class at UC-Santa Cruz in 2009: "The sophisticated prose of *The Book of Salt* invites readers to reflect upon their own privilege and the exclusionary practices engendered by labels of race, sexuality, or history. In Monique Truong's words, she 'alienates readers without them knowing it'" (Pelaud 39). Fitting Bình in familiar, exotic tropes, however, counteracts this alienation.

embellishment and withholding to illuminate the representational limits of literature for ethnic American writers.

Bình's insistence on his right to embellish or withhold his story also underscores his vulnerability as a queer, racialized laborer in the 1930s. He resents his forcible inclusion in even an identifiably queer archive in part because the stakes of visibility for his queerness are different from those for his white, American, lesbian employers who are partly protected by fame, gender, and class. While other characters read Bình as queer in the novel, Bình resists GertrudeStein's impulse to formalize his story and his queerness in narrative. Truong evokes a different context of visibility for Bình, in addition to his diasporic, class, and racial positioning: queerness and its varying historical relationships to privacy, performance, and compulsory visibility ("outing"). Bình's insistence on controlling his story resonates with the personal and political importance of queer individuals' control over how they share their sexual identification(s). To privileged liberal subjectivities—GertrudeStein, but also to many readers and critics in the twenty-first century—the visibility may be desirable, but to multiply marginalized subjects like Bình, inclusion in a queer archive may be yet another burden to bear. In refusing readers a coherent narrative or full insight into Bình's character, however, Truong focuses critical attention on why audiences desire access to historical and literary spaces of privacy, and to whose benefit.

Truong's formal play in *The Book of Salt* is her experiment in writing about forgetting. Just as Le allows Nam's father to narratively forget in "Love and Honor," Truong allows Bình to slip out of the fiction he tells, uncaptured by her narrative; he remains historically illegible. She works to adapt her form to the novel's content, privileging forgetting, invisibility, and ephemerality and leaving her readers unsure of whom or what to trust. Through Bình, *The Book of Salt* proposes a literary form that offers privacy rather than exposure, and ephemerality rather than the preservation GertrudeStein—and, generally, literary studies—seeks. In addition to the myriad alternative archives scholars theorize as means of accessing and recognizing historically marginalized subjects and histories, Truong proposes readers and literary scholars find critical space for reading practices that afford subjects privacy from the demands of representation.

Truong makes clear the stakes and potential appropriations of representation and narrates potential political reasons subjects may have for evading literary or historical documentation. Complementing and tempering efforts to rediscover stories and individuals and to close gaps in historical and archival records, her critique of literary practices that reinscribe the authority of written and photographic documentation reminds readers that while literature can be used to entertain, to remember, and to include, it is also deployed to assuage guilt, to trivialize behavior, to evade responsibility, to contain and limit individuals and experiences, and for various other purposes that fall short of the idealized democratization of fiction and the archive. Along with the other writers in these chapters, Truong expresses an abiding faith in literature even as *The Book of Salt* asks readers to question the foundations of literary study by examining the politics of readers' access to literature.

The Book of Salt's publication, for instance, diegetically—and extradiegetically, given publishers' resistance to Bình's vocabulary—illustrates how literature reinforces the status quo. Truong's use of narrative privacy draws attention to the ways in which the novel is itself a privileged form of documentation and means of preservation. Along with the other fictions in these chapters, *The Book of Salt* provokes reflection on the potentially oppressive nature of literature from within, and raises critical questions: how might writers write and readers read novels without "capturing" subjectivities in texts? Without privileging and reinscribing the authority of textual records? Hartman argues that narrative replication of trauma, while empowering and bearing witness to marginalized or erased experiences, also offers readers low-risk voyeurism into historical trauma. Hartman shares this concern with Cheng, who worries readers can too easily find closure in narrative, or absolution in their personal acts of witnessing. Much as Treuer in *The Translation of Dr. Apelles* critiques white Americans' use of romantic narratives about Natives as a salve for something broken inside of themselves, Truong indicts readers in her depiction of Bình's prospective employers, who seek in Bình's story a consumable form of pain and exile that does not require any political commitments, not a reminder of an ongoing, persistent crisis in which they are complicit. Rather than allowing readers an opportunity to move beyond their own complicities in ongoing issues of racism, sexism, and homophobia, Truong narratively evades closure.

Truong is certainly not alone in her endeavor to illuminate the perils of narrative. Cheyenne and Arapaho writer Tommy Orange, for example, similarly declines resolution in *There, There* (2018), his debut novel, which takes its title from Gertrude Stein's famously decontextualized characterization of Oakland. In ironic resonance with GertrudeStein's own depiction of Paul Robeson in Truong's novel, Orange places the decontextualization of language and stories in the same violent genealogy as genocidal US policies (39). Further, Dene, one of the novel's protagonists, crafts an episodic, multivoiced documentary of indigenous life in Oakland, a film that shares its form with the novel, which explores the same topic through close personal vignettes. Speaking of the film, a character observes of Dene: "sometimes we risk putting too much of the director's vision on stories. I like that he's going to allow the content to direct the vision" (42). Parallels between the film's and the novel's structure extend the critique of editorial overreach to Orange, as well, inviting questions about novelists' power to control and revise the stories their characters tell, embellish, or withhold.

Similarly, Percival Everett's *Erasure* (2001) critiques black authors who sate publishers' and readers' thirst for particular narratives of impoverished, imperiled blackness. Frustrated with the tepid reception of the literary fiction he writes, the novel's protagonist proves a point by pseudonymously publishing a novel, titled *My Pafology*, that satirizes popular depictions of blackness and is met with critical acclaim. Everett reproduces *My Pafology*, later retitled *Fuck*, in full within the pages of *Erasure*, offering a diegetic study of readers' and authors' responsibilities in creating and consuming written narratives. Kiese Laymon, Valeria Luiselli, and other writers similarly explore the perils of narrative for the characters within their pages.

The introspective nature of metafiction gives authors a diegetic stage for self-critical examination of their roles in literature; the texts throughout these chapters leave it to reading audiences, however, to contend with characters' widespread anxieties about their readership. Apelles, Bình, de la Fe, EMF, and certain Fool's Hip patrons, for example, anticipate extractive, exploitative readers who will twist stories to suit their own purposes. Other characters, like Little Merced and Nam's father, resent the pity and dismissal they expect from those looking down on the page. While playful—the characters are, of course, entirely fictional—the lengths to which characters go to protect themselves from how they expect they'll be read should give readers, especially literary critics, pause. Narrative privacy requires literary critics to understand literature as something other than the passive subject of privileged study; reading vulnerably, as the characters suggest, entails recognizing the critiques literature offers its readers or moments when certain readers are unwelcome. Doing so means recognizing the complicated, layered politics of visibility and privacy on the page, through history, and in the world around us.

CONCLUSION

In a dedication that also serves as an epigraph to his novel, Salvador Plascencia writes, "And to Liz, who taught me that we are all of paper." In writing themselves and their reading audiences into the fiction they craft, the other writers in this volume appear not only to concur, but to insist that real-world problems might be worked out, in some measure, on the page. The attention these writers clearly pay to their roles in this—their self-deprecation, their careful critique of their positionality, their indictment of uncritical audiences—indicates a generation of writers that is not only engaged in the vital, urgent task of reimagining ethnic and indigenous privacy and visibility in the US, but that has created in narrative privacy a new form to meet the challenges of a new century.

Their attention to their works' literariness—their metafictionality—also allows authors an opportunity to address audiences' roles in the stakes of narrative privacy. In the context of twenty-first-century discussions of privacy and surveillance, metafictionally positioning readers as subjecting characters to unwanted—perhaps unwarranted—surveillance calls into question the innocence of curiosity and the privilege of access to others' stories and lives. For example, texts such as *The Translation of Dr. Apelles* and *The People of Paper*, among others throughout this volume, suggest a genealogical link between curious readers' access to characters' lives and the institutions and policies, such as ethnography and government surveillance, so thoroughly questioned in twenty-first-century literature for violating the human right to privacy. The connection is certainly playful—characters are, after all, not human, and as Apelles assures us, "books are meant to be read"—but it also carries a serious critique of historical and ongoing practices of invasive surveillance of people of color and indigenous people in the US.

Importantly, the primary texts of *The Politics of Privacy* are not singular in their endeavor, but are instead indicative of a much broader formal pattern across contemporary fiction by writers of color and indigenous writers.[1] The rich range of narrative privacy in contemporary fiction opens possibilities for working through some of the most pressing issues of the present moment on the page by contextualizing questions of privacy and visibility historically and socially, and by provoking deeper introspection on the part of authors, publishers, and readers.

However, I open the conclusion with Plascencia's dedication to Liz—"And to Liz, who taught me that we are all of paper"—precisely because it precludes resolution. While those of us who write, read, teach, and study literature may take Liz's lesson as an homage to the power of language, the fiction in these chapters supply ample evidence to the contrary. Being of paper, for example, makes one more vulnerable not only to the whims of omniscient narrators and invasive authors—as well as the social processes they represent—but also more generally, as the physical material of paper is fragile and thus worrying as a metaphor. Merced de Papel, the literal person of paper in *The People of Paper*, for example, disappears without a trace once she is turned to pulp by rain and fire retardant:

---

1. Other contemporary writers navigate twenty-first-century pressures of visibility and storytelling through narrative privacy. For example, in *I'm Not Saying, I'm Just Saying* (2013), Matthew Salesses's narrator pauses three-quarters of the way through the novel to reflect, "I knew this was the point in the novel where the protagonist is revealed to the reader by an object. Where, if you pay close attention, you know the protagonist has changed before he does" (111). Checking on readers' progress and breaking the fourth wall by being self-aware as a character, Salesses's narrator reminds readers of the structures of power and access to information inherent in a work of literature. Mario Alberto Zambrano structures *Lotería* (2013) around the titular card game, requiring of readers a particular form of cultural knowledge. He shares this formal move with Nina Marie Martinez, who similarly organizes ¡*Caramba!: A Tale Told in Turns of the Card* (2004) by chapters responding to *lotería* cards interspersed throughout the text. Just as Zambrano shares the "Rules of the Game" as the first chapter of his novel, Martinez shares, in her novel's front matter, a description of the card game: "La Lotería: A game of chance, not unlike bingo, only the cards come with images as well as numbers and dichos to make the wise wiser." Both authors provide tools for readers to learn—if they choose—the skills required to understand the cultural context of their narratives. Valeria Luiselli, Lily Hoang, Mauro Javier Cardenas, Alejandro Zambra, Tan Lin, Manuel Muñoz, Toni Jensen, Percival Everett, and other contemporary artists similarly engage with the politics and craft of literature in their metafictional meditations on privacy and visibility.

> On a rare stormy Los Angeles morning, Merced de Papel pressed the brakes of her automobile. Her car slid across Wilshire Boulevard, stopping only after crashing into the grille of an oncoming Chevy. The ambulance took away the driver of the Impala, untangling him from his steering wheel and wiping the blood that covered his face and mouth. The second driver was never found. The cleaning crew came, sprayed fire retardant over the two vehicles, and then scraped away shreds of wet paper that clung to the shattered windshield and hood, some of the pulp falling to the asphalt and washed into the gutters by rainwater. As with all people made of paper, there was no official record of Merced de Papel's death, no death certificate or funeral announcement; even the accident report refused to acknowledge her. (197–98)

An undocumented person of paper, Merced de Papel is wiped away by a cleaning crew, an anxiety echoed in the metaphor Nguyen's narrator uses to articulate his fear about power imbalances in representation industries: "not to own the means of representation is also a kind of death. For if we are represented by others, might they not, one day, hose our deaths off memory's laminated floor?" (187). Paper is less resilient than flesh, more easily manipulated, erased, or destroyed, rendering problematic its conflation with living humans. For example, in "Love and Honor," Nam equates his father to the leaves of paper on which his story was typed, reflecting that in burning the manuscript his father "had destroyed himself" (Le 28). Further, the characters who populate the fiction in these chapters would largely prefer to escape the confines of the page, or at least the gaze of reading audiences. As chapter 4 outlines, conflating humans with their documents has had disastrous consequences throughout US history into the present day. Liz's dedication, therefore, may be more cold comfort than a rich affirmation of literature's potential to advance social justice in the world.

Plascencia's epigraph, on the other hand, might be understood as ironic, opening a novel that critiques the conflation of representation (characters) and reality (humans). Allowing representations to stand in for lived realities, as Jodi Melamed notes in her critique of liberal multiculturalism, renders unnecessary the actual presence of people of color and indigenous people (37). In a paradox central to this volume, the metafictional deployments of narrative privacy not only in *The People of Paper* but in the fictions throughout these chapters at once criticize this conflation and invite readers to draw equivalences between representation and reality by breaking diegetic boundaries and narratively mimicking historical patterns of observation and surveillance as well as contemporary, post-9/11 gazes. Fully complicit in the process these texts critique, I demonstrate this formal paradox by staying close to the page, tending toward the literal, and awarding volition to figments of authors' imaginations. Paradoxes are constitutive of narrative privacy, however, given the contradictory and competing nature of its critical questions: how might literature reshape visibility by asserting privacy as a political tool? How might authors refuse visibility in a moment when representation has never been more important? How do fictions remain private even as they circulate in the literary marketplace, where they are meant to be purchased and read? In part, these fictions respond by metafictionally drawing readers' gazes inward to illuminate the limits of literature. In doing so, they direct our gaze outward to the extratextual: the world outside of the book where Federico de la Fe and Little Merced seek asylum, where Apelles and Bình look when they break the fourth wall, where words have material consequences on the lived experiences of people of color and indigenous people.

If the authors throughout these chapters cultivate spaces of narrative privacy by strategically withholding information and resisting readers' gazes, many of Charles Yu's short stories, in contrast, might be understood as disclosing themselves in excess. Throughout his body of work, Yu contends with the limits of literature and of literary study by underscoring the importance of narratives for finding meaning in our lived experiences while also insisting on the distinction between fiction and reality. In "Realism," for example, the first-person narrator recounts his recursive conversations with his mother who, nearing death, becomes enthralled with the idea of literary realism and the possibilities it affords. She asks the narrator, a writer, to cast her in a realistic story so she can find meaning in her life. "I want to go through an experience," she explains, "I want to have an epiphany" (104). Reading a lengthy tome of literary criticism titled *Realism,* she offers her son ideas for her story: "'I want to try out all of these new emotions I learned about,' she says. 'I want to feel weltschmerz. I want to feel malaise, six kinds of it. I want to feel ennui'" (104). The narrator's frustration with his inability to write the sort of realism his mother desires—which, he learns, is more of a compelling narrative than a realistic account of their lived experiences—culminates in a metacritical turn at the end of the story. In response to his mother's fear that he will not write her into the sort of realistic story that gives her life purpose before her impending death, the narrator concedes failure:

> All stories are failed stories, I say. All real stories are stories that failed at being the ideal story.
>
> I try to make things happen. I try to drive us toward something, anything. I have no great secret to tell her, nothing that will tie it all together. I'm

not smart enough to do it. Some stories have no beginning or end or middle. Some stories do not exist. There are some places you can't get to.

I give up.

"I can't do it," I say. "I can't make this into a story." (110)

Yu's story ends with his narrator's confession, abruptly abbreviating the story's mediation on the relationship between literary realism—as understood not just by the narrator's mother, a reader, but also by the literary scholar who authored *Realism*—and life itself.

Formally, "Realism" appears to replicate the literary mode at its center. Readers learn nothing but the mundane details of the narrator's life as they relate to his mother. The story's recursive nature—the narrator apologizes at several points for repeating himself, a critique his mother also levels—mimics the writing process, leaving in place passages that revision might remove or smooth over. "Realism" formally resists such revision, however, insisting on revealing itself even in failure; the revisions required to reduce repetition, emphasize identifiable narratives, and improve clarity would likely entail the story's almost complete erasure. The narrator explains the specific limitations of his task: "I can't reach out, go above it, tell a larger story, a story-within-a-story. I can't cheat. Not if she wants realism" (107). The story's realism, in other words, succeeds in replicating the difficult project of representing life on the page even if it fails to mimetically represent those lives. Still, a story about the insufficiency of literature, about the limitations of representation, and about the incongruency between narrative and life is certainly recognizable as a failed story, particularly ending, as it does, with the author's admission of failure. However, the narrator's failure is in not recognizing until it was too late that his mother's search for meaning, experiences, and feelings could not actually be worked out on the page in a literary register. What she needed were the lived interactions and experiences her son tried to represent; any story he crafted, no matter how realistic, would be insufficient to effect the necessary material changes. In literalizing the limits of literature, Yu joins the other authors in this volume in distinguishing the literary from the living and in underscoring the urgency—for authors, for readers, for literary critics—to look up from the page.

The political aim of narrative privacy in its ultimate turn outward to the extraliterary is to highlight the transferability of literary critique to the world in which we live. Narrative privacy encourages readers, especially privileged audiences, to look differently by questioning who expects and receives access to information, from whom, and at what cost: what historical and political legacies condition our access and subjects' availability? What are the power dynamics in any given representational context? Necessarily a lens rather than a prescription, narrative privacy acknowledges that the answers to these questions shift not only according to specific contexts but also the social, political, and historical positions of both viewing agent and subject.

Taking seriously the effect words have on the living provokes sincere questions about the utility of a formal move like narrative privacy in a society in which people of color and indigenous people remain underrepresented in positions of power—literally and literarily—while at the same time racial and indigenous visibility remains highly mediated. For instance, one need only to recall a conservative commentator's recent charge to LeBron James to "shut up and dribble" after James spoke out about social issues (Kelly). Black men enjoy national visibility as athletes, but not as political individuals (or, specifically, as black men). My aim in these chapters is to illuminate the potential of narrative privacy not only to name the formal maneuver contemporary writers use to navigate this representational bind, but also to open up new reading strategies for literature and approaches—with respect to privacy—to lived efforts toward social justice. As a formal strategy, narrative privacy teaches readers how to see literature differently in order to help us read more closely and, more importantly, in order to see the world around us more deliberately and to recognize the politics—the power differentials, the material consequences—of how we look. Publicly asserting privacy—in long historical contexts but also our present moment—is a powerful political statement that disrupts conventional structures of visibility and access. Rather than a depoliticized recusal from the important work toward visibility for people of color and indigenous people, narrative privacy is a tool for recognizing historical, colonial institutions of inequality as well as for navigating our present moment.

Following the lead of the authors in *The Politics of Privacy*, I understand contemporary fiction as asking where privacy fits into struggles for social justice, even as those struggles necessitate visibility and exposure. For example, new technology, wider access to the internet, and social media have enabled much more democratic, decentralized forms of visibility that do not face the same issues of mediation as traditional outlets. In the past several years, cell phone cameras have allowed individuals not only to digitally witness acts of police brutality or public racism, but also to disseminate those images and videos across social media networks. While this uptick in visibility has become a primary means of igniting social justice movements, it remains to be seen whether such documentation achieves tangible social justice. For example, Philando Castile's 2016 shooting by a St. Anthony, Minnesota, police officer during a traffic stop was live-broadcast and narrated via Facebook by his partner, Diamond Reynolds, also in the vehicle. Despite videographic evidence of the event, the police officer, Jeronimo Yanez, was acquitted (Mannix). Other deaths of black men, including Eric Garner and Walter Scott, have also been recorded and disseminated without producing substantive change; when the intimate details of these men's deaths are broadcast without attendant justice, the value of visibility comes into question. As activists have queried, in what way do these acts of violence serve as modern-day lynchings? Without aiding legal justice, the deaths become spectacles that reinforce racist practices; they serve, therefore, as social policing for black people, people of color, and indigenous people. Narrative privacy would have us consider the politics of how and why we look at video evidence of violence—surely different for every viewer—rather than accept visibility as unqualified progress.

Even nonviolent, well-meaning demands for access might bear additional examination. For example, access to college, to scholarships, or to internship programs often relies on essays mining students' lives for stories of hardship. Nested in the well-intentioned impulse to reward those youths who have overcome extraordinary challenges is the familiar demand for access to their stories; once again, some of the most vulnerable are asked to reveal themselves to powerful audiences in exchange for recognition or opportunities. Similarly, people with disabilities who do not look "sick enough" and impoverished individuals who do not appear "poor enough" are often compelled to divulge the specific nature of their disability or to perform familiar representations of poverty to gain social acceptance or even material assistance from social or governmental organizations. Without advocating for the dismissal of educational, social, or governmental programs that recognize the unevenness of privilege and the particular challenges of communal and individual life experiences, we might still denaturalize their attendant expectations of access to individuals' and communities' stories. When recounting his employers' interest in his life story, Bình observes, "the honey that they covet lies inside my scars" (19). Narrative privacy puts critical pressure not only on the practice of covetousness but also on the desirability of honeyed stories of trauma, marginalization, and adversity. Following the authors throughout this volume, reading the world through narrative privacy encourages audiences to invite critique of why—in any given situation—we desire access to another.

More broadly, in using literary form to cast readers into various viewer roles, narrative privacy encourages introspection into how and why we look at the world around us as well as the conditions under which we make representations visible and accessible. For instance, in an interview on NPR's *Fresh Air*, Treuer condemns what he characterizes as "trauma porn," which is, he explains, "basically trotting out hardship which provides a kind of catharsis, right? There's a cathartic reaction on the part of the reader to it, this sort of—this unleashing and this unburdening of emotion, like, oh, my God—of pity and fear. And then once unburdened, you know, the reader is—their burden is lightened. They've expiated whatever guilt they have, right?" (Treuer and Davies). Trauma porn and its ideological cousins, such as poverty porn, rez porn, inspiration porn, and the like, exist not just in literature but, perhaps more problematically, in charity campaigns, celebrity publicity stunts, religious missionary accounts, and even in forms of tourism such as tours through socioeconomically depressed areas, urban ethnic enclaves such as Chinatowns,[2] or disaster zones. As indicated in the description of these representations as "porn," such visual or textual depictions are voyeuristic and entertaining—honeyed—in quality, meant to arouse emotional responses in the viewer. Often, in emphasizing the vast power differentials between viewer and viewed, the source elicits support—charities, for instance, ask for financial support, as do politicians who may also ask for votes—so therefore justifies the risk of invading subjects' privacy.

Importantly, narrative privacy is not antirepresentational, but contemplative; profound change often requires shocking representations, and privacy is very often an unnecessary luxury in the face of vast need. Recent examples of Puerto Rico's humanitarian crisis after Hurricane Maria, Flint, Michigan's water crisis, and the ongoing humanitarian crises in ICE facilities on the US–Mexico border, all disasters that remain largely invisible to the national imaginary, for instance, immediately come to mind. In allowing characters to metaleptically speak back to and challenge their author–characters and reading audiences, however, narrative privacy works through these representational challenges on the page, providing a pedagogical stage in which readers practice contending with the historical and ongoing conditions of visibility of fictional characters without real rights.

The fictions throughout this volume take a necessarily visible, commodified, exposed form in commercial literature, suturing their physical existence in the world with the critiques they level on the page. They put their visibility and consumability in historical, political, and social contexts, recognizing issues of access and power that have worked against people of color and indigenous people throughout history up to our present, post-9/11 moment. As they do so, they craft spaces of privacy to remind readers of the limits of our access, preserving space for self-care, for political organizing, and for personal and communal privacy; their lessons of paper should inform our engagement

---

2. Here I think specifically of Yoonmee Chang's *Writing the Ghetto: Class, Authorship, and the Asian American Ethnic Enclave* (2010).

with the world around us. Even as they maintain a healthy degree of cynicism, skepticism, and suspicion—and how can they not, given the weight of history?[3]—their participation in commercial fiction markets and communities testifies to an abiding faith in the power of narrative to effect meaningful social and political change in the world.

---

3. Here I invoke Lisa Brooks's language from "At the Gathering Place," the Afterword of *American Indian Literary Nationalism* (2006).

WORKS CITED

Aarseth, Espen J. *Cybertext: Perspectives on Ergodic Literature*. Johns Hopkins UP, 1997.

Abbott, H. Porter. *The Cambridge Introduction to Narrative*. 2nd ed. Cambridge UP, 2008.

Allen, Paula Gunn. "Special Problems in Teaching Leslie Marmon Silko's *Ceremony*." *American Indian Quarterly*, vol. 23, no. 4, 1990, pp. 379–86.

Aranda, José F. Jr. *When We Arrive: A New Literary History of Mexican America*. U of Arizona P, 2003.

Bal, Mieke. *Narratology: Introduction to the Theory of Narrative*. U of Toronto P, 1985.

Banita, Georgiana. *Plotting Justice: Narrative Ethics and Literary Culture After 9/11*. U of Nebraska P, 2012.

Barker, Joanne. *Native Acts: Law, Recognition, and Cultural Authenticity*. Duke UP, 2011.

Barth, John. "The Literature of Exhaustion." *The Friday Book: Essays and Other Non-Fiction*. The Johns Hopkins UP, 1984. 62–76.

———. "The Literature of Replenishment." *The Friday Book: Essays and Other Non-Fiction*. The Johns Hopkins UP, 1984. 193–206.

Behar, Ruth. "Ethnography and the Book That Was Lost." *Ethnography*, vol. 4, no. 15, 2003, pp. 15–39.

Belcourt, Billy-Ray. "Fatal Naming Rituals." *Hazlit*, 19 July 2018, https://hazlitt.net/feature/fatal-naming-rituals.

Benfey, Christopher. "Ordering In." *The New York Times*, 6 Apr. 2003.

Berkhofer, Robert. *The White Man's Indian: Images of the American Indian from Columbus to the Present*. Random House, 1978.

Bieder, Robert E. *Science Encounters the Indian, 1820–1880: The Early Years of American Ethnology*. U of Oklahoma P, 1986.

Blackburn, Venita. "The People of Paper vs. Light Boxes/Rant on Racism." *Loosely Literary Blog Mostly About Liquor*, 6 Oct. 2013, https://literarylush.wordpress.com/2010/10/06/the-people-of-paper-vs-light-boxesrant-on-racism.

Bolaki, Stella. "'It Translated Well': The Promise and the Perils of Translation in Maxine Hong Kingston's 'The Woman Warrior.'" *MELUS*, vol. 34, no. 4, 2009, pp. 39–60.

Breuninger, Kevin. "NFL Bans On-Field Kneeling During the National Anthem." *CNBC.com*, 23 May 2018, https://www.cnbc.com/2018/05/23/nfl-bans-on-field-kneeling-during-the-national-anthem.html.

Brooks, Lisa. "Afterword: At the Gathering Place." *American Indian Literary Nationalism*. U of New Mexico P, 2006. 225–52.

Brown, Kimberly Juanita. *The Repeating Body: Slavery's Visual Resonance in the Contemporary*. Duke UP, 2015.

Brown, Wendy. *Edgework: Critical Essays on Knowledge and Politics*. Princeton UP, 2005.

Browne, Simone. *Dark Matters: On the Surveillance of Blackness*. Duke UP, 2015.

Calloway, Colin G. *First Peoples: A Documentary Survey of American Indian History*. Bedford/St. Martin's, 2008.

Chacon, RosaMaria. "Making Space for Those Unruly Women of Color." *Review of Education, Pedagogy and Cultural Studies*, vol. 28, nos. 3–4, 2006, pp. 381–93.

Chang, Yoonmee. *Writing the Ghetto: Class, Authorship, and the Asian American Ethnic Enclave*. Rutgers UP, 2010.

Chavez, Leo R. *The Latino Threat: Constructing Immigrants, Citizens, and the Nation*. Stanford UP, 2008.

Cheng, Anne Anlin. *The Melancholy of Race: Psychoanalysis, Assimilation, and Hidden Grief*. Oxford UP, 2000.

Cheung, King-Kok. *Articulate Silences: Hisaye Yamamoto, Maxine Hong Kingston, Joy Kogawa*. Cornell UP, 2003.

Chiu, Monica. *Scrutinized! Surveillance in Asian North American Fiction*. U of Hawaii P, 2014.

Chow, Rey. *Primitive Passions: Visuality, Sexuality, Ethnography, and Contemporary Chinese Cinema*. Columbia UP, 1995.

Chuh, Kandice. *Imagine Otherwise: On Asian American Critique*. Duke UP 2003.

Coffman, Chris. "The Migrating Look: Visual Economies of Queer Desire in The Book of Salt." *Texas Studies in Literature and Language*, vol. 56, no. 2, 2014, pp. 148–80.

Cotera, María Eugenia. *Native Speakers: Ella Deloria, Zora Neale Hurston, Jovita Gonzalez, and the Poetics of Culture*. U of Texas P, 2008.

Cox, James H. "The Past, Present, and Possible Futures of American Indian Literary Studies." *Studies in American Indian Literatures*, vol. 20, no. 2, 2008, pp. 102–12.

Dávila, Arlene. *Latinos, Inc.: The Marketing and Making of a People*. 2nd ed. U of California P, 2012.

Deloria, Philip. *Playing Indian*. Yale UP, 1998.

Deloria, Vine Jr. *Custer Died for Your Sins: An Indian Manifesto*. U of Oklahoma P, 1969.

Donahue, James J. "Introduction: Narrative, Race, and Ethnicity in the United States." *Narrative, Race, and Ethnicity in the United States*. Eds. James J. Donahue, Jennifer Ann Ho, and Shaun Morgan. The Ohio State UP, 2017, pp. 1–12.

Dubrofsky, Rachel E. and Shoshana Amielle Magnet, eds. *Feminist Surveillance Studies*. Duke UP, 2015.

Duvall, John N. and Robert P. Marzec, eds. *Narrating 9/11: Fantasies of State, Security, and Terrorism*. Johns Hopkins UP, 2015.

Edwards, Naomi. "Melancholic Ghosts in Monique Truong's *The Book of Salt*." *WSQ: Women's Studies Quarterly*, vol. 40, nos. 3 & 4, 2012, pp. 167–86.

Elias, Amy J. "Postmodern Metafiction." *The Cambridge Companion to American Fiction After 1945*. Ed. John N. Duvall. Cambridge UP, 2012. 15–29.

Elliot, Michael A. *The Culture Concept: Writing and Difference in the Age of Realism*. U of Minnesota P, 2002.

Eng, David. *The Feeling of Kinship: Queer Liberalism and the Racialization of Intimacy*. Duke UP, 2010.

European Commission. "What Are My Rights?" *European Commission*. https://ec.europa.eu/info/law/law-topic/data-protection/reform/rights-citizens/my-rights/what-are-my-rights_en.

Evans, Brad. *Before Cultures: The Ethnographic Imagination in American Literature, 1865–1920*. U of Chicago P, 2005.

"Factsheet on the 'Right to be Forgotten' Ruling." *European Commission*. http://ec.europa.eu/justice/data-protection/files/factsheets/factsheet_data_protection_en.pdf.

Fadda-Conrey, Carol. *Contemporary Arab-American Literature: Transnational Reconfigurations of Citizenship and Belonging*. New York UP, 2014.

Fanon, Franz. *Black Skin, White Masks*. Trans. Richard Philcox. Grove Press, 2008.

Fishkin, Shelley Fisher. "Interview with Maxine Hong Kingston." *American Literary History*, vol. 3, no. 4, 1991, pp. 782–91.

Franzen, Jonathan. "Jonathan Franzen: What's Wrong with the Modern World." *The Guardian*, 13 Sept. 2013, https://www.theguardian.com/books/2013/sep/13/jonathan-franzen-wrong-modern-world/print.

Freiert, William K. "An Ojibwe Daphnis and Chloe: David Treuer's The Translation of Dr. Apelles." *Mediterranean Studies*, vol. 21, no. 1, 2013, pp. 57–66.

Fung, Catherine. "A History of Absences: The Problem of Reference in Monique Truong's *The Book of Salt*." *Novel*, vol. 45, no. 1, 2012, pp. 94–110.

Fusco, Coco. *English Is Broken Here: Notes on Cultural Fusion in the Americas*. The New Press, 1995.

Gass, William. "Philosophy and Form of Fiction." *Fiction and the Figures of Life: Essays*. Jaffrey, NH, David R. Godine, 1979, pp. 3–26.

Gates, Henry Louis Jr. *Loose Canons*. Oxford UP, 1992.

Geertz, Clifford. *The Interpretation of Cultures*. Basic Books, 1973.

Goellnicht, Donald C. "'Ethnic Literature's Hot': Asian American Literature, Refugee Cosmopolitanism, and Nam Le's The Boat." *Journal of Asian American Studies*, vol. 15, no. 2, 2012, pp. 197–224.

González, Rigoberto. *Crossing Vines: A Novel*. U of Oklahoma P, 2003.

Green, Rayna. "The Pocahontas Perplex: The Image of Indian Women Culture." *Unequal Sisters: A Multicultural Reader in U. S. Women's History*. Eds. Ellen Carol DuBois and Vicki L. Ruiz. Routledge, 1990, pp. 15–21.

Gross, Terry. "Author Viet Thanh Nguyen Discusses 'The Sympathizer' and His Escape from Vietnam." *Fresh Air. NPR*, 17 May 2016, https://www.npr.org/2016/05/17/478384200/author-viet-thanh-nguyen-discusses-the-sympathizer-and-his-escape-from-vietnam.

Hartman, Saidiya V. *Scenes of Subjection: Terror, Slavery, and Self-Making in Nineteenth-Century America*. Oxford UP, 1997.

Henley, Jon. "French Angry at Law to Teach Glory of Colonialism." *The Guardian*, 15 Apr. 2005.

Ho, Jennifer Ann. "Afterword: Intersections and Future Connections." *Narrative, Race, and Ethnicity in the United States*. Eds. James J. Donahue, Jennifer Ann Ho, and Shaun Morgan. The Ohio State UP, 2017. 208–18.

Hoberek, Andrew. "Introduction: After Postmodernism." *Twentieth Century Literature*, vol. 53, no. 3, 2007, pp. 233–47.

Holsinger, Paul M. "And Babies." *War and American Popular Culture: A Historical Encyclopedia*. Greenwood Press, 1999. 363.

Hong, Terry. "Q&A with Viet Thanh Nguyen." *Bloom*, 8 Apr. 2015, https://bloom-site.com/2015/04/08/qa-with-viet-thanh-nguyen/.

hooks, bell. "Eating the Other: Desire and Resistance." *Black Looks: Race and Representation*. Between the Lines, 1992. 21–40.

Huggan, Graham. *The Postcolonial Exotic: Marketing the Margins*. Taylor and Francis, 2002.

Huynh, Matt. "The Boat." Digital Graphic Adaptation of "The Boat" by Nam Le. *SBS*. 2015, http://www.sbs.com.au/theboat/.

Jansen, Anne Mai Yee. "(Dis)Integrating Borders: Crossing Literal/Literary Boundaries in *Tropic of Orange* and *The People of Paper*." *MELUS*, vol. 42, no. 3, 2017, pp. 102–28.

Jones, Norman W. "Eucharistically Queer?: The Postsecular as Transnational Reading Strategy in The Book of Salt." *Studies in American Fiction*, vol. 41, no. 1, 2014, pp. 103–29.

Jones, Shane. *Light Boxes*. Penguin, 2010.

———. "Now that Dave Eggers Has Been Accused of Plagiarism We Finally Have Something in Common." *Vice*, 8 Oct. 2013, https://www.vice.com/en_us/article/exm48a/now-that-dave-eggers-has-been-accused-of-plagiarism-we-finally-have-something-in-common.

Jones, Stephen Graham. *The Bird Is Gone: A ~~Monograph~~ Manifesto*. Fiction Collection 2, 2003.

Justice, Daniel Heath. "Currents of Trans/national Criticism in Indigenous Literary Studies." *American Indian Quarterly*, vol. 35, no. 3, 2011, pp. 334–52.

Kelly, Lyn. "Lebron James Lashes Back at Fox News Host's 'Just Shut Up and Dribble' Comment." *TieBreaker.com*, 18 Feb. 2018, https://www.tiebreaker.com/lebron-fox-news-shut-dribble/.

Kennedy, Virginia. "Conversation with David Treuer." *Studies in American Indian Literatures*, vol. 20, no. 2, 2008, pp. 47–63.

Kim, Sue J. "What Asian American Studies and Narrative Theory Can Do for Each Other." *Narrative, Race, and Ethnicity in the United States*. Eds. James J. Donahue, Jennifer Ann Ho, and Shaun Morgan. The Ohio State UP, 2017. 13–26.

King, Thomas. *Green Grass, Running Water*. Bantam Books, 1993.

Kingston, Maxine Hong. *The Woman Warrior: Memoirs of a Girlhood Among Ghosts*. Vintage International, 1976.

Kirwan, Padraig. "Language and Signs: An Interview with Ojibwe Novelist David Treuer." *Journal of American Studies*, vol. 43, no. 1, 2009, pp. 71–88.

Klopotek, Brian. *Recognition Odysseys: Indigeneity, Race, and Federal Tribal Recognition Policy in Three Louisiana Indian Communities*. Duke UP, 2011.

Kroeber, Karl. "A Turning Point in Native American Fiction? A Review of Native American Fiction: A User's Manual." *Twentieth Century Literature*, vol. 54, no. 3, 2008, pp. 388–95.

Krupat, Arnold. *Ethnocriticism: Ethnography, History, Literature*. U of California P, 1989.

Le, Nam. "The Boat." *The Boat*. Vintage Books, 2008. 230–72.

———. "Love and Honor and Pity and Pride and Compassion and Sacrifice." *The Boat*. Vintage Books, 2008. 3–28.

Lee, Christopher. "Asian American Literature and Resistances of Theory." *Modern Fiction Studies*, vol. 56, no. 1, 2010, pp. 19–39.

The Lego Movie. Directed by Phil Lord and Christopher Miller. Warner Brothers, 2014.

Lewis, Leslie W. *Telling Narratives: Secrets in African American Literature*. U of Illinois P, 2007.

Lord, Nate. "What is GDPR (General Data Protection Regulation)? Understanding and Complying with GDPR Data Protection Requirements." *Data Insider*. DigitalGuardian.com, 19 June 2018, https://digitalguardian.com/blog/what-gdpr-general-data-protection-regulation-understanding-and-complying-gdpr-data-protection.

Lott, Eric. *Love and Theft: Blackface Minstrelsy and the American Working Class*. Oxford UP, 1993.

Lowe, Lisa. *Immigrant Acts: On Asian American Cultural Politics*. Duke UP, 1996.

"LPTape 1." *Demontheory.net*, 4 Jan. 2011, https://www.demontheory.net/lptape-1/.

Lye, Colleen. *America's Asia: Racial Form and American Literature, 1893–1945*. Princeton UP, 2004.

Lyons, Scott Richard. "Battle of the Bookworms." *Indian Country Today*, 10 Aug. 2007.

MacPherson, Myra. *Long Time Passing, New Edition: Vietnam and the Haunted Generation*. Indiana UP, 2001.

Magnuson, Stew. "Military Technology Considered for U. S. Border Surveillance." *National Defense Magazine*, Aug. 2010, https://www.nationaldefensemagazine.org/archive/2010/August/Pages/MilitaryTechnologyConsideredForUSBorderSurveillance.aspx.

Mannix, Andy. "Police Audio: Officer Stopped Philando Castile on Robbery Suspicion." *Star Tribune*, 12 July 2016, http://www.startribune.com/police-audio-officer-stopped-philando-castile-on-robbery-suspicion/386344001/#1.

Mannur, Anita. "The Book of Salt by Monique Truong." *Gastronomica: The Journal of Food and Culture*, vol. 4, no. 3, 2004, pp. 120–21.

Marcus, George E. and Michael M. J. Fischer. *Anthropology as Cultural Critique: An Experimental Moment in the Human Sciences*. U of Chicago P, 1986.

Martinez, Nina Marie. *¡Caramba!: A Tale Told in Turns of the Card*. Alfred A. Knopf, 2004.

Mayer-Schönberger, Viktor. *Delete: The Virtue of Forgetting in the Digital Age*. Princeton UP, 2009.

McLean, Adrienne L. *Being Rita Hayworth: Labor, Identity, and Hollywood Stardom*. Rutgers UP, 2004.

Meadlo, Paul. Interview with Mike Wallace. *CBS Evening News*. CBS. VTNA. 24 Nov. 1969.

Melamed, Jodi. *Represent and Destroy: Rationalizing Violence in the New Racial Capitalism*. U of Minnesota P, 2011.

Meléndez, A. Gabriel. *Hidden Chicano Cinema: Film Dramas in the Borderlands*. Rutgers UP, 2013.

Miller, D. A. *The Novel and the Police*. U of California P, 1988.

Million, Dian. "Felt Theory: An Indigenous Feminist Approach to Affect and History." *Wicazo Sa Review*, vol. 24, no. 2, 2009, pp. 53–76.

Minh-ha, Trinh T. *Woman, Native, Other: Writing Postcoloniality and Feminism*. Indiana UP, 1989.

Mize, Ronald L. and Alicia C. S. Swords. *Consuming Mexican Labor: From the Bracero Program to NAFTA*. U of Toronto P, 2011.

Mizruchi, Susan. *The Rise of Multicultural America: Economy and Print Culture, 1865–1915*. North Carolina UP, 2008.

Morrison, Toni. *Playing in the Dark: Whiteness and the Literary Imagination*. Vintage, 1993.

Mulvey, Laura. "Visual Pleasure and Narrative Cinema." *Screen*, vol. 16, no. 3, 1975, pp. 6–18.

Ng, Fae Myenne. *Bone: A Novel*. Hyperion, 1993.

Nguyen, Viet Thanh. *The Sympathizer*. Grove Press, 2015.

Obama, Barack. "Remarks by the President on Trayvon Martin." *The White House of President Barack Obama*, 19 July 2013, https://obamawhitehouse.archives.gov/the-press-office/2013/07/19/remarks-president-trayvon-martin.

Olivas, Daniel. *The Book of Want: A Novel*. U of Arizona P, 2011.

Oliver, Kendrick. *The My Lai Massacre in American History and Memory*. Manchester UP, 2006.

Ovalle, Priscilla Peña. *Dance and the Hollywood Latina: Race, Sex, and Stardom*. Rutgers UP, 2011.

Palumbo-Liu, David. *Asian/American: Historical Crossings of a Racial Frontier*. Stanford UP, 1999.

———. "Introduction." *The Ethnic Canon: Histories, Institutions, and Interventions*. U of Minnesota P, 1995. 1–30.

Parrott, Jill M. "Power and Discourse: Silence as Rhetorical Choice in Maxine Hong Kingston's The Woman Warrior." *Rhetorica: A Journal of the History of Rhetoric*, vol. 30, no. 4, 2012, pp. 375–91.

Pelaud, Isabelle Thuy. *This is All I Choose to Tell: History and Hybridity in Vietnamese American Literature*. Temple UP, 2011.

PEN America. "The PEN Ten with Rigoberto González." PEN America. *PEN.org*, 3 June 2014, https://pen.org/the-pen-ten-with-rigoberto-gonzalez/.

PEN American Center. *Chilling Effects: NSA Surveillance Drives U. S. Writers to Self Censor*. PEN America. *PEN.org*, 12 Nov. 2013, http://www.pen.org/chilling-effects.

PEN American Center. *Global Chilling: The Impact of Mass Surveillance on International Writers*. PEN America. *PEN.org*, 5 Jan. 2015, https://www.pen.org/sites/default/files/globalchilling_2015.pdf.

"Perry Authorizes More Border Security Funding, Virtual Border Watch Program." Justice and Public Safety. *Govtech.com*, 1 June 2005, https://www.govtech.com/public-safety/Perry-Authorizes-More-Border-Security-Funding.html.

Phelan, James. *Living to Tell About It: A Rhetoric and Ethnics of Character Narration.* Cornell UP 2005.

Plascencia, Salvador. *The People of Paper.* Bloomsbury, 2005.

Plato. *Selected Myths.* Ed. Catalin Partenie. Oxford UP, 2004.

Pratt, Mary Louise. *Imperial Eyes: Travel Writing and Transculturation.* Routledge, 2002.

Quintana, Alvina E. "Ana Castillo's *The Mixquiahuala Letters*: The Novelist as Ethnographer." *Criticism in the Borderlands: Studies in Chicano Literature, Culture, and Ideology.* Eds. Héctor Calderón and José David Saldívar. Duke UP, 1991, pp. 72–83.

Rand, Naomi R. "Surviving What Haunts You: The Art of Invisibility in Ceremony, the Ghost Writer, and Beloved." *MELUS*, vol. 20, no. 3, 1995, pp. 21–32.

Rebolledo, Tey Diana. *Women Singing in the Snow: A Cultural Analysis of Chicana Literature.* U of Arizona P, 1995.

Reid, Margaret. *Cultural Secrets as Narrative Form: Storytelling in Nineteenth-Century America.* The Ohio State UP, 2004.

Robinson, Douglas. "The Translator as Lover." *California Literary Review*, 24 Apr. 2007.

Rodríguez, Sylvia. "The Tourist Gaze, Gentrification, and the Commodification of Subjectivity in Taos." *Essays on the Changing Images of the Southwest.* Eds. Richard Francaviglia and David Narrett. Texas A&M UP, 1994. 105–26.

Roiphe, Emily Carter. "With Quiver & Quill." *Star Tribune*, 20 Aug. 2006.

Rosaldo, Renato. *Culture and Truth: The Remaking of Social Analysis.* Beacon Press, 1989.

Rosner, Helen. "The Absurdity of Trump Officials Eating at Mexican Restaurants During an Immigration Crisis." *The New Yorker*, 22 June 2018, https://www.newyorker.com/culture/annals-of-gastronomy/the-unsurprising-absurdity-of-kirstjen-nielsen-and-stephen-miller-eating-mexican-food-during-a-border-crisis.

Said, Edward. *Culture and Imperialism.* Vintage Books, 1994.

Saldívar, Ramón. "Historical Fantasy, Speculative Realism, and Postrace Aesthetics in Contemporary American Fiction." *American Literary History*, vol. 23, no. 3, 2011, pp. 574–99.

———. "The Second Elevation of the Novel: Race, Form, and the Postrace Aesthetic in Contemporary Narrative." *Narrative*, vol. 21, no. 1, 2013, pp. 1–18.

Salesses, Matthew. *I'm Not Saying, I'm Just Saying.* Civil Coping Mechanism, 2013.

Sarris, Greg. *Keeping Slug Woman Alive: A Holistic Approach to American Indian Texts.* U of California P, 1993.

Seaman, Donna. "No Reservations." *Los Angeles Times*, 27 Aug. 2006.

"Sergeant Ronald Haeberle." *Biography: Selected Men Involved with My Lai.* PBS.org, http://www.pbs.org/wgbh/americanexperience/features/biography/mylai-biographies/.

Silva, Kumarini. *Brown Threat: Identification in the Security State.* U of Minnesota P, 2016.

Simpson, Audra. *Mohawk Interruptus: Political Life Across the Borders of Settler States.* Duke UP, 2014.

———. "On Ethnographic Refusal: Indigeneity, 'Voice' and Colonial Citizenship." *Junctures*, vol. 9, 2007, pp. 67–78.

Smith, Linda Tuhiwai. *Decolonizing Methodologies: Research and Indigenous Peoples.* Zed Books, 1999.

Sommer, Doris. *Proceed with Caution, When Engaged by Minority Writing in the Americas.* Harvard UP, 1999.

Song, Min Hyoung. *The Children of 1965: On Writing, and Not Writing, as an Asian American.* Duke UP, 2013.

Sontag, Susan. *Regarding the Pain of Others.* Picador, 2003.

Sternstein, Aliya. "Obama Requests Drone Surge on U. S.-Mexico Border." *Defense One. Defenseone.com,* 9 July 2014, https://www.defenseone.com/threats/2014/07/obama-requests-drone-surge-us-mexico-border/88303/.

Streitfeld, David. "For Viet Thanh Nguyen, Author of *The Sympathizer,* a Pulitzer but no Peace." *The New York Times,* 21 June 2017, https://www.nytimes.com/2016/06/22/books/viet-thanh-nguyen-prizewinning-author-of-the-sympathizer-still-wrestles-with-apocalypse-now.html.

Tagg, John. *The Burden of Representation. Essays on Photographies and Histories.* U of Minnesota P, 1993.

Tang, Amy C. *Repetition and Race: Asian American Literature After Multiculturalism.* Oxford UP, 2016.

Tatonetti, Lisa. "The Both/And of American Indian Literary Studies." *Western American Literature,* vol. 44, no. 3, 2009, pp. 276–88.

Taylor, Christopher. "North America as Contact Zone: Native American Literary Nationalism and the Cross-Cultural Dilemma." *Studies in American Indian Literature,* vol. 22, no. 3, 2010, pp. 26–44.

Teuton, Christopher B. "Theorizing American Indian Literature: Applying Oral Concepts to Written Traditions." *Reasoning Together: Native Critics Collective.* Eds. Craig S. Womack, Daniel Heath Justice, and Christopher B. Teuton. U of Oklahoma P, 2008, pp. 193–215.

Toklas, Alice B. *The Alice B. Toklas Cook Book.* Harper Perennial, 2010.

Toobin, Jeffrey. "The Solace of Oblivion." *The New Yorker,* 29 Sept. 2014, https://www.newyorker.com/magazine/2014/09/29/solace-oblivion.

Treuer, David. *The Translation of Dr. Apelles.* Vintage, 2008.

Treuer, David and Dave Davies. "Prisoners of War and Ojibwe Reservation Make Unlikely Neighbors in 'Prudence.'" *Fresh Air.* NPR, 23 Feb. 2015, https://www.npr.org/sections/interviews/.

Troeung, Y-Dang. "Forgetting Loss in Madeleine Thien's Certainty." *Canadian Literature,* vol. 206, 2010, pp. 91–109.

The Truman Show. Directed by Peter Weir. Paramount Pictures, 1998.

Truong, Monique. *The Book of Salt.* Haughton Mifflin Company, 2003.

———. "Interview with Monique Truong." *Readers Read,* May 2003.

Ty, Eleanor. *The Politics of the Visible in Asian American Narratives.* U of Toronto P, 2004.

United States. House of Representatives. Committee on Armed Services, Armed Services Investigating Subcommittee. *Investigation of the Mai Lai Incident.* 91st Cong., 2nd sess. Apr-Jun 1970. https://congressional.proquest.com.ezproxy.lib.utexas.edu/congressional/docview/t29.d30.hrg-1970-ash-0001?accountid=7118.

Vargas, Jennifer Harford. *Forms of Dictatorship: Power, Narrative, and Authoritarianism in the Latina/o Novel.* Oxford UP, 2017.

Vizenor, Gerald. *Fugitive Poses: Native American Indian Scenes of Absence and Presence.* U of Nebraska P, 1998.

———. "Preface." *Manifest Manners: Narratives on Postindian Survivance.* U of Nebraska P, 1999.

Vorgefuehl. "Some Rushed Thoughts on Plagiarism." *SelfDoubtAmerica.Blogspot.com*, 31 Mar. 2009.

Walker, Alice. *In Search of Our Mothers' Gardens: Womanist Prose*. Harcourt, 1983.

Wallace, David Foster. "*E Unibus Pluram*: Television and U. S. Fiction." *Review of Contemporary Fiction*, vol. 13, no. 2, 1993, pp. 151–94.

Warrior, Robert. "Native Critics in the World: Edward Said and Nationalism." *American Indian Literary Nationalism*. U of New Mexico P, 2006, pp. 179–223.

Waugh, Patricia. *Metafiction: The Theory and Practice of Self-Conscious Fiction*. Routledge, 1984.

Weaver, Jace. *That the People Might Live: Native American Literatures and Native American Community*. Oxford UP, 1997.

"WTF!?! Virtual Surveillance———Texas Live Border Cams?!?!? TPTB Want Us to Watch and Report . . . But They Are Watching Us!!!" *Godlike Productions*, 12 June 2010, https://www.godlikeproductions.com/forum1/message1097912/pg1.

Yeager, Patricia. "Consuming Trauma: or, The Pleasures of Merely Circulating." *Extremities: Trauma, Testimony, and Community*. Ed. Nancy K. Miller and Jason Tougaw. U of Illinois P, 2002, pp. 25–51.

Yost, David. "Apelles's War: Transcending Stereotypes of American Indigenous People in David Treuer's The Translation of Dr. Apelles." *Studies in American Indian Literatures*, vol. 22, no. 2, 2010, pp. 59–74.

Young, Michael. "Homemade Penguin Light Box." *HTMLGiant*, 11 Aug. 2009.

Yu, Charles. "Realism." *Sorry, Please, Thank You*. Pantheon, 2012.

Zambrano, Mario Alberto. *Lotería: A Novel*. Harper Perennial, 2013.

Zhuang, Yi. "Building a Complete Tweet Index." *Engineering Blog. Twitter.com*, 18 Nov. 2014, https://blog.twitter.com/2014/building-a-complete-tweet-index.

INDEX

9/11, 6, 8, 13, 15, 17, 17n20, 18, 24–25, 26, 65–68, 96, 98, 111, 119, 186; post-9/11 literature, 2, 14, 17, 18n20, 31, 100; post-9/11 surveillance, 17, 18, 25, 31, 67, 68, 69, 70–71, 73, 181, 191. *See also* surveillance

Abbott, H. Porter, 21, 21n26, 50, 73
acknowledgement (tribal sovereignty), 147n3. *See also* federal recognition
Alice B. Toklas Cook Book, The (Toklas), 28, 144, 169, 172–73
Anaya, Rudolfo, 9
"and babies," 92, 92n24
anthropology, 29–41, 53n40, 154; anthropologists as characters, 95, 97, 99, 100–104; archetypes, 32–35, 37, 39, 41, 44; as colonial surveillance, 27, 29–30, 36–39, 50, 107n2; history of discipline, 29–30, 34n9, 35–37, 38–41; and indigenous peoples, 30, 30n3, 31, 38, 44n31, 50, 1–52, 53n40, 101; as institutional authority, 31, 35, 38, 38n18, 38n19; and literature, 31, 41–44. *See also* ethnographic gaze; ethnographic surveillance; ethnographic voyeurism; ethnography; the Lone Ethnographer; native informant; staking limits

anti-documentary desire, 141, 144, 151–52, 157, 158. *See also* documentary desire
antirepresentational, 4, 13, 112, 151n10, 186
Apelles (historical figure), 52–53
Apocalypse Now (Coppola), 28, 104, 106, 134
archives, 9, 28, 46, 49, 89, 97, 143–45, 150–51, 154, 154n14, 157, 161, 162, 163, 169–70, 173, 175–76
Armed Forces Investigating Subcommittee (My Lai), 82. *See also* Department of Defense; My Lai; US Army; Vietnam War
author-character, 7, 27, 68, 103, 106, 110, 114, 120, 130, 132, 186
authoritarian, 115
authority, 4, 136, 172; of author, 6, 8, 75, 79n14; institutional, 29, 30, 32n6, 33, 34, 35, 37, 38, 38n19, 92, 145, 147, 151, 166, 171; of written narrative, 10, 28, 143, 145, 146, 166, 171, 175, 176

Banita, Georgiana, 18n20, 66, 66n2, 73, 100
Barker, Joanne, 147–48
Barth, John, 6, 7n7, 74n8
Behar, Ruth, 34, 34n12, 39, 39n21, 40, 40n23, 41

Belcourt, Billy Ray, 154n14

Benedict, Ruth, 35, 40n25

betrayal, 81, 119, 120–23, 124, 125–26, 137, 138, 139, 163, 170; authorial, 82, 113, 114, 115, 123; colonial, 68, 82; cultural, 121, 124, 126–27; gendered, 76n10, 82, 121–23, 126–27

Bieder, Robert E., 34n10

Bird is Gone: A Monograph Manifesto, The (Jones), 26, 27, 67, 68, 94–104

birthers, 71–72

Bitter in the Mouth (Truong), 164n23

Black Lives Matter, 72

Boas, Franz, 34n9, 35, 39, 39n22

"Boat, The" (Le), 26, 29n1, 32, 59–64, 94, 153, 154. See also *The Boat* (Le)

Boat, The (Le), 67, 93, 106. See also "The Boat" (Le); "Love and Honor and Pity and Pride and Compassion and Sacrifice" (Le)

Bone (Ng), 149, 149n9, 151n10

Book of Salt, The (Truong), 28, 141, 144, 150–53, 155–77

Borges, Jorge Luis, 7n7, 130n22

Brooks, Lisa, 41n26, 187n3

Brown, Kimberly Juanita, 17n18

Browne, Simone, 17n18, 67

Bureau of Indian Affairs (BIA), 98, 147, 148

Calloway, Colin G., 98

Calvino, Italo, 7n7, 74n8, 130n22

Campaspe (historical figure), 52–53

captivity, 42, 257, 161, 174. See also capture

capture, 83n16, 88, 157, 168, 173, 175, 176. See also captivity

¡Caramba!: A Tale Told in Turns of the Card (Martinez), 180n1

Cardenas, Mauro Javier, 180n1

carnations, 79

Castile, Philando, 184

Cha, Theresa Hak Kyung, 151–52

Chang, Yoonmee, 38n16, 42, 43, 43n28

Chavez, Leo, 70n4, 72, 72n5, 146

Cheng, Anne Anlin, 9, 11, 12, 14, 17n19, 43n28, 94, 151, 152, 153, 153n12, 176

Cheung, King-Kok, 16, 16n16, 17n19

Chiu, Monica, 17n18

Chow, Rey, 30, 34, 35n13, 36, 37n15, 69, 69n3, 111n7

Chuh, Kandice, 10, 11, 43, 43n28

citizenship, 21, 31, 35, 38n19, 65, 70–71, 75, 77, 145, 146, 148, 149, 149n7

civil rights, 2, 8, 10, 12, 12n13, 13, 14

commercial literature, 2, 3, 6, 27, 41, 55, 68, 88, 104, 105, 107–9, 111, 112, 113, 116, 118, 119, 125–26, 128, 129, 138, 140, 155, 186–87

Cooper, James Fenimore, 49n36

Cotera, María Eugenia, 35, 39n22, 40n25

critical race narratology, 19, 19n23, 21. See also narrative studies; narratology

Crossing Vines (González), 26, 29n1, 31, 54–59, 84, 100, 160, 161

cultural appropriation, 8n8, 104, 109, 113, 120

culture/intellect divide, 42–43

curiosity, 4, 26, 30, 32, 33, 39, 58, 59, 60, 62, 63, 64, 68, 69, 80, 93, 94, 102, 104, 105, 107, 113, 119, 127, 153, 156, 158, 171, 173, 179

Daphnis and Chloe (Longus), 45–46, 50, 50n37, 51, 52, 112

Dávila, Arlene, 110, 110n5

Delilah, 126–27

Deloria, Ella, 39n22, 40n25

Deloria, Vine, 32, 33, 34, 37, 38, 39, 41, 44

Department of Defense, 27, 67. See also Armed Forces Investigating Subcommittee; US Army; Vietnam War

Department of Homeland Security, 70–71

Dick, Philip K., 7n7

Dictee (Cha), 151, 151n10

diegesis, 21, 50, 52, 73, 74, 74n8, 78, 81, 82, 83, 91, 102, 106, 107, 116, 119, 120, 125, 127, 130, 131, 154, 168, 176, 177, 181

documentary desire, 12, 158. See also anti-documentary desire

Dubrofsky, Rachel E., 17n18

Elias, Amy J., 6, 6n4, 10n11

Elliot, Michael A., 42, 43n29

Ellison, Ralph, 25

Eng, David, 12, 17n19, 43n28, 143, 143n1, 150, 151, 166n27, 166n28, 168n32, 169n34, 170, 171 ethnography, 26, 29–32, 41, 60, 105, 109, 174, 179; as a way of looking, 17, 26, 27, 29–32, 34, 41–44, 50, 59–60, 70, 144; autoethnography, 37n15; in *Crossing Vines*, 54–59; ethnographic imperative, 11, 11n12, 26, 31, 41–43, 55, 59, 64, 90, 91, 106, 114, 144; ethnographic voyeurism, 26, 31, 32, 44, 44n32, 50, 54; history of discipline, 26, 29–32, 34–41; and institutional authority, 17, 27, 29–32, 34–41, 70, 144; and literature, 7n7, 11, 31, 32n5, 41–44, 50, 52, 54, 91, 108–9, 114, 116, 129, 136; and power, 29–32, 33n7, 34–41; and refusal, 30, 40–41; in *The Translation of Dr. Apelles*, 45, 46–48, 50, 52. See also anthropology; ethnographic gaze; ethnographic surveillance; ethnographic voyeurism; The Lone Ethnographer; native informant; staking limits

ephemerality, 77, 144, 157, 160–62, 171, 173, 175

erasure, 16, 106, 123n20, 144, 147, 148, 152, 153, 171, 183

Erasure (Everett), 177

ergodic literature, 46n35

ethnic studies, 1, 9, 10, 12, 19, 27

European Commission, 18n21

European Union General Data Protection Regulation, 18

Evans, Brad, 41–42

Everett, Percival, 7, 24, 177, 180n1

exoticism, 106, 107, 107n1, 114n11, 174. See also Huggan, Graham

Fadda-Conrey, Carol, 25n31

Fanon, Franz, 3n1, 163n21

Federal Bureau of Investigation (FBI), 27, 67, 68, 95–100

federal recognition, 147–49

Fishkin, Shelley Fisher, 16n15

flowers, 73, 76–78, 82, 124, 126, 132

focalization, 60, 61, 62, 66

folklore, 30n3, 38, 54

forgetting, 5, 47, 58, 61, 62n44, 64, 84, 87, 88–90, 92, 93, 118, 119, 124, 128, 141, 143, 144, 154, 156, 161, 166n28, 175

fourth wall, 6n4, 7, 7n6, 26, 95, 168, 180n1, 182

Franzen, Jonathan, 66n1

free papers, 145–46

Freiert, William K., 50n37, 52n39

Fung, Catherine, 170n35, 171

Fusco, Coco, 8n8, 69n3, 109–10, 111n6

García Márquez, Gabriel, 130n22

Garner, Eric, 185

Gass, William, 6n3

Gates, Henry Louis Jr., 8, 8n9

gaze, 62, 63, 73n5, 75n9, 79, 104, 107n1, 137, 153, 181; cinematic, 7n6, 108; colonial, 3n1, 36n14, 44, 163n21; ethnographic, 33n8, 36, 37, 44, 50, 60; readerly, 5, 26, 32, 44, 46, 50, 60, 67, 68, 69, 83, 85, 94, 107, 127, 181, 182

Geertz, Clifford, 34n9, 39

General Allotment Act of 1887, 148

Goellnicht, Donald C., 2, 23, 60, 61, 88, 89–90, 92, 94, 118, 118n14, 128

González, Rigoberto, 26, 29n1, 31–32, 54–59, 60, 64, 84, 160. See also *Crossing Vines*

Green Grass, Running Water (King), 46n34, 74n8

Haeberle, Ronald, 86, 91–93

happiness, 49, 51, 132, 140–41, 162

Hartman, Saidiya V., 90n22, 111n6, 153, 154, 176

haunting, 170, 171n36

Hayworth, Rita, 76, 76n10, 82, 106, 121–24, 133

Hiawatha, The (Treuer), 53

historical catachresis, 150–51, 152, 168, 170, 171. See also Eng, David

Ho, Jennifer Ann, 19, 20

Hoang, Lily, 7, 180n1

Hollywood, 28, 74n8, 76, 104, 106–9, 111n6, 122–24, 129, 131, 133–41

hooks, bell, 69n3, 112, 118, 119, 128n21

Huggan, Graham, 107, 107n1, 112, 114n11. See also exoticism

Hurston, Zora Neale, 9n10, 39n22

I'm Not Saying, I'm Just Saying (Salesses), 180n1

Immigration and Nationality Act of 1965, 14

innocence, 4, 30, 50, 52, 58, 112, 131, 138, 172, 172n37, 179

inspiration porn, 186
invisibility, 2, 3, 4, 8, 14, 17, 17n19, 69, 75, 78, 110, 151, 160, 162–63, 164n22, 168, 175, 186. See also visibility

James, LeBron, 184
Jansen, Anne Mai Yee, 74, 78n13, 80, 116
Jensen, Toni, 7, 100, 180n1
Jones, Norman, 165, 165n26, 166n27, 168n32, 169n33, 169n34
Jones, Shane, 129–33
Jones, Stephen Graham, 26, 27, 66–69, 73, 94–104, 144; interview with, 68–69, 102–3. See also *The Bird is Gone: a Monograph Manifesto*

Kim, Sue J., 19–20
Kingston, Maxine Hong, 9, 15, 16, 16n15, 16n16, 174
Klopotek, Brian, 146–47
Krupat, Arnold, 37n17, 42

Last of the Mohicans, The (Cooper), 49n36
latino threat narrative, 146
Laymon, Kiese, 24, 177
Le, Nam, 26–29, 31–32, 59–64, 66, 67, 68, 69, 73, 83, 84–94, 95, 103–4, 105–8, 113–20, 126–28, 134, 140, 141, 143, 153, 154, 160–61, 175, 181. See also "The Boat" (Le); "Love and Honor and Pity and Pride and Compassion and Sacrifice" (Le)
Lee, Chang-Rae, 38n16
Lee, Christopher, 43n30
Lego Movie, The (Lord, Miller), 74
Life magazine, 92, 93n26
Light Boxes (Jones), 129–33
Lin, Tan, 7, 180n1
literature, limits of, 3, 144–45, 169–71, 175, 182, 183
Lone Ethnographer, the, 32–34, 41, 43, 44. See also anthropology; ethnography
Lotería (Zambrano), 180n1
"Love and Honor and Pity and Pride and Compassion and Sacrifice" (Le), 84–94, 100, 101, 102, 104, 106, 107n1, 110, 113–19, 126, 127, 128, 135, 136, 140, 141, 143, 160–61, 174, 175, 177, 181. See also *The Boat* (Le)

Lowe, Lisa, 17n19, 38n19, 149, 149n7, 149n8, 151n10
Luiselli, Valeria, 7, 177, 180n1
Lye, Colleen, 38n18, 38n19, 111n6, 172n37

Magnet, Shoshana Amielle, 17n18
la Malinche, 82, 106, 121–23, 127
manifest manners, 46
Martin, Trayvon, 72
Martinez, Nina Marie, 180n1
Mayer-Schönberger, Viktor, 18
McLean, Adrienne L., 122
McSweeney's, 129
Meadlo, Paul, 91–92
Melamed, Jodi, 5n2, 9–11, 13, 38, 181
Meléndez, A. Gabriel, 107n2, 108, 109, 133n27
memory, 32, 37n15, 53, 54, 61, 63, 81, 87–89, 91, 92, 93, 94, 113, 118, 118n14, 119, 123, 128, 137, 140, 141, 155, 158, 162, 163, 164, 165, 181. See also remember
metafiction, 2, 3, 5, 6–8, 14, 21, 24, 27, 31, 55, 67, 68, 69, 75, 84, 102n35, 106, 108, 115, 116, 119, 120, 125, 131, 133, 139, 150, 166, 168, 177, 179, 180n1, 181, 182. See also metanarrative; self-referential fiction
metalepsis, 74n8, 81, 186
metanarrative, 14. See also metafiction; self-referential fiction
Million, Dian, 2, 4
Minh-ha, Trinh T., 16, 32n6, 34n11, 36, 39n20, 145n2, 154
Mize, Ronald L., 70, 70n4, 75, 76n11, 112n9, 146
Mizruchi, Susan, 110
mocumentary, 7n6, 74
Momaday, N. Scott, 9
Morrison, Toni, 9, 25, 111n6
multiculturalism, 2, 10–13, 20, 22, 38, 85, 110, 111, 111n6, 112, 136, 181
Mulvey, Laura, 17n19, 36, 37n15, 69, 111n7
Muñoz, Manuel, 180n1
My Lai, 62n44, 68, 85, 86–88, 90–94, 102, 116, 118, 135, 143. See also Armed Forces Investigating Subcommittee; US Army; Vietnam War

narrative privacy, 2–3, 4, 5–6, 8, 13, 14–16, 21, 24–28, 29n1, 41, 45, 47, 49, 53, 54, 59–60, 61, 62, 64, 67, 85, 89, 92–94, 102, 104, 127, 134, 135, 143–45, 149n9, 150–51, 153–57, 168, 169, 176, 177, 179, 180–86; and ethnographic contexts, 31–32, 53, 55; and the marketplace, 106–8, 110, 116, 126–28, 140; as self-destruction, 5, 27, 68, 84, 88–89, 127, 144, 181; and surveillance, 64, 91. *See also* privacy

narrative studies, 19–22. *See also* critical race narratology; narratology

narratology, 19–21. *See also* critical race narratology; narrative studies

native informant, 26, 30, 31, 37, 38, 39n22, 43, 45, 46, 47, 51, 53, 55; authors positioned as, 26, 31, 38, 41, 50, 113, 116. *See also* anthropology; ethnography

Ng, Fae Myenne, 149, 149n9, 150, 151n10

Nguyen, Viet Thanh, 28, 106–9, 115, 134–41, 181; interview with, 14, 117, 135, 139, 140–41. See also *The Sympathizer*

Obama, Barack, 71–72

objecthood, 37n15

Office of Federal Acknowledgement (OFA), 147

Olivas, Daniel, 120

omniscience, 46, 48, 50, 51, 66, 73, 74, 78, 80, 82, 83, 112, 112n8, 120, 121, 124, 125, 127, 168, 180; as surveillance, 65, 68, 78, 79, 79n14, 83, 119; war on, 27, 73, 74–75, 78, 79n14, 83, 107, 107n2, 119, 124

opaqueness, 16, 36, 54, 154, 154n14

Orange, Tommy, 176, 177

Ozawa v. United States, 38, 38n19

Ozeki, Ruth, 74

Page Law of 1875, 149, 149n7

Palumbo-Liu, David, 10, 44n31, 69

paper sons, 149–50

Pasadena, 77, 132

Pelaud, Isabelle Thuy, 167, 173–74

PEN America, 65

People of Paper, The (Plascencia), 5, 26, 27, 67–84, 89, 100, 101, 102, 103, 104, 128, 139, 140, 141, 143, 144, 153n13, 160, 174, 177, 179, 180, 181, 182; and commodification, 106–7, 110, 114, 115, 119–27, 129 (see also selling out); and Light Boxes controversy, 129–34. *See also* surveillance; war on

Perry, Rick, 70–71

petals, 77, 132, 170

Phelan, James, 19n22, 21n26

photography, 109, 158–60, 162, 165; and audiences, 60n43, 83n16; distribution of photographs, 83n16; novelty of, 55, 158; photographs as artifacts, 57, 158–59; resistance to, 144; theories of, 159, 159n19; Vietnam War, 85, 86, 91–93; as violation, 57, 158–59

Pine Ridge, 97–98, 101

plagiarism, 131–32

Plascencia, Salvador, 5, 14, 26, 27, 28, 66, 67–84, 94, 95, 102, 103, 104, 106–8, 112, 112n8, 113, 115, 119–20, 123, 123n19, 123n20, 124, 125–30, 131, 131n26, 132, 133, 153n13, 160, 169, 179–81; harassment of, 129–34; publishing, 129. See also *The People of Paper*

Plessy v. Ferguson, 38, 38n19

Pocahontas, 82, 106, 121, 122, 123n18, 127

postmodernism, 6–8, 10–11, 21, 140

poverty porn, 186

Pratt, Mary Louise, 3n1, 25, 30, 42, 69n3, 153

privacy, 1–8, 13–19, 24–29, 30–32, 36–37, 47–49, 52–55, 57–60, 62, 63–67, 70–75, 79–85, 89–90, 92, 93, 105–7, 120, 126, 127–29, 134, 141, 143–45, 150, 154, 156, 158, 160, 162, 163, 164, 170–75, 179–80, 182, 184–86. *See also* narrative privacy

Pynchon, Thomas, 7n7

Quintana, Alvina, 42, 43n28

racial profiling, 65, 70, 72, 75, 120, 133, 146, 184

reading vulnerability, 5, 20, 21, 23, 26, 54, 133, 177. *See also* vulnerability

"Realism" (Yu), 182–83

Rebolledo, Tey Diana, 43n28, 121, 122n18

recovery projects, 9, 10, 12, 17, 28, 145, 150–53; successful examples of, 9n10

refusal, 1, 6, 40, 41, 72n6, 85, 92, 113n10, 119, 128, 148, 149, 181, 182; by characters, 41, 47, 53, 54, 62, 78n13, 81n15, 83, 104, 114,

119; literary, 14, 16, 23n29, 103, 106, 111, 151, 175

remembering, 46n34, 54, 56, 58, 63, 64, 82, 86, 87, 90, 92, 118, 144, 154, 159, 162, 172n37, 176. *See also* memory

reviewers, 7n7, 11, 30, 50, 130n23, 131, 150, 174

Reynolds, Diamond, 185

rez porn, 186

Right to be Forgotten, 18

Robeson, Paul, 171–72, 173, 176

Rodríguez, Sylvia, 10

Rosaldo, Renato, 33, 34, 34n9, 37, 39, 41, 44, 44n32, 152

sadness, 75, 78, 80, 84, 127, 130, 130n22, 130n23, 155n16, 168, 174; commodification of, 27, 78, 79n14, 80, 84, 119, 120, 121, 125–26, 127

Said, Edward, 4, 174

Saldívar, Ramón, 10n11, 12n14, 13, 115, 115n12, 116, 125, 127, 128, 140

Salesses, Matthew, 180n1

San Francisco earthquake, 149

Sarris, Greg, 23, 24

SB 1070, 70, 146

Scott, Walter, 185

secrets, 15, 16, 16n15, 17n19, 26, 62, 128, 154, 156, 167, 169, 173, 182

self-referential fiction, 7, 8, 14, 15, 23, 24, 107n1, 115, 127. *See also* metafiction; metanarrative

selling out, 121–22, 125; one's community, 5, 107, 114, 120, 121, 125, 126, 133, 138; and publishing, 84, 106, 107, 114, 119, 121, 125, 126, 127, 129, 133; and trauma, 90. *See also* sellout

sellout, 114, 121, 123, 124, 125, 137, 139. *See also* selling out

silence, 2, 3, 4, 14, 15–17, 55, 61, 63, 64, 87, 92, 93, 93n25, 107, 110, 118, 134, 168

Silko, Leslie Marmon, 9, 30n4

Silva, Kumarini, 17n18, 25, 70

Simpson, Audra, 30n3, 31, 33n7, 34, 39–40, 42

Smith, Linda Tuhiwai, 4, 29, 33n8, 35, 36, 36n14, 37, 40, 43n28, 44, 50, 69n3, 109, 109n4, 110, 111n6

Song, Minh Hyoung, 10n11, 13, 42, 43, 85, 86, 107, 113, 113n10, 114, 116, 117, 129, 135, 156n18

Sontag, Susan, 60n43, 159, 159n19

sovereignty (indigenous), 22, 98, 146–49

spectacle, 72, 111, 134, 140, 150, 154; of cultural viewing, 108; media, 2, 72n5, 146; race as, 28, 72, 72n5, 104, 107, 108, 109, 111, 111n6, 114n11, 138; of surveillance, 72, 72n5; of violence, 2, 135, 185

staking limits, 31, 40, 40n23, 40n25, 47, 57, 57n42, 61, 91

Stein, Gertrude, 28, 144, 150, 155, 155n15, 159, 168, 169, 170, 176

surveillance, 4, 6, 16, 30, 36, 66–73, 75, 94, 94–96, 100, 103, 112, 113, 115, 115n13, 116, 133, 153, 156, 160, 180, 181; border, 27, 64, 67, 68, 69–76, 120, 133, 146, 186; ethnographic, 17, 29, 30, 36, 36n14, 37, 44, 64, 95, 97, 104, 107n2, 179; narrative, 26, 66–69, 74, 75–76, 78, 95–97, 102, 103, 107, 119, 130, 132–33, 156, 160, 167, 179; state, 17, 18, 18n20, 19, 24, 26, 27, 30, 64–73, 75, 75n9, 78, 79–80, 82, 84, 85, 88, 91, 92, 95–99, 102, 103, 104, 105, 111, 116, 119, 133, 144, 156, 160, 179; studies, 17, 17n18, 17n19, 67; technology, 64, 66, 67, 69, 72, 73, 75, 95, 102, 106, 144. *See also* spectacle of surveillance

suspicion, 4, 40n25, 49, 55, 65, 71, 76, 102, 140, 141, 144, 146, 156, 158, 165, 174, 187

Swords, Alicia C. S., 70, 70n4, 75, 76n11, 112n9, 146

Sympathizer, The (Nguyen), 14, 28, 104, 106, 114, 134–41, 181

Tale for a Time Being, A (Ozeki), 74

Tang, Amy C., 12, 13, 20, 111, 136

Texas Border Sheriff's Coalition (TBSC), 70

There, There (Orange), 176

to-be-looked-at-ness, 37, 37n15

Toklas, Alice B., 28, 144, 150, 155, 155n15, 159, 168, 169, 170, 172–73

tourism, 77–78, 95, 103–4, 123, 132, 186

translation, 10, 14, 26, 34, 36, 37, 40, 41, 42, 43, 45–50, 53, 54, 61, 113, 121

Translation of Dr. Apelles, The (Treuer), 26, 29n1, 31, 32n5, 45–54, 83, 107n1, 112, 155, 158, 168, 174, 176, 177, 179, 180, 182 trauma, 12, 15, 60, 61–64, 83, 92–94, 148, 153, 160, 162; compulsory performance of, 185; post-9/11, 18n20; readers' access to, 2, 4, 32, 60, 62, 64, 85–87, 90, 93–94, 119, 126, 168, 176, 185, 186; representation of, 3, 4, 27, 59, 60, 61–62, 64, 68, 85–90, 92–94, 106, 113, 116, 117, 119, 119n15, 126, 154n14; theorizations of, 60n43, 61, 64, 90, 90n22, 176; "trauma porn," 185–86

Treuer, David, 26, 29n1, 31, 45–54, 57, 64, 68, 83, 91, 107n1, 112, 155, 158, 168, 169; interview with, 14, 45n33, 53–54, 185–86; professional background of, 32n5, 53n40. See also *The Translation of Dr. Apelles*

Troeung, Y-Dang, 64, 90, 90n22, 153, 169n34

Truman Show, The (Weir), 74n8

Trump, Donald, 70, 71, 72

Truong, Monique, 28, 141, 144–45, 150–69, 175–76; and history, 169–72, 175; and publishers, 173–74. See also *The Book of Salt*

Twitter, 18, 72

Ty, Eleanor, 24, 69, 111, 114

universities, 4, 22n27, 30, 35, 152, 185; in *Crossing Vines*, 54–56; and expansion of ethnic and indigenous studies, 9; and liberal multiculturalism, 8–9, 10–12

US Army, 27, 68, 85, 86, 88, 91, 92. See also Armed Forces Investigating Subcommittee; Department of Defense; Vietnam War

USA PATRIOT Act, 70–71

Vargas, Jennifer Harford, 115, 115n13, 129

Vietnam War, 85, 91, 106. See also Armed Forces Investigating Subcommittee; My Lai; US Army; Vietnam War

visibility, 1–5, 8, 16, 28, 41, 64, 66n2, 105, 109n4, 133, 177, 180, 182, 184–86; compulsory, 3, 4, 5, 26, 29–31, 69, 175; ethnographic, 27, 29–31, 36, 37n15, 44; racial and indigenous, 1–3, 8–14, 17–18, 24–25, 26, 54, 67, 69, 73, 90n21, 107, 110–11, 114n11, 144, 159, 160, 175, 179, 184–86; to readers, 8, 60, 62, 64, 67, 145, 153–54, 180n1, 182, 185, 186; visibility studies, 17–18, 69. See also invisibility; surveillance

Vizenor, Gerald, 17n19, 36, 36n14, 46, 47, 83n16, 100

volition, 16n16, 37, 44, 74, 78, 79, 84, 119, 132, 133, 168, 182; war for, 27, 78, 119

voyeurism, 44n32, 47, 50, 51, 59, 60, 67, 68, 83, 90n22, 153, 176, 186; ethnographic, 26, 31, 32, 44, 44n32, 50, 54

vulnerability, 3, 5, 30, 48, 59, 66, 68, 84, 126, 175, 180, 185. See also reading vulnerably

Walker, Alice, 9, 9n10

Wallace, David Foster, 7, 7n7, 130n22

Wallace, Mike, 1, 92n24

War on Drugs, 70

Warrior, Robert, 41n26

Waugh, Patricia, 6

Weaver, Jace, 44n31, 51–53

Welch, James, 9

Woman Warrior, The (Kingston), 15–16, 174

Yeager, Patricia, 4

Yost, David, 49n36, 50, 51, 52n39, 53n41, 112

Yu, Charles, 182, 183

Zambra, Alejandro, 7, 180n1

Zambrano, Mario Alberto, 180n1

www.ingramcontent.com/pod-product-compliance
Lightning Source LLC
Chambersburg PA
CBHW020332240426
43665CB00043B/450